Reformed Worship

Reformed Worship

Howard L. Rice and James C. Huffstutler

Geneva Press
Louisville, Kentucky

Illustration of Advent prayer wreath on p. 198 is by Earleen Dudley; drawing of fish and loaves construction on p. 200 is by Mary Newman. Tune for "Advent Candles" on p. 202 is by James C. Huffstutler.

Book design by Sharon Adams
Cover design by Lisa Buckley

First edition
Published by Geneva Press
Louisville, Kentucky

This book is printed on acid-free paper that meets the American National Standards Institute Z39.48 standard. ∞

PRINTED IN THE UNITED STATES OF AMERICA

01 02 03 04 05 06 07 08 09 10 — 10 9 8 7 6 5 4 3 2 1

Library of Congress Cataloging-in-Publication Data

Rice, Howard L.
　　Reformed worship / Howard L. Rice and James C. Huffstutler.—1st ed.
　　　　p.　cm.
　　Includes bibliographical references and index.
　　ISBN 0-664-50147-8 (alk. paper)
　　1. Reformed Church—Liturgy.　I. Huffstutler, James C., 1938– II. Title.

BX9427 .R53 2001
264'.042—dc21

00-065454

Contents

Introduction

No subject is more important but more divisive for churches today than worship. People once assumed that they knew what worship should be like and they had their expectations fulfilled Sunday after Sunday in a predictable order, but now every worship leader and planner knows that at least two congregations are present each Sunday morning: people who expect a repeat of what they have come to expect, and people who are longing for change—for something new and different.

Often the pastor is caught between these conflicting sets of expectations, and sometimes both sides take the pastor to task. If too many changes are made, the "traditionalist" contingent will be unhappy and, since these folks usually have the money, the budget will suffer. People who want change will not be satisfied because the changes didn't go far enough. If too few changes are made, the church may find itself dwindling in numbers and graying in appearance until it withers and dies without doing anything to try to stop the disease or heal it. Many congregations would, in fact, rather die than change.

The Causes of the Change

Recognizing this need for change and the resulting tension is not enough. We must also recognize the issues that create the need for change:

1. Churches have been faced with a crisis of meaning. Secularism has taken its toll, and a sense of the holy has been reduced to the desire for relevance at all costs. The long-present enthusiasm for worship is now gone, and a general sense exists that something is missing. Church leaders recognized this problem even when they resisted doing anything about it.

2. The crisis of language has become self-evident. Words change meaning, which is particularly true of English, a highly flexible and adaptable language largely because of its multiple roots in both Saxon (Germanic) and Norman (French). As use of the Revised Standard Version of the Bible became common in worship, all the standard assumptions about the use of Shakespearean

or the King James English were challenged. "Thee" and "thou" began to sound archaic and quaint; hymns and prayers were adapted to meet this change. The word "man" was no longer commonly understood to refer to everyone. Women made it clear that they felt excluded by much of the language used in worship. Worship planning meetings often became a battle between those who wanted to preserve the old language and those who demanded changes.

3. The Second Vatican Council changed the face of Roman Catholicism, thereby challenging Protestants. We Protestants have often measured our worship by contrasting it to everything "Catholic." If Catholics knelt for prayer, then we did not. If Catholics had weekly Communion, we could not. Because of its connection to Rome, even the cross was a suspect symbol for many Protestants. Now all that has been upset. Rome revolutionized itself. The Mass was put in the language of the people, the sermon was restored to a central place in worship, the hymns of Protestantism were sung with gusto, the altar was moved out from the wall to stand in the midst of the people as a table, lay participation was now common, and in some congregations the cup was given to the people. Rome seemed to have adopted the agenda of the Protestant Reformation. Protestants could no longer measure what they did by how they contrasted with things Catholic. The response was slow but real: Protestants began to increase the frequency of Communion, display the cross, adopt more formal prayers and, in other ways, move toward an ecumenical consensus in which Catholic and Protestant were more and more alike.

4. We increasingly have become a society in which people are reluctant, even unwilling, to surrender autonomy to any person or institution. Institutional loyalty has declined radically, and people quite easily change churches when they find something they like more. Growing churches provide worship that appeals to people and gives them what they are looking for—generally, informality in language, dress, and style. Newly composed "praise songs" accompanied by guitar and electronic keyboard with congregational clapping and swaying are replacing the old hymns. The consumer mentality that has come to dominate American society now applies to worship as well; many people seek out churches that offer them what they want. They move from the congregations and denominations of their upbringing in search of something that "grabs" them.

5. In an electronic age, people respond to a bombardment of their senses. People who have been raised with television, particularly, are easily bored with worship that offers little to the senses and does not touch their feelings. Reading is less popular, so successful churches replace hymnals with projection screens. People draw together and sing lustily. Some pastors have aban-

doned their sermon texts and moved out from behind the pulpit, preaching without notes.

Other people, seeking a more sensory worship style, have moved into the most highly liturgical churches where the incense, candles, vestments, and ceremony provide them with a richly textured setting for worship that is filled with awe and reverence. Many young Protestants have become attracted to Eastern Orthodoxy, for example.

The Results

Many Reformed congregations today are anxious about the loss of membership. The younger members (those under forty-five) are conspicuous by their absence. Fewer people are present on Sunday morning, and those who attend often seem more drawn by institutional loyalty and habit than anything else. Church leaders are generally discouraged; they know something is wrong, but they feel caught between the warring factions in their own congregations. Besides, most pastors were not trained to think about worship very seriously, and they may have avoided any course in worship in their seminary education.

Denominations have tried to respond to the changes. Each of the Reformed denominations—the United Church of Christ, the Reformed Church in America, the Presbyterian Church (U.S.A.), the Christian Reformed Church, and the Disciples of Christ—has produced new worship materials and new hymnals within the last twenty years. These new materials all recognized changes in language; for example, "you" has replaced "thee," and "people" has replaced "men." New music appears in the hymnody, including hymns from Roman Catholic and Lutheran sources, folk songs, hymns from different ethnic traditions, and newly written hymns that speak in a very modern idiom. The liturgical materials represent the ecumenical consensus of more formal services for Communion and Baptism and include more verbal participation of the people in the liturgy itself through spoken responses, shared prayers, processionals, and other acts.

Implications for Reformed Protestants

The challenges and changes have been particularly difficult for Protestants within the Reformed family of denominations. These churches have placed great emphasis upon the thoughtful proclamation of the Word, particularly in the reading of scripture and its interpretation in the sermon. Word-centered worship appeals to the mind of the worshiper, sometimes to the neglect of the emotions. Partly because of this emphasis, the flight of the young from

Reformed congregations has been particularly noticeable, and the feeling that something is wrong is very deep.

In response, some congregations have, in the rush to be popular, abandoned their tradition entirely. They look and feel like Pentecostal congregations. People who have not joined this rush to change often feel left behind and apologetic for their staid and dull style, probably feeling vaguely guilty about what they cannot bring themselves to do. In some cases, congregations have tried to have one service that carried on the tradition and another—called "contemporary" or "informal"—that tries to adopt changes. The result is two congregations that share a building and staff but are otherwise somewhat suspicious of each other.

Because Reformed congregations are not bound to follow a particular order of worship from a standardized liturgical source, some pastors and other leaders have felt quite free to experiment with new materials; others have hung on to old ways because they are comfortable. Within the limits of constitutional responsibility, congregations are free to experiment or to cling to the tried-and-true.

Most Reformed congregations in the United States have very little shared sense of a healthy tradition that reaches back farther than the way grandmother used to do it. When people ask to sing the "good old hymns," they do not request Geneva chant, or even Reformation hymns, but the songs of the late nineteenth-century revival movement. Printed prayers are suspect because they seem too formal and lacking in spirit. People who have no understanding of the historic roots of their tradition can more easily abandon it altogether or cling defensively to "the way we have always done it" without thinking about "why we do it."

The Purpose of This Book

This book is written in the hope that it will help pastors and congregational leaders appreciate the Reformed tradition in which they find themselves and find values in that tradition that enable them to make appropriate changes and meet contemporary needs, but still be faithful to the core ideas that make them a unique part of the Christian community. We believe that the Reformed tradition of worship has an important contribution to make toward the whole church and should have a significant voice in ecumenical discussions. This contribution can happen only if its pastors and people have a healthy pride in who they are. Self-deprecating titles such as "the frozen chosen" reflect a low self image, as do the frequent efforts to abandon nearly all elements of the tradition by copying the methods of others.

At present, no single book does what this book sets out to accomplish: explain the history of the Reformed liturgical tradition and apply it to the actual setting of worship in congregational life. This combination of theory and practice is made particularly clear in the background of the authors: One is a pastor and the other is a retired seminary professor. Neither of us claim to be either totally theoretical or wholly functional, but we have tried to express our unique point of view even when we have had to struggle to find agreement between ourselves. We hope that readers will find themselves enlightened in understanding and renewed in appreciation for the elements in worship that proclaim the glory of God and offer the hope of human transformation.

The book is intended for use in congregation classes that are seriously seeking understanding of our Reformed heritage, by pastors and worship leaders and planners, and in seminary instruction.

Overview

The book begins with historical background and moves to concrete discussions about current issues. The first chapter briefly summarizes the shape of the Reformed tradition: those central elements identifiable in all branches of that tradition. Chapters 2 and 3 deal with history. Chapter 2 treats the history of Christian worship up until the Reformation, in order to demonstrate the catholicity of the Reformed tradition. The Protestant Reformers never intended to start from scratch; they assumed the value of the centuries-long tradition of the church catholic and built upon it, correcting it where in their minds it erred. John Leith, in his important book *Introduction to the Reformed Tradition*, tells of a Lutheran (it could just as easily have been a Presbyterian or Methodist) who, when asked where his church was before the Reformation, responded by asking where was his face before he washed it. Chapter 3 begins with the sixteenth-century Reformation itself and takes the story to the present day. Of necessity, these chapters present a very abbreviated history. Readers who wish for more in-depth historical treatment are invited to explore the bibliography.

Chapters 4, 5, and 6—on Baptism, the Lord's Supper, and the Service for the Lord's Day—are both historical and practical. They discuss issues commonly faced by congregational leaders and make some concrete suggestions for dealing with them. In chapters 7 through 10, we become even more practical, dealing with the elements of music, prayer, the setting for worship, and the church year. In each case, resources are provided as well as a background for understanding a way through the struggles now faced in many churches.

In chapters 11, 12, and 13, we discuss the wedding, the funeral, and other special occasions for worship, and, again, we provide specific resources for those who plan and conduct these services.

In chapter 14 we discuss the style of worship and the difficulty of remaining true to our Reformed tradition as we work to find a balance between traditional and contemporary styles. The book concludes with a bibliography and an index.

Comments and Explanations

You will not find the prayers and litanies in this book in the liturgical materials printed by any denomination. We assume that readers will make themselves familiar with those excellent resources. We have, rather, sought to provide some new materials that can be used to supplement what is in print.

In the litanies and prayers, a Greek cross and boldface are used to mark the people's parts. Boldface is commonly used for this purpose, and the crosses are used to encourage those who design worship to pay more attention to the design of the bulletin. Too often, pastors and worship planners have ignored the visual effect of what we put in the hands of the people, and we hope to assist in the process of changing this situation.

In most cases we used *The Oxford Dictionary of the Christian Church* (3rd edition) for purposes of standardization of dates and spelling of names.

No book is ever written by the authors alone. We are in debt to many people who have helped to make this book possible. The congregation of First Presbyterian Church of San Bernardino, California, has in many ways been a laboratory for the testing of materials included here during the thirty-seven years Jim Huffstutler has served as pastor there. The campus community of San Francisco Theological Seminary also served as a laboratory, since Howard Rice taught worship there for twenty-nine years and conducted worship as chaplain. The students challenged his assumptions, eagerly accepted his insights, and cooperated in the development of campus worship, which included weekly Communion services. Without the encouragement and forgiveness of these two communities, we would never have developed our present skill or interest in worship.

We also owe a debt of gratitude to people who contributed prayers and worship materials to this book: the Reverend Jeffrey S. Gaines of Seventh Avenue Presbyterian Church, San Francisco; the Reverend Nan Jenkins, pastor of First Presbyterian Church, Elgin, Texas; and the Reverend James Robie, pastor of Faith Presbyterian Church, Rohnert Park, California, wrote and offered selections that give life to this book.

Stephanie Egnotovich, our editor, was both encouraging and demanding of us. She made a great many helpful criticisms and concrete suggestions that greatly improved the quality of the writing. Many thanks also to Tommy Jane Roberts and Nancy Rice for their review of the manuscript.

Our families endured hours of listening to us on our computers, huddled over the keyboard and somewhat distant from family activities. We thank them for their patience.

1

The Characteristics
of Reformed Worship

The branch of Protestantism known by the name "Reformed" derives its name from its motto, "The Church Reformed, Always Being Reformed by the Word of God." This family of churches owes its existence to the Reformation, which began in Zurich, Switzerland, under the leadership of Ulrich (Huldreich) Zwingli, and continued in Geneva under John Calvin. Geneva became a refuge for persecuted Protestants from all over Europe. When these people were able to return to their homes, they took with them a form of church life that Calvin shaped. The Reformed tradition thus took root in many parts of Europe: Switzerland, France, Hungary, Germany, the Netherlands, England, and Scotland.

The Protestant Reformation coincided with the development of the nation-state, and as a result, Reformed churches became identified with the nations in which they founded themselves. Each of these "national churches" sought to adapt the common traditions to the particular needs of the local setting. This adaptability is a hallmark of the Reformed tradition that has continued as Reformed missionaries have spread that tradition to other parts of the world. In Brazil, Indonesia, Korea, Mexico, Guatemela, Malawi, Congo, Egypt, the Sudan, and Kenya, large Reformed populations are expressing their own forms of adaptation in their own particular setting. No aspect of church life is more varied than its worship.

In polity, most Reformed churches practice government by elders or pres-byters, who, with the pastors, transact the business of the church in corporate governing bodies, variously named consistory, session, association, classis, conference, synod, and presbytery. Certain exceptions exist: the Hungarian Reformed Church has bishops, and the Congregational and Disciples traditions have a polity in which each congregation exercises considerable autonomy.

In their theology, Reformed churches express their debt to John Calvin, with their strong emphasis on the providence and sovereignty of God, the centrality of the whole biblical record, the necessity of a public and private faith, and above all, a thoughtful and tough-minded effort to be obedient to God on earth.

In its worship, the Reformed tradition is considerably more diverse and harder to distinguish. A researcher looking at the bulletins of twenty different Reformed congregations within the United States today would find everything from a modified revival service to a slightly altered form of Episcopal Morning Prayer. Communion might be observed weekly, monthly, or quarterly.

In addition to this historical heritage, two forces have shaped Reformed Protestant churches in the United States: (1) the Great Awakenings, which were efforts to evangelize the unchurched population, putting the sermon and altar call at the conclusions of the service and leaving us with a pattern for worship that has persisted long after revivals ceased and their fervor died down; and (2) a middle-class ethos that assumes more or less successfully that we can free ourselves from the constraints of the past and live fresh and new in the moment without concern for history. These two influences have tended to produce a kind of rootless attitude that sees little to be gained from the dim past. In most Protestant denominations, tradition has come to mean only that which we remember, or "the way our grandparents did it." As middle-class Americans, Reformed Protestants are often indistinguishable from the broader American culture.

Tradition should encompass more than our collective memory. Tradition is a feeling for, and appreciation of, that which goes back far beyond our own parents and grandparents. The most serious arguments about worship in our churches usually surround issues such as the singing of a particular hymn, the way of serving Communion, the placement of the offering in the order of worship, or the arrangement of the chancel furnishings, particularly the location of the American flag. These debates are not about tradition but instead are about familiar habits that may have no theological meaning whatsoever.

The power of any tradition is its ability, if it is deep enough, to save us from cultural captivity; tradition can enable a group of people to withstand fads, yet have the power to adapt to changing times and circumstances. "The church reformed and always being reformed" does not mean doing anything at all just because it seems new and perhaps fun. The basis for all ongoing reformation is the biblical record; we seek reformation for ourselves and our congregations in being faithful to that record as it is best understood today. Rooted in the biblical tradition, we can move into the future with as few extraneous holdovers from the past as possible. We should strive for this kind of holy irrelevance about what Christians do together in worship.

Reformed Protestants have never had a single litrugy, in part because of the variety of ways in which the Reformation occurred and the various personalities involved. From Zwingli came the emphasis upon the Word preached as central to worship. Zwingli had little use for anything besides the sermon. He was deeply suspicious of what he called the "seductive" power of music, and he banned all forms of visual arts, whitewashing the murals on church walls. To Zwingli, the Word is the primary sacrament; the Lord's Supper is not central but is, rather, a way of enacting the Word and a way of keeping a living reminder of it. The primary purpose of the Lord's Supper was educational, and quarterly observance was sufficient.

Calvin, in contrast, believed that music has the power to inflame the human heart with spiritual zeal and he worked to that end. He actively recruited musicians for the church in Geneva and set them to work producing new melodies for singing the Psalms. For Calvin, the two types of prayer were spoken and sung. Late medieval church music had been anything but the prayer of the people. Melodies from that time were too complicated for anyone but trained musicians and often obscured the text. In reaction, Calvin sought to restore singing without accompaniment or harmony. The point of the music, he believed, was to carry the text, not to draw attention away from it. The music was directed at the ability of the congregation; simple chant best fit this need because it did not require musical training and was sung in unison.

Because Calvin sought to *reform*, not *replace* the church, he wanted to preserve the historic structure of the Mass. He believed in weekly Communion and unsuccessfully argued for it throughout his life with the City Council of Geneva. Calvin insisted on a basic bare outline for worship: "No assembly of the church should be held without the Word being preached, prayers being offered, the Lord's Supper administered, and alms given" (*Institutes*, IV.xvii.44). He believed that the Word of God, which is Jesus Christ, is best presented in two ways: the Word proclaimed and the Word enacted. Calvin believed that to receive the bread and the wine was to participate in the reality and presence of the risen Christ, and he made a point of telling future generations that they should not follow the Genevan model of monthly Communion because it was defective.

The differences between Zwingli and Calvin continue to provoke conflicting points of view and modes of action in the church today. Zwingli, for instance, served Communion to the people while they were seated in their pews, while Calvin urged the people to come forward and be served standing around the table. Differences such as this are reflected in a continuing conflict in many congregations. Most Reformed Protestants are likely to be either predominantly Zwinglian or predominantly Calvinist in their attitudes toward worship. For example, when someone says, "Communion is *only* a memorial," that person speaks as a true Zwinglian. On the other hand, one who seeks weekly Communion is a true Calvinist.

Because Zwingli and Calvin were both committed to scriptural faithfulness, they were willing to make adaptations and concessions as necessary to meet particular situations, because for them, only the Word of God is absolute. Neither suffered from a lack of conviction. Both emphasized the reading and preaching of scripture as central, and because this emphasis coincided with the increase in the literacy rate, the church became a *hearing* church as distinct from a *seeing* church. People came to speak of *going to hear the sermon* rather than *going to worship*.

For both reformers, the Word included both the reading and hearing of scripture. Because the sermon was an explication of scripture, scripture-sermon was always referred to as one act, always preceded by prayer for right hearing and followed by a bidding prayer that summed up the themes of the scripture for the day. The sermon had a sacramental character, for to preach was to offer forgiveness and new life in Christ, to present the risen and living Christ himself. Because the medieval lectionary was made up of small bits of scripture taken out of context, both Zwingli and Calvin rejected it and opted for preaching through entire books of the Bible, chapter by chapter, so that the people could follow and be instructed.

The desire to keep scripture central reinforced the starkness of Reformed worship, originally a reaction against medieval ceremonial excesses and nervousness about idolatry. The result has been a fear of signs and symbols and a tendency to treat people like disembodied minds rather than whole persons. While visual presentations can get out of control when improperly interpreted, the audible word without a visual counterpart lacks concreteness. Fortunately, as if to check his own tendencies, Calvin expressed great appreciation for the power of the symbols of bread, water, and wine.

The Reformation emphasis upon the centrality of the Word and the simplicity of the setting and service were reinforced in the seventeenth century in Great Britain by Puritanism, and on the continent of Europe by Pietism. Both of these movements, which occurred at about the same time, sought to promote a form of spirituality that was direct, immediate, and personal, but they also opposed any practices that seemed artificial. Calvin, for example, did not object to kneeling for prayer, the sign of the cross, or candles; he considered such matters to be nonessentials and believed they could be left to local custom. As the Reformed church grew and spread, however, its position was often that of a minority people, struggling for its very existence against an opposing monarch. In France, the Reformed church lived through a century of intense persecution. In Hungary, it suffered from barbaric slaughter from both Rome and Islam. In Italy and Spain, Protestantism was rendered almost extinct. In Holland, the struggle against Roman Catholicism was part of the struggle against Spanish domination. In Scotland and England, much of the Protestant struggle was against traditions associated with the monarchy.

The result of these battles was a centuries-long period of rejection for those images and practices identified with Rome or with Canterbury: the sign of the cross, the liturgical year, kneeling for prayer, anointing the sick, fasting, weekly Communion, and private confession. None was rejected because of scriptural teaching or theological consideration, but because these practices carried "Catholic" overtones. James Hastings Nichols, the great church historian who had a long and distinguished career at Princeton Theological Seminary, concludes his chapter on the reformers with these words:

> These liturgies must be interpreted against the background of massacre and torture, of galley slaves, kidnapped children, the wheel and the gallows, the smell of burning flesh and hair. The ceremonial lines of robed monks chanting, the tapers, the images of the Virgin, the crucifixes used to escort the martyrs to the stake, were recognized and permanently classified as devil worship. . . . The stress on human incapacity and sin and absolute dependence upon God's mercy has often seemed extreme to those of their descendants whose lines have fallen in more pleasant places. . . . The kind of aesthetic consideration that moves most historians of liturgy did not interest these churches. Their concern was for reality in worship and true obedience.[1]

The end result has been a liturgical tradition that can be easily understood as starved for sensory satisfaction. The starkness of most Reformed buildings and liturgies sometimes shocks people of other traditions. A visitor may take a while to discover beauty in the simplicity.

Certainly, the Reformed tradition that arose out of Switzerland takes the mind seriously. From Zwingli and Calvin to the twentieth-century theological giants—Barth, Brunner, and the Niebuhr brothers—the Reformed tradition has been rigorously academic. This emphasis on intellect has produced a tradition that seeks to be faithful to scripture and to the most noble aspirations of the human mind, and seeks to address the whole of the human situation: political, economic, family, and spiritual. As Nichols noted:

> The worship of these churches has been the vehicle of a highly verbal, emotionally disciplined, intellectually critical mentality. It has never appealed widely to sub-literate groups, either in the West, or on the mission field. But with its limitations and in part because of them, it has still an important calling in the science-dominated technological society where Christian liturgy and symbolism are so widely problematical. For the Reformed have always laid chief weight on what is most crucial, the actualization of fully responsible personal existence before God.[2]

The single most important contribution of the Reformed tradition to the twenty-first century could be that it dares to celebrate a thoughtful faith, to combine mystery and rationality in a way that causes the worshiper to think about what faith means in the complex world of life and work. In the midst of so much activity that has cheapened worship—causing it to become little more than "feel-good religion"—surely an important place exists for this tradition.

Characteristics of Reformed Worship

In spite of the diversity among Reformed churches, their common tradition has six distinctive characteristics.

1. *A focus on community:* The Reformed tradition understands the church as a rigorously maintained community that takes seriously the church as a people covenanted together; the people are responsible for one another, and worship is never just a private matter. The sacraments belong to the whole church and are administered under the authorization of a governing body.

2. *The involvement of the people:* The singing of the people—until quite recently unaided by any musical instruments—has always been a thrilling event, and the singing of hymns and responses continues to be the people's major role in worship. Hymnals can be understood as the chief liturgical texts. Participation of the people also included study during the preaching. In fact, many early Reformed church buildings had desklike ledges in the pews so the people could take notes during the sermon. In many churches people customarily bring their Bibles and take notes in the bulletin. At its best, preaching is not a monologue. For congregations, passively watching the performance of others is a quite recent phenomenon.

3. *Simplicity:* The focus of attention in Reformed worship is on the Word of God rather than on persons or objects. This focus has, at times, led to the kind of starkness in both architecture and the form of worship about which Nichols wrote. Church furnishings were intended to be useful rather than merely decorative. The central focus was upon the pulpit and the table. The service omitted unnecessary frills, and the language was that of the people. Scripture was always to be interpreted, and often only one passage of scripture was read and preached upon. Calvin was concerned about the danger of reading scripture without comment, lest the people either pay no attention or come away with the wrong message. John Knox began reading both an Old and a New Testament lesson, and he made the practice common among Scottish Presbyterians.

4. *The combination of Word and sacrament:* The Reformed understanding of the sacraments as the enactment or sealing of the Word means that the Lord's Supper stands alongside the preached Word. Both bear testimony to Jesus

Christ, the living Word. Martin Luther once said that God has given us five senses and we are ungrateful if we use fewer in worship. Much of the emotional impoverishment of worship today is because worship centers upon the "Word heard" and excludes all the senses but hearing; worship is thus reduced to something like a lecture or forum. Restoring the balance of both Word and sacrament is an important key to the renewal of Reformed worship.

5. *The importance of the Psalms:* Early Reformed Protestants were known for their knowledge of and love for the Psalms. The Psalms were sung at every service of worship. The people generally knew many psalms by heart and could recite them in times of crisis. The Psalms represent the deepest spirituality of the scriptures. They are prayers of praise and lament that express the full range of human emotions and enable people to give expression to their own emotions. The Psalms are also a principal connection between public and private worship. As they are sung and prayed corporately, people are able to use them in their own private devotion. The Psalms can prevent us from being caught up in the pressure to put on a performance. The Reformed insistence upon worship as glorifying God means that we do not ask who we are or why we are gathered, but that we proclaim the goodness and grace of God. The Psalms enable us to do this.

6. *Adaptability:* The Reformed tradition has always welcomed change. Its very motto, "the church Reformed always being reformed by the Word of God," suggests anything but rigidity. Its adaptability has enabled the Reformed tradition to become at home in many different cultures and to adjust to rapid social change, as demonstrated by its welcome of democratic ideas as well as its openness to science and medicine. This tradition can move forward into the future without the burden of being stuck in the past. In fact, churches are free to experiment with new forms of worship when they are sufficiently grounded in a faith that keeps them from becoming vapid.

These six characteristics of Reformed worship provide the basis upon which a relevant and meaningful worship life can be sustained today. In this post–Vatican II world, the Roman Catholic Church has changed dramatically, and Protestants no longer need to live in negative reaction to Rome. In fact, Catholics have incorporated many of the principles of the sixteenth-century reformers: restoring the place of the people, emphasizing the reading and preaching of the Word, simplifying the service in the language of the people. Protestants are free to receive gifts from the Roman Catholic tradition as well.

Today, a growing liturgical consensus among many different denominations is reflected in current liturgical practices: frequent celebrations of Communion, gathering about the table, anointing the sick, spontaneous prayers of petition and intercession by the people, kneeling for prayer, fasting—these are just a few. The Reformed tradition has much to bring to this ecumenical mix. Reformed worship has nurtured people for centuries, enabled them to struggle for freedom, strengthened them in tribulation and oppression, assisted them in finding meaning in their lives, and helped them discover God's gracious intent in a confusing world.

2

From the New Testament to the Reformation

Calvin, Zwingli, and the other Reformers did not imagine that they were founding a totally new church. They believed that they were, instead, correcting the errors of the church catholic and therefore purifying that ancient institution. Because of this conviction, they took seriously all that had transpired from the time of the New Testament until their own, honoring many of the great saints and writers of those centuries and building their own theology of worship on what their predecessors thought and did. The Reformers also insisted upon the centrality of scripture and, therefore, sought to draw all their ideas and actions from the Bible. Reformed worship is built upon these pre-Reformation foundations.

The Tradition of Israel

The first Christians were Jews who spoke either Aramaic or Greek. The inheritance they brought to their new faith was steeped in Hebrew words and phrases, common worship patterns in temple and in synagogue, and long-standing traditions that marked them as a distinct people.

The Idea of Covenant

Central to the self-understanding of the early Christians was the Sinai event, which determined their attitude toward God, themselves, and the rituals that formed their worship tradition. Five features of the Sinai tradition were particularly important to these early Christians and shaped their theology and liturgy:

1. The initiative in the covenant lay with God, who called the people out of bondage and brought them to Sinai, gave them the Law, and then led them to the land of promise. All worship was understood as human response to divine initiative.

2. The calling of Israel was into a covenant, a relationship that bound Israel together as a people with their God. The covenant was with their ancestors in the past and with generations yet to come. All the people of Israel were involved in the covenant and were responsible for living it out, even though they had not themselves taken part in the Sinai event.

3. Signs and symbols represented the covenant. The most important signs included circumcision, the ark of the covenant, the Law, the land of promise, the altar of sacrifice, and the Temple itself. These signs were all external realities, representing something that could neither be seen nor touched.

4. The people ratified the covenant and renewed it in every generation. The primary symbol of ratification was blood sacrifice. Because blood was understood to be life, it represented the seriousness of the covenant. Blood sacrifice was practiced by Israel and all of its neighbors, but Israel was unique in that no human sacrifice was permitted. Instead only animals were sacrificed.

5. Israel's responsibility for covenant faithfulness always included an ethical/moral dimension. Ritual alone could not satisfy the demands of covenant. God required ethical action.

A Sense of Sacred Time

The first Christians also inherited a sense of time from their Jewish roots. Time was conceived as more than a turning of the days and seasons; it was marked by moments of remembering God and God's acts in their history. Central to this concept of time was the Sabbath, which gave a weekly rhythm to life. Israel understood the Sabbath to be rooted in creation itself, a part of God's gracious provision for humankind (Exod. 20:8–11). Thus, to remember the Sabbath was to pause from labor as God did, to restrain greed and give thanks for what God has provided. Sabbath also had a deaconal function (Deut. 5:12–15). Israel was reminded of its own time of slavery by remembering to provide rest for those people who labored in its midst. Because in slavery Israel had no rest, giving rest to others was a way of giving thanks for freedom. The Sabbath also had an eschatological focus, pointing to God's final consummation of history, the great "Day of the Lord," which would be a Sabbath rest for all creation.

Israel had inherited the chief agricultural festivals of its neighbors, but in each case they attached historical memory to the seasonal festival. The Feast of Tabernacles (Booths) was originally a harvest festival of olives and grapes, celebrated in the fall (September or October). Very early, the practice of making small huts in the field was established; this tradition perhaps was rooted in the practical purpose of bringing the harvest in quickly before the rains came. To Israel, these huts served as a reminder of the wilderness wanderings, when the people had no settled homes (Lev. 23:43). This fall celebration was also connected with the beginning of the new year, for the fall rains represented the beginning of the new year as the earth was once more renewed. Certain psalms were linked to this festival by their reference to the rain:

> Rain in abundance, O God, you showered abroad;
> you restored your heritage when it languished. . . .
> (Ps. 68:9)

> As they go through the valley of Baca
> they make it a place of springs;
> the early rain also covers it with pools.
> (Ps. 84:6)

> He it is who makes the clouds rise at the end of the earth;
> he makes lightnings for the rain
> and brings out the wind from his storehouses.
> (Ps. 135:7)

The new year festival was also a time for renewing the covenant. This covenant renewal ceremony celebrated God as monarch over Israel. A detailed description of this covenant renewal ceremony appears in Joshua 24. A series of psalms also came out of this celebration, all of which speak of the kingship of God (Psalms 94–100). Ultimately this larger festival was split into three parts: new year, the Day of Atonement, and the Feast of Tabernacles itself.

The barley festival, celebrated in March or April, was originally the second great pilgrimage festival. During this seven-day festival, Israelites ate only unleavened bread made with new grain. This harvest festival was quickly associated with the Exodus, the unleavened bread representing the bread eaten in haste during the departure from Egypt. By the time of the New Testament, the festival called Passover was a celebration of deliverance, a memorial of what God had done. As the ancient story of the departure was retold, it provided a clue for understanding Israel's destiny. An ancient rabbinic saying makes this clear, "Each person should feel as though he himself had gone forth from Egypt." Deuteronomy 6:20–21 provides a clue for the centrality of remembering: "When your children ask you in time to come, 'What is the meaning of the decrees and the statutes and the ordinances that the LORD our God has commanded you?' then you shall say to your children, 'We were Pharaoh's slaves in Egypt, but the LORD brought us out. . . .' "

Passover links the past, present, and future: to remember the past is to set the present in a new light and to transform the future by providing hope. To remember the Exodus event is much more than simply recall. Remembering involves recapturing the event, participating in its original meaning, and becoming involved with those who were its original participants, so that this event from the past can shed light upon the present.

The third festival, celebrated in May or June, was connected with the wheat harvest. The Israelites called it the Festival of Weeks or First Fruits. By the time of Jesus, Hellenistic Jews called it Pentecost because it came fifty days after Passover. Connected with the giving of the Law at Sinai, the celebration is described briefly in Leviticus 23:15–21.

Sacred Space

Just as time was hallowed, so was space. Although Israel never narrowly conceived of God as localized in one place, the sacred places of encounter with God—the mountain, the wilderness, and the Temple—were hallowed. The mountain, symbol of the meeting between Moses and God, always held a special, sacred position. One of the names for God, "El Shaddai," may well mean "God of the mountain." Throughout the Hebrew scriptures, the mountain is a symbol for the holy. Wilderness also became a sacred symbol because there God fed the people with manna.

Above all places, the Temple had the special character of sacred space. Israelites believed that God, in a way that transcended all human understanding, dwelled in the "Holy of Holies" in the middle of the Temple. Only the stark emptiness of this shrine could suggest its meaning. In the darkness dwelt the treasure of the nation, the ark of the covenant. Even after the destruction of the Temple and its rebuilding after the exile, Israelites thought this spot was especially holy although it was now completely empty, since the ark of the covenant was lost during the exile and never replaced. This space was so holy that only the high priest could enter it, and only once a year.

The Temple was the scene of continuous sacrificial action. As a reminder of the God who appeared to Moses in fire, the altar fire was kept permanently ablaze, for the Temple liturgy centered upon sacrifice. Every morning at daybreak, incense was offered as the symbol of prayer, then an unblemished lamb was sacrificed, and then the meal offering was made while psalms were sung. Prayers were recited and offerings received. The same pattern took place at sunset.

Priests who were set apart from others conducted the Temple worship. Although born into the priesthood as Levites, the priests were consecrated for their particular service. Exodus 29 describes the service for their consecration. They were given special garments for their service (Exod. 28:40–43).

Probably about the time of the destruction of Jerusalem and the exile into Babylonia, the synagogue came into being in order to preserve both the Torah and the people from absorption or extinction. The synagogue became the cultural, religious, educational, and social center of Jewish life and remains so to the present day. Because a synagogue could be established at any place [only ten males were required, a "minyan"], the synagogue had the advantage of being easily transplanted in a wide variety of settings. Divorced from the sacrifice that occurred in the Temple, ordered worship centered upon the reading of scripture and prayer. The offering of prayers in the synagogue was deliberately timed to coincide with the offering of sacrifice in the Temple.

In the synagogue, the scrolls of the Law were treated with reverence, because through the words written on them, God addressed the people. Before verses from the Law were read, people recited the following versicle: "Blessed art thou, O God, giver of the Torah." The entire Torah (five books of the Law) was read through once every three years. All synagogues, no matter how geographically scattered they were, were united by these common readings. The leader chose the reading from the Prophets or Writings, which was meant to complement the reading from the Torah. After the readings, the rabbi or another person present was invited to interpret the reading. The readings climaxed with the recitation of the *Shema* (Deut. 6:4–5), the great confession of Israel's faith: "Hear, O Israel, the LORD is our God, the LORD alone. You shall love the LORD your God with all your heart, and with all your soul, and with all your might."

Summary

The first Christians brought with them from their Jewish heritage

1. An understanding of God as active in human events
2. The idea of a covenant people whose duty to God included both ritual response and ethical behavior
3. The Psalms as hymnal and prayerbook
4. A sacred calendar of festival days and a weekly Sabbath
5. A set-apart priesthood
6. A sacred scripture, publicly read and interpreted
7. The importance of blood sacrifice, and especially the sacrifice of the lamb, slain in offering to God
8. The idea of sacred space: God dwelling with the people, accessible yet transcendent

Worship in the New Testament

The New Testament describes no single, common worship pattern. Instead, we have incomplete descriptions, fragments of hymns, and hints of a variety of very different forms of worship. During the time of the composition of the New Testament (from ca. A.D. 54 until A.D. 125), worship was still evolving.

At first, Christians maintained the familiar pattern of Temple worship. They sought to maintain their identity with both their heritage and their new-found faith in Jesus by combining regular Temple worship with informal house worship. In the Book of Acts we read: "Day by day, as they spent much time together in the temple, they broke bread at home and ate their food with glad and generous hearts . . ." (Acts 2:46). By combining these two forms of worship, they were being faithful followers of Jesus, who continued to respect the Temple throughout his ministry. Yet the first Christians supplemented traditional forms of worship with unique forms that they developed for themselves. Ultimately the destruction of the Temple in A.D. 70 resolved the issue of Temple worship.

Among Hellenistic Christians—that is, people who were either culturally assimilated Jews who had become Greeks or Gentiles who had accepted Christianity—no sense of the Temple and its rituals existed. Thus, new forms of worship arose easily. These Christians could easily see all previous rituals as having been completed and fulfilled in Jesus. The Temple itself became a symbol for Christ. Just as the old Temple on Mount Zion was the symbol of God's dwelling with humanity, so Christ was understood as the primary symbol of God's dwelling among people.[1]

The Temple also became the symbol of the Christian community itself. Paul used this metaphor repeatedly. Because the Christian community centered on the risen Christ, its character is that of being Christ's body on earth. The sacrificial symbolism of the Temple ritual was transformed into an understanding of Christ as the Lamb slain, whose blood replaces all Temple sacrifices.

The synagogue quite easily became the natural place of worship for those Jews who lived away from Palestine, among the Greeks, and who had become Hellenized. When Paul entered a town, he would go first to the synagogue, because he could get a hearing there. The pattern of synagogue worship in Christian worship became the "Liturgy of the Word." The reading and commentary on sacred texts, together with prayers and the singing of psalms, was the pattern for early Christian worship. Christians very reluctantly let go of their attachment to the synagogue, only when forced out.

For two important reasons, worship in homes was necessary to maintain the identity of this new sect within Judaism. First, Christians—often called "People of the Way"—had no legal status in the Roman Empire. House worship was thus necessary as a refuge from persecution. Second, house meetings produced a sense of community and the intimacy of a family gathering. Everyone had a name and could be cared for. The phrase "breaking bread in their homes" (Acts 2:46) means more than it says, although the members did share meals together. More important, the phrase refers to the beginning of the celebration of Communion, which was observed at least weekly and perhaps daily and became the most distinctive characteristic of Christian worship.

Without question, early New Testament Christians celebrated on the first day of the week. The Gospel writers appear quite deliberate in their recounting of Jesus' healings on the Sabbath. The old, seventh-day Sabbath was replaced by the Lord's Day on the first day of the week. The new "Sabbath" that the Messiah (Christ) brings was a day of release from bondage to evil, sin, pain, and suffering.

The Gospels all recount the resurrection as an event that took place on the first day of the week. Jesus' resurrection inaugurates the new era, the so-called "eighth day," which was the anticipated Day of the Lord, and was now understood to be fulfilled. Luke's recounting of the two disciples on the road to Emmaus on the first day of the week, breaking bread together with the risen Christ, is the prototype of the Christian Lord's Day (Luke 24:13–35).

The synagogue pattern of preaching upon the read text became a general Christian pattern. So, too, Christians quickly adopted the idea of two readings, one to interpret the other. Christian preaching sought to connect Jesus with the Torah to demonstrate that he was the Promised One of Israel. Examples of preaching that seek to make this connection include Peter's sermon at Pentecost and Stephen's sermon, both in Acts.

The Corinthian correspondence gives a good example of early Christian worship in its Gentile setting. The desire for freedom from Jewish customs was sometimes expressed in forms of speech such as prophecy and ecstatic utterance (speaking in tongues, for example), which came from the Greco-Roman mystery religious practice. Paul urges these Christians to be more orderly in their worship. When he tells them, "When you come together, each one has a hymn, a lesson, a revelation, a tongue or an interpretation" (1 Cor. 14:26), Paul seems to be responding to worship in which there was a great deal of individual participation and in which leadership was widely shared. The hymns he refers to might have been psalms or new hymns written to give expression to the new Christian faith. Some of these early hymns still exist: the Song of Mary or "The Magnificat" (Luke 1:46–55), the Song of Zechariah or "Benedictus" (Luke 1:68–79), and the Song of Simeon or "Nunc Dimittis" (Luke 2:29–32). These three hymns all use the psalm form with Christian content. Other Christian hymns reflect a different literary form, such as the two hymns to Christ in Philippians 2:5–11 and Colossians 1:15–20, and the hymns in the Book of Revelation: the "Sanctus" (4:8) and the hymn of praise to Christ (5:9).

The two unique rituals of early Christianity were Baptism and the Lord's Supper. Both appear to be assumed as normative by the authors of the

Epistles and the Gospels alike. Both are also the result of a mix of Jewish origin and Gentile culture. Baptism is related to circumcision and the Lord's Supper to Passover.

Before proceeding, remember that no single pattern applies to New Testament worship. Its fluidity is its chief characteristic. By the close of the New Testament, however, the normative Sunday pattern of worship, whether in a home, an assembly hall, or out of doors, was probably eucharistic.

Worship in the Post–New Testament Period

It was less than 250 years from the time of the last writings in the New Testament until the legalization of Christianity under Emperor Constantine. This relatively short period of time saw radical changes in the shape of the church and its worship. From the point of view of our discussion, five important changes occurred:

1. The canon of the New Testament became, generally speaking, fixed in its present form, although with some modifications from one region to another.
2. A form of church government with bishops as chief officers became normative.
3. Women were gradually excluded from positions of authority.
4. Creeds were written and enforced to combat heresy within the church and persecution from without.
5. Fixed forms of worship developed. Applications of these forms still varied, but a movement toward standardization began.

Very little was actually written down about the ways these early Christians worshiped, and only fragments of liturgical texts remain. Two reasons for this lack of documentation of early worship are that: (1) periods of persecution required that the church keep its life secret, and (2) fluidity remained a hallmark of the shape of the church's practice.

The texts that do exist come from the end of the first century and the early second century. Clement's Letter to the Corinthians (A.D. 96–100) referred to the offering of sacrifices in the elements of the Lord's Supper. He also mentions the use of the "Sanctus" ("Holy, Holy, Holy") as part of the liturgy. In A.D. 112, Pliny, the Proconsul of Bythinia, in a letter to Emperor Trajan asked what to do about the people called "Christian." In his letter, he described their behavior: they would meet before dawn on a fixed day of the week, sing a hymn to Christ their god, and bind themselves by a "sacramentum" or oath to do no wrong. Then, he wrote, later that day they would meet again for a meal together. At about the same time, Ignatius, the bishop of Antioch, wrote letters to churches in which he mentioned that Sunday, the first day, had been chosen to take the place of the Sabbath, the seventh day. Christians were clearly breaking from their Jewish roots.

Sometime between A.D. 130 and 150, *The Teaching of the Twelve Apostles*, or *Didache*, was written. This document was lost in history, not recovered until 1875, and unknown to the Protestant Reformers. It gave directions for ordering the affairs of the church and contained a eucharistic prayer that included the words of institution from Paul's letter to the Corinthians (1 Cor. 11:23–26). At the time the *Didache* was written, the full meal was still included in worship, with separate prayers for the bread and cup at the beginning of the meal and a longer prayer at the end. The evidence of a meal shows the continuing power of the Passover service, which was also a meal. The *Didache* also warned that only the baptized should take part in the sacrament, and indicated that Wednesdays and Fridays were fast days.

In about A.D. 140, a Palestinian convert to Christianity named Justin described two types of worship found in Rome. One came after the annual initiation of the catechumens, and the other was held weekly. Justin wrote that on the Lord's Day, Christians gathered in one place, and the president, a person set apart, led them in worship. The service included reading from the prophets and from the "memoirs" of the apostles (probably the Gospels), an interpretation by the presider (a sermon), psalms and hymns, and a time of free prayer open to all participants. Then he writes:

> We salute one another with a kiss when we have ended the prayers. Then is brought to the president of the brethren bread and a cup of wine. And he takes them and offers up praise and glory to the Father of all things, through the name of the Son and of the Holy Ghost, and gives thanks at length that we are deemed worthy of these things at his hand. When he has completed the prayers and thanksgivings, all the people present assent by saying "Amen."[2]

Justin's writing indicates that the full meal (agape) was now clearly separated from the Eucharist. He also says, "We call this food 'eucharist.' " Thus, by now, eating and drinking were limited to those who believed and had been baptized. Deacons would distribute the elements to all who were present and carry them to the absent. Without any further explanation, Justin also says that the bread and wine are the flesh of Jesus.

In about A.D. 200, Irenaeus wrote that Christians were a priestly people who offered a new covenant sacrifice to God. Arguing in a tract against the Gnostics, he wrote: "When the bread from the earth receives the invocation of God, it is no longer common bread, but eucharist, having both an earthly and a heavenly reality."[3]

The most complete description of worship in the Roman Empire is from the theologian Hippolytus of Rome, in about A.D. 215, in *The Apostolic Tradition*. (Hippolytus was martyred in A.D. 235.) He identified two settings for the liturgy: one for the consecration of the bishop and another for the initiation of catechumens after their baptism. Although he included examples of prayers that might be used in these liturgies, he emphasized that the presider should not memorize them but should pray according to his own ability.[4]

Hippolytus' Great Prayer of Thanksgiving is in three parts: thanksgiving, remembering, and invoking of the Holy Spirit. These three parts of our present eucharistic prayer, in nearly all traditions, are thus very ancient. Hippolytus does not introduce them as a new idea but rather seems to assume that they are common in the Christian community.

According to Hippolytus, the passing of the peace preceded the Great Prayer. In the Easter liturgy he writes that three cups were consecrated: one of wine mixed with water to represent the blood of Christ on the cross, a second of milk mixed with honey to represent the land of promise now realized, and the third, that of water alone as a sign of baptism. Only the bishop gave the people the bread, but the deacons gave them the three cups.

We can see that the meal had, by this time, evolved from a full meal to a ritualistic meal with prayers that were becoming stylized but not yet set, except for the words of institution. The basic pattern or order of the service had also been established and now included

1. The great thanksgiving
2. Breaking of bread
3. Reception of bread and cup by all

A form of priesthood had also emerged, although the congregation still participated in the prayers and dialogues and responded with spoken "Amens."

The Legalization of Christianity

In A.D. 313, the Emperor Constantine lifted the legal ban against Christian worship, and Christians were free to worship in public. In A.D. 321, Constantine declared that Sunday was a day of rest, which meant that Christians could extend their services for as long as they desired. In 380, Emperor Theodosius proclaimed Christianity as the official religion of the Roman Empire. Christian worship, almost at once, became a state ritual as well as a religious ritual. Once Christianity was legalized, changes in worship occurred quickly, and great crowds began to pour into the churches. Some Christians, especially those who had been imprisoned or tortured during the earlier persecutions, were shocked at how easily the church seemed to accommodate itself to these new converts and how little was demanded of them as penance. Some very serious souls retreated into the wilderness to escape what they perceived as the worldliness and secularization of the church.

Most Christians, however, stayed within the church and were happy with the changes. The church became rich from the offerings of the faithful, and church interiors showed signs of that increasing wealth. Walls were painted with great frescoes and mosaics, marble altars took the place of simple tables, and jeweled crosses replaced wooden ones. Ritual and symbol assumed an increasingly important educational function and thus became even more important. As the knowledge of Greek declined and the Christian faith spread throughout the Empire, the liturgy was translated into a number of different languages.

In the West, the change in language brought changes in the name of the liturgy. The service was sometimes known as "the offering" because of the offering of the prayers and gifts of bread and wine. Another designation for the service was "*missarum solemnia*" or the ceremony of dismissals, which referred to the dismissal of the catechumens after the sermon and the dismissal of the rest of the people after Communion. Eventually, this term was abbreviated to simply the one word, "mass," which became commonly used, even though by the fifth century everyone in southern Europe had been baptized and the dismissal of catechumens had been dropped.

Ambrose, bishop of Milan from 374 to 397, in his sermons on the sacraments, included actual prayers whose form appears to have been quite set. He wrote that the bread and wine in Communion are only bread and wine before the words of institution are said, but after the words are spoken they are the body and blood of Christ.[5] Ambrose explains no further how this happens, but his clear emphasis is upon the power of the spoken words. Augustine of Hippo in his *Sermons* echoes the same theme: that the bread on the altar is sanctified by the word of God and thus is the body of Christ.

Augustine was the first to clearly define a sacrament as a visible sign of an invisible (or inward) reality. He said a visible sign resembles the thing it signifies and is thus given the name of the thing. Augustine maintained that a sign must be identified by a word spoken about it, which makes it a visible word.

In the East, Cyril of Jerusalem did not emphasize the importance of the words of institution but instead put the center of liturgical action at the point at which the Holy Spirit is invoked. To Cyril, the prayer for God's spirit was the locus of the power that transforms the bread and wine and sanctifies them.

Thus, an early difference between Eastern and Western forms of Christianity is that in the West the power was focused on the word spoken and in the East upon the invocation of the Holy Spirit.

In the Western church, the missionary movement to northern Europe made no concessions to local languages. Unlike the Eastern Orthodox churches, which translated the Bible and liturgies into the Slavic languages of the people, Western missionaries continued to use the unfamiliar Latin in worship, and as a result, the Mass became for most people, a performance they watched rather than a liturgy in which they participated. Even in Italy, the spoken language was no longer Latin, so the liturgy was said on behalf of the people rather than with them.

A new development in the West was the rise of the private mass, offered by a solitary priest with no congregation present. This practice began in the monasteries and in the mission territories to which the monks traveled. Originally, the monasteries were lay institutions, and visiting priests led the liturgy for the lay brothers, but in the sixth century, the missionary monks were ordained. Soon monasteries became filled with many priests who could not all gather about the altar to celebrate the liturgy together, so those who wanted to celebrate were forced to do so privately.

The differences between Eastern and Western Christianity developed gradually, but as time went on the two forms became increasingly distinct. In the East, the vernacular was used and the congregation participated in verbal responses and Amens to the prayers of the deacon. There were no solitary masses, and the invocation of the Holy Spirit became the key to Eastern spirituality, which was centered in prayer more than in scripture. Both bread and wine were given to the people, and a sense of mystery was maintained, partly by the use of the iconostasis (a screen composed of icons), which separated the celebrant from the people rather like the Holy of Holies in ancient Israel.

In the West, by contrast, the use of Latin was normative and the people became little more than spectators; the Mass became a priestly matter in which the people were not necessary. Only the bread was given to the people for fear they would spill the wine and thus desecrate the blood of Christ. The centrality of the words of institution kept the focus at a rational level. The theme of the Mass centered on the crucifixion, and thus the mood was somber, even funereal.

The Theology of Holy Communion

The theology as well as the practice of the Eucharist slowly changed. The Mass was understood to represent the redemptive death of Christ and, in some mysterious way, to reenact it. But opinion differed on the specifics. Some scholars insisted that the real flesh and blood of Christ must be physically present on the altar during the Mass. By the power of the words of institution, the bread and wine were changed into the body and blood of the incarnate Christ.

Others were careful not to be so absolute about this matter. Yet, nearly everyone insisted that faith was central to the experience of this spiritual reality. One person might spiritually eat the flesh and drink the blood of Christ because of faith, while another would not because of the lack of trust.

Berengar of Tours, in the middle of the eleventh century, challenged this interpretation of Christ's presence and offered his own explanation. To Berengar, things were what they appeared to be, and since the bread and wine did not change their appearance after the words of institution, they must still be bread and wine. Therefore, Christ's presence had to be a spiritual presence, not a physical presence. Berengar used Augustine's definition of a sacrament as a "sign of a sacred reality" to support his position, arguing that the bread and wine were signs of Christ's body and blood, not identical with it.[6] In 1059 a council of bishops cited Berengar for heresy; he was forced to sign an oath admitting that the bread and wine are not only the sacrament but also the true body and blood of Christ and that they are taken by the hands of the priest and torn by the teeth of the faithful, not simply as a sacrament but as a reality.

The development of this theology led to an increased sense of reverence for the elements. For a long time, some of the bread had been reserved in a cupboard near the altar as food for the journey into the next world and was carried to the dying. Bishops had been accustomed to bowing toward the reserved sacrament before beginning the liturgy. Now, priests began to genuflect in reverence whenever they passed in front of the altar to give the reserved sacrament more reverence. The sacrament was placed in a tabernacle on the altar and a light was kept lit to remind people who entered the space that Christ was present. Priests were required to genuflect every time they touched the host. Since, it was reasoned, Christ was equally present in both bread and wine, priests stopped giving the wine to the people out of fear of spilling even a drop and thus desecrating Christ's body.

In the twelfth century, the scholastics—scholars who were skilled in the use of logic—began to examine the theology and practical issues surrounding the sacrament, including questions such as, "At what point in the Mass does the sacrifice take place?" and "How are the bread and wine changed into the body and blood of Christ?" The scholastics proposed three different explanations:

1. According to one view, the substance of Christ was added to the material elements when the words of consecration were spoken. This view came to be known as "consubstantiation" since both realities were present together.
2. Others appealed to the idea that two substances could not occupy the same space. During the consecration, therefore, they argued, the bread and wine are annihilated by the power of God and the body and blood of Christ take their place. Critics of this idea noted that the elements still looked like bread and wine.

3. A third view, known as "transubstantiation" and using Aristotelian philosophy as its starting point, taught that a substance was anything that could exist on its own; it was a reality in its own right. Living things were substances, but their size, shape, and color were not substances because they could not exist on their own but were rather accidental properties that could change. Sometimes these properties of appearance changed, as when a person gained weight or a leaf turned color. Sometimes, though, substances themselves changed from one thing to another, as when a person died and became a corpse, or when wood burned and turned into ash, or when flour and water turned into bread. In the natural world, substance changes involved changes in the accidental properties as well.

Transubstantiation insisted that during the Mass, the substance of the bread and wine changed into the substance, or reality, of Christ's body and blood. The visible properties or accidents did not change, making for a unique instance in which the substance changed but the properties remained the same. When, for example, wood changed to ash, all the properties also changed and when green leaves turned color and fell from a tree, their properties changed. Transubstantiation accepted the commonly held belief that Christ was present in the sacrament, but did not have to explain how Christ could fit into the elements or how he could be both in heaven and on the altar. The change was not physical but metaphysical; that is, the change occurred in the reality that could be perceived by faith even if not perceived by the senses.

Thomas Aquinas was the most important interpreter of transubstantiation. For him, the consecrated elements were both sacrament and reality since they both signified the body and blood of Christ and were, in fact, that which they signified. The church accepted Aquinas's teaching, which became orthodox doctrine. In reality, most people neither appreciated nor understood the subtleties of Aquinas's philosophical reasoning, but simply believed by faith that the elements had been transformed.

In any case, the awe surrounding the elements was so great that most common people feared that receiving communion might bring damnation upon them if they ate unworthily. People began attending mass without communing, and the church had to urge them to take communion at least once a year at Easter, when receiving the bread was understood to be one's Easter duty. In 1415, the Council of Constance defended giving only the bread to the people and also replaced real bread with wafers that could be placed directly on the tongue, all of this to avoid the sin of spilling the body and blood of Christ.

By the time of the Protestant Reformation, the Mass in the West had become a priestly action, a miracle in which Christ was believed to be actually present, a performance or reenactment of Christ's sacrifice, and a spiritual benefit for those who did not even attend. Thus masses that provided grace could be said on behalf of the sick or even the dead.

In reaction to what they saw as the excesses of a theology that overemphasized the sacredness of the elements of bread and wine, the Protestant Reformers tried to return to what they understood was a biblical pattern for Communion. They insisted that the people had to be present and participate in worship and sought to make the sacrament more like a meal. The common agenda for the Reformation was closely tied to a call for new thinking about the sacrament that was more clearly connected to the biblical accounts.

3

From the Reformation to Today

The Protestant Reformation of the sixteenth century comprised a series of events that together brought about the division of Western Christianity into Protestantism and Roman Catholicism. The events that gave birth to this split in the church included: (1) protest against a powerful church, which many sensitive people began to see as corrupt beyond hope; (2) a struggle for independence from the central power of Rome by monarchs throughout Europe; and (3) a challenge to the theological underpinnings of the Roman Catholic sacramental system made possible by the increase of learning in the Renaissance, serious study of scripture, and a recovery of the writings of some early church theologians. Some early Reformers predated the Reformation itself; the earliest was Peter Waldo, a French merchant who began preaching in the twelfth century and gathered a band of followers. Waldo was forbidden to preach by the archbishop of Lyon and was later excommunicated, but his followers continued the movement he began, moving to the Waldensian Valleys of Italy, where they became known as Waldensians. Later pre-Reformation leaders were Jan Hus (1372–1415) in Bohemia, and John Wycliffe (1330–1384) in England. Each began to protest against what he perceived as abuses of Roman Catholic power, and each was excommunicated and effectively silenced, leaving a scattering of followers to come after them. Martin Luther differed from these earlier Reformers only in that he succeeded, having been protected by a prince in Germany.

The usual dates set by many historians for the Reformation begin with the threat to excommunicate Martin Luther in 1520 and his actual excommunication on January 3, 1521, and end with the excommunication of Elizabeth I of England in 1570. This fifty-year period coincided with the invention of movable type in the printing press and the Renaissance, marked by a burst of new learning throughout Europe. The mid-sixteenth century was a time of extended and extensive criticism of the Catholic Church from within, and of reform efforts that sought to eliminate abuses of power by the clergy and the church hierarchy. At the same time, the unity of the Empire and papal authority were breaking apart, and the nation-states of Europe were developing. Monarchs, eager to achieve independence for themselves, often sided with the Reformers and used the Reformation for their own political purposes.

By the time the Reformation ended, Europe was divided into predominantly Roman Catholic countries: Spain, Portugal, Italy, Poland, and France; predominantly Protestant countries: Norway, Sweden, Denmark, Holland, and Great Britain; and countries divided by region or ethnic group such as Ireland, Switzerland, Hungary, and Germany. The new nation-states, whether Catholic or Protestant, were quite independent of papal power.

Nevertheless, the Reformation was primarily a movement seeking religious renewal, spiritual integrity, and an experiential relationship with Jesus Christ, without arbitrary interference from the institutional church or the clergy. The Reformers were eager to renew the worship of the church because they understood that public worship is the heart of the Christian life and that character of worship has a great deal to do with the way that life is nourished and sustained. Therefore, the Reformers, different though they were in many ways from one another, were united in their belief that worship had to be reformed.

Certain liturgical reforms were common to all the major Reformers:

1. Rejection of the doctrine of transubstantiation (as they understood it) and, thus, the adoration of the elements.
2. Restoration of the practice of giving the cup to the people.
3. Use of the language of the people (vernacular) in worship.
4. The centrality of the reading and preaching of the Word.
5. Elimination of private masses; congregational participation was necessary for worship.
6. Regular and frequent Communion by the people.

Despite this wide liturgical agreement, the Reformers disagreed with each other about theological matters and about the government of the church, so that the Reformation produced distinct branches and was never a unified movement. At times, for instance, Lutheran and Reformed Protestants fought with each other, and both of them fought against the Anabaptists.

Martin Luther (1483–1546)

Martin Luther's *The Babylonian Captivity of the Church* was probably the single most important document of the Reformation, and it determined the basic outline of all Protestant thought about worship. Most of what Luther said was not disputed by other Reformers, and was taken for granted by Calvin in Switzerland, Bucer in Germany, and Cranmer in England, among others.

Luther extended to the subject of worship his insistence upon grace as a free gift not earned through any human effort, and he was very critical of the medieval sacramental system. He saw the sacraments as a means of human achievement whereby believers earned grace for themselves, and he finally came to reject four altogether as not genuine: confirmation, ordination, marriage, and extreme unction. He concluded that they did not meet the qualifications of a sacrament for three reasons:

1. Jesus did not institute them nor command them of his disciples.
2. They did not apply equally to all believers.
3. They did not act out the central meaning of the gospel.

Luther denied any essential difference between clergy and laity and stressed the priesthood of all believers. Ordination, he believed, conferred no special power or indelible character and was for functional purposes only. This position undercut the role of the priest as the one who plays a sacrificial role in the Mass at the same time that it elevated the role of baptism as a kind of ordination into the priesthood of all believers, who were to serve each other. Luther wrote:

> Why could not Christ confine his body within the substance of bread, just as in the accidents? Fire and iron are two substances, yet they are so mingled in red-hot iron that any part is at once iron and fire. What prevents the glorious body of Christ from being in every part of the substance of bread?[1]

Seeking to find a way to speak about the mystery of God's action, Luther settled upon the ancient teaching of consubstantiation: the body and blood are fully within the bread and wine (in, with, and under the elements). The power of the Word makes this happen, for God's word is always true, and when the words are spoken they must be accepted with a believing heart and not subjected to unnecessary speculation.

The risen Christ shares in the character of God who is everywhere at once; thus Christ can be ubiquitous, everywhere at one time, in heaven at the right hand of God and on earth in every crumb of the bread of the Mass. Luther insisted upon the real presence, but he also believed that this presence is not realized except as the people partake of the elements by faith. Christ's presence in the elements is not a miracle apart from faith.

In 1521, Luther appeared at the Castle Church of Wittenberg without vestments and performed a purified Mass without the liturgy of consecration and elevation of the elements, in German, and with both bread and wine given to the people. This radical action produced a storm of activity because many people believed that Luther had cast his lot in favor of a radical reformation. When the response to his action became violent and people smashed statues, Luther backed away from his radical stance and preached moderation. He said we must distinguish between what is commanded in scripture and what is left free for us to decide (pictures, images, fasting, vestments, etc.). Liturgy provides order and stability, which were important for Luther in a time of potential social chaos. Because scripture provides no clear rubrics, we must exercise freedom with cautious responsibility.

In spite of Luther's counsel, some of his followers continued their excesses, and so, in 1523, in part to curb these excesses, he issued instructions on the Order of Worship:

1. There should be no worship without a sermon.
2. Daily services of the Word should be added to the weekly Mass.
3. The congregation must be present and participate in worship.
4. Hymnody should be written and sung by the people.
5. The people must notify the minister and be examined in their faith if they intend to take Communion.

Luther drew a distinction between worship as sacrifice and worship as God's gracious gift in Christ. The one-time sacrifice of Christ is sufficient for all time. Any notion of sacrifice on the part of the people implies both an angry God and the idea that people could earn God's favor by works of righteousness.

In the German Mass of 1532, Luther retained some elements of the medieval Mass: the vestments, altars, candles, and images. He believed that, so as not to disturb the faith of people who depended upon these external helps, they should remain for a time, but ultimately the altar would be moved out from the wall and would then become a table. As a monk who was steeped in the medieval Mass, Luther prized a sense of the historic continuity of the Mass throughout the ages, and he maintained that too much innovation is difficult for weaker believers.

Luther's major liturgical reforms were

1. The elimination of the offertory
2. An extensive paraphrase of the Lord's Prayer
3. An exhortation for right reception replacing the preface in the order for the Mass
4. The elimination of the prayer of consecration in the service for Communion; only the words of institution were spoken as the elements were distributed

Huldreich Zwingli (1484–1531)

Huldreich, or Ulrich, Zwingli was the first Swiss reformer. His powerful personality had a tremendous impact upon the Reformation in German-speaking Switzerland and beyond. He was a humanist scholar who had great faith in the scripture as the ground of all human activity. As a preacher and organizer, he set the agenda for the Reformation in Switzerland as "reformed, always being reformed according to the Word of God." Upon his arrival in Zurich, Zwingli observed a liturgical practice that was common to southwest Germany and German-speaking Switzerland, the Prone or Pronaus. Conducted before the mass, the Prone was a short service in the vernacular that centered upon a sermon on the gospel.

Ulrich Surgant, a priest in Basel where Zwingli had studied, had published a Prone service in 1506. Zwingli adopted this service from 1519 to 1523 in Zurich but changed the liturgical Gospel of the lectionary to a method of preaching consecutively from one Gospel at a time, returning to the ancient practice of Augustine and other early church figures. He did not change the Mass itself; perhaps, as a priest, he was reluctant to part with the form of the Latin Mass to which he was deeply attached.

In 1523, a few months before publication of Luther's *Formula Missae*, Zwingli published his first work on worship, *An Attack on the Canon of the Mass*. In it he wrote of his opposition to sacrifice and presented the alternative idea of remembrance, which is central to his theology of the Eucharist. We remember, he argued, an act that took place on the cross once and for all. We do not, in any way, repeat that act, which was a unique and singular act of God on our behalf.

Zwingli rejected transubstantiation and insisted that eating and drinking was an occasion for believers to reaffirm their faith:

> And when in the thanksgiving, in company with the congregation, you partake of the two elements of bread and wine, all that you do is to confess publicly that you believe in the Lord Jesus Christ; . . . to feed on him is simply to believe on him.[2]

The principal difference between Zwingli and both Luther and Calvin was that Zwingli drew a line of separation between the physical and the spiritual. He believed that nothing in the physical world could be a manifestation of the spiritual, and he wrote, "No external element or action can purify the soul."[3]

For Zwingli, the only means of grace was the Word. The Lord's Supper was not a means of grace or even a norm for worship but another method of applying the Word to our hearts, a method of teaching us by dramatic action. The key is remembrance of something essential that Jesus did. In fact, Zwingli believed there was a certain danger in the sacrament, for it might lead to super-stitious dependence upon the physical objects of bread and wine as signs to point to the divine. Therefore, for Zwingli, quarterly observance was suffi-cient, for it preserved the memorial aspect without fostering dependence.

In 1525 he published *Action or Use of the Lord's Supper,* in which he declared that the Lord's Supper was to be celebrated only on the three great Christian festivals of Christmas, Easter, and Pentecost, and on the festival of the patron saints of Zurich, Sts. Felix and Regula (September 11).

On Easter Sunday of that year, Zwingli celebrated a revised Communion service that was cleansed of all the elements to which he objected. The emphasis in the service was upon the sharing of the bread and cup by all the people who were gathered around the table set up in the nave. Ministers faced the people across the table, wearing black academic gowns, not as priests, but as fellow members of the Body of Christ. The people recited the Gloria, the Creed, and Psalm 113 (Hallel Psalm). There was an exhortation for the right reception of the gifts and a prayer for the people's faith, but no prayer of con-secration nor other words were spoken when the bread and wine were dis-tributed. The reading of the words of institution was followed by silence. The people remained seated, passing the elements to one another while an assis-tant read from the Gospel of John, chapter 13. This dramatic, innovative service had great power and quickly became normative for the quarterly celebrations in Zurich.

Zwingli's distrust of the material world led in 1524 to the cleansing of the Zurich churches, disposing of relics, whitewashing paintings, removing stat-ues, discarding vestments, and removing the pipe organs. There was to be no more music. People were to hear the Word only. Nothing physical was to detract from the Word.

Zwingli also introduced a new Sunday service that same year (1525), which became the weekly norm. Centered upon sermon and scripture, the service, like the Prone, was completely disconnected from the Eucharist. The service had no music; silence and simplicity set the mood, but oddly it preserved the Hail Mary and the commemoration of the dead. Zwingli's service ended with the Confes-sion of Sin and Pardon as a response to the hearing of the Word. He maintained that we dare not confess until we have heard the gracious promise of the gospel.

In summary, Zwingli's significance for Reformed worship was fivefold:

1. He separated Communion from the normal Sunday worship.
2. His services set forth the centrality of remembrance for Communion: it is a memorial.
3. He abandoned the lectionary in favor of reading entire books of the Bible in sequence *(Lectio continuo).*
4. He rejected the physical world as revelatory or able to convey the spiritual, and thus he rejected visual symbolism (only the Word was salvific).

5. He was rigorously theological; even prayers were precise theological state-ments rather than simple devout petitions; that is, they were didactic rather than devotional.

Conflict between Zwingli and Luther

Zwingli's ideas shocked Martin Luther; they sounded to him like those of Anabaptist spiritualizers, dissolving the objective character of the sacrament into subjective experience. In a sermon on the sacrament, Luther insisted that the real presence is essential; he insisted that we must believe Christ's words, "This is my body."

In 1529, Luther and Zwingli, with several of their colleagues, met in Mar-burg, and though the two sides reached agreement on fourteen articles of faith—including justification by faith, the person of Christ, and the rejection of transubstantiation—they could not reach agreement on the issue of Christ's presence in the Lord's Supper. Their failure to agree set the division into Lutheran and Reformed branches of Protestantism.

The Strasbourg Reformers

In 1524, Diebold Schwarz, at the Cathedral of St. Lawrence in Strasbourg, celebrated a German Mass like the one Luther had proposed but had not as yet celebrated. The Mass was in German, the offertory was removed, all the prayers in the Canon that implied sacrifice were removed, and the people were given both bread and wine.

Schwarz's reformation of the Mass was more conservative than Luther's, but it began a process of change. It retained vestments and elevation of the host, but it introduced a congregational prayer of confession in place of the priest's *Confiteor* (Lat., "I confess"; the usual beginning of the confession in the Mass). The whole service was said audibly so that the people could hear and not depend upon the ceremonies to know what was going on.

Martin Bucer (1491–1551) moved from a Zwinglian pattern of worship to one that combined Luther's insights with those of other Reformers. In 1524 Bucer recommended a ritual like Zwingli's with some modifications, such as the inclusion of a declaration of pardon and the reading of the words of insti-tution. In 1539 he developed a more complete order of service that made Schwarz's German Mass into a more Protestant service by implementing the following changes:

1. He substituted the title "Lord's Supper" for "Mass."
2. He called the altar the "altar-table" or simply "table."
3. The priest became known as the parson or minister.
4. Vestments were abolished in favor of the academic gown.

5. The Gospel was read *Lectio continuo*, thus eliminating the lectionary.
6. The liturgical year was discontinued except for major festivals of Christ's life.
7. In place of the Offertory, he used Romans 12:1ff—"self-sacrifice" to replace the idea of the sacrifice of the elements.
8. Weekly Communion was the rule, but by 1538, a practice of Morning Prayer and Sermon was developed for the parish churches that only celebrated Communion monthly. The cathedral continued to practice weekly Communion.

This shift to monthly rather than weekly celebration was soon widely adopted. Why did it happen so quickly? For three reasons: (1) the strong and powerful influence of Zwingli, even after his death; (2) the long-standing custom in Roman Catholicism of infrequent Communion out of fear of damnation; and (3) enthusiasm about the power and centrality of preaching among newly literate people.

Bucer retained the historic structure of the Mass and the liturgy of the Communion service, even when Communion was not served. No separate and distinct order for morning worship without Communion developed, as Zwingli had maintained. The significance of this action was to establish the Lord's Supper as normative even when it was not being served, and to remind everyone of the centrality of the Lord's Supper.

A number of Bucer's guiding principles strongly influenced Calvin:

1. The belief that sharing of the bread and cup by the whole people of God is the heart of the Communion service. The emphasis is more upon the sharing than consecrating.
2. The idea of Communion as a covenant meal that binds the whole community together under a common discipline.
3. The words of institution proclaimed as promises of the gospel rather than as a formula for consecration.
4. The idea that the sermon and sacrament belong together.

Bucer began the order of Communion with a corporate confession of sin. The Decalogue followed the pardon or absolution, not to convict people of sin, but to bring the faithful to true piety and to teach people who have been forgiven how to live as Christians. The prayer for illumination came before the reading/preaching of scripture. Bucer distinguished between the "external" word and the "internal" word that can only be heard through the action of the Holy Spirit. The Creed was sung after the sermon as a response to the Word and as a sign of commitment leading to the sacrament. Prayers of intercession followed the Creed and were part of the consecration prayer.

Bucer focused the Great Prayer of Thanksgiving on the consecration of the people rather than the elements of bread and wine; he prayed that the people might receive the goodness of God with faith.

> Grant that we may yield ourselves with whole hearts and a true faith to Thy Son, our only Redeemer and Savior; and forasmuch as He hath not only offered His body and blood unto Thee upon the Cross for our sin, but willeth also to give it unto us for food and drink unto eternal life, grant that we, with our whole eager desire and true devotion may receive His goodness and gift and with true faith partake of and enjoy His True Body and True Blood.[4]

Communion was received kneeling or standing, the people going forward to and gathering about the Lord's Table.

John Calvin (1509–1564)

John Calvin was the product of Renaissance humanism. He was educated at the University of Paris and studied law at Orleans and Bourges. When he arrived in Geneva in 1536, the Genevan reformer Guillaume Farel had already simplified Zwingli's preaching service and made it normative for each Sunday. Farel also had adopted Zwingli's method of preaching through whole books of the Bible in sequence, thereby abandoning most of the liturgical calendar in order to give continuity in preaching, treating each passage in its full context. He preached from the Gospels on Sundays and from the Old Testament and the Epistles on weekdays. For a congregation of biblically illiterate people, this method of preaching was of great educational value.

Calvin was unhappy with the divorce that had taken place between Word and Sacrament and wanted to restore the Eucharist to its centrality in worship and to its primitive simplicity. In 1538 the Council expelled Calvin and Farel for their political activities in support of such changes, and Calvin moved to Strasbourg. There Bucer gave Calvin permission to conduct the sacrament monthly in the French refugee congregation. He translated Bucer's service into French, making some adaptations in the process:

1. He introduced a long paraphrase of the Lord's Prayer.
2. He had the Decalogue sung in meter, with the *Kyrie* sung after each Commandment.
3. He had the *Nunc Dimittis* sung after Communion.
4. He "fenced the Table" (that is, announced who could receive the sacrament) after a long exhortation.
5. He adapted Farel's "Reformed *Sursum Corda*" to read:

   Therefore, lift up your heart on high, seeking the heavenly things in heaven, where Jesus Christ is seated at the right hand of the Father, and do not fix your eyes on the visible signs, which are corrupted through usage.[5]

In 1541 Calvin, no longer out of political favor, returned to Geneva and in 1542 produced a Genevan service that was a simplified version of the Strasbourg rite. As a compromise with the Genevan magistrates, he omitted the words of absolution and substituted an assurance of pardon; he also omitted the sung Decalogue and *Kyrie*, placed the words of institution before the consecration prayer as scriptural warrant for the sacrament, instead of after, and added the *Nunc Dimittis*, sung in meter.

While in Strasbourg, Calvin had published eighteen psalms and three canticles. Now he used the talents of musicians Louis Bourgeois and Claude Goudimel (Palestrina's teacher) and the poetic ability of Clement Marot to prepare an expanded psalter. Psalm singing has been a mark of Reformed worship from that time on.

In the *Institutes*, he outlined his liturgical goal that "the Supper could have been administered most becomingly if it were set before the church very often, and at least once a week" (*Institutes* IV.xvii.43), and he proposed a particular order of worship:

1. The service "should begin with public prayers (said or sung)."
2. After this, a sermon should be given.
3. Then when the bread and wine have been placed on the table, the minister should repeat the words of institution of the Supper.
4. Next he should recite the promises that were left to us; he should excommunicate all who are debarred. He should pray that the Lord teach and form us to receive this sacred food with faith and thankfulness of heart and make us worthy of such a feast. Here psalms should be sung or something read, and in a seemly order the believers should partake of the most holy banquet, the ministers breaking the bread and giving the cup.
5. When the Supper is finished, there should be an exhortation to sincere faith and confession of faith, to love and behavior worthy of Christians.
6. At the last, thanks should be given and praises sung to God.
7. "When these things are ended, the church should be dismissed in peace" (IV.xvii.43).

Calvin continued to urge frequent celebration of the sacrament:

It was not ordained to be received only once a year, rather it was ordained to be frequently used among all Christians in order that they might frequently return in memory to Christ's passion, by such remembrance to sustain and strengthen their faith and urge themselves to sing thanksgiving to God and to proclaim his goodness; finally by it to nourish mutual love, and among themselves give witness to this love, and discern its bond in the unity of Christ's body (IV.xvii.44).

In spite of his urgings, Calvin was never able to gain support for weekly Communion. The fear of eating and drinking to one's damnation lingered in spite of his efforts to teach otherwise, and the power of preaching was so inspiring that the people wanted to hear more. Although he tried to rotate Communion services among the different churches of Geneva, monthly Communion was the best that Calvin could achieve.

Calvin brought the bread and wine to the table during the singing of the Creed (Great Entrance) so as to represent the gifts of the people and also to avoid exposing the elements to the people until the Word had validated the sacrament. He sought to avoid adoration of the elements. Reading the words of institution before the prayer of consecration is a significant symbol. Calvin believed that in both of the sacraments, Christ's command to "do this" is central. We obey him in observing these sacraments.

Calvin tried to stand between what he saw as Luther's literalism and Zwingli's memorialism. In his *Short Treatise on the Lord's Supper* (1540) he commented on the conflict between Lutheran and Reformed: "I could wish that the memory of it could be quite abolished, so far am I from desiring to relate it at length."[6] He defended Luther:

> [w]hile condemning transubstantiation, he said that the bread was the body of Christ, insofar as it was united with him. Further, he added some similes which were a little harsh and rude. But he did so as by constraint, because he could not otherwise explain his meaning. For it is difficult to give an explanation of so high a matter, without some impropriety of speech.[7]

But he could also criticize Luther:

> It was Luther's duty in the first place, to make it clear that he did not intend to set up such a local presence as the papists imagine; second, he should have protested that he did not mean the sacrament to be adored in stead of God; and third, he should have abstained from the similies so harsh and difficult to conceive.[8]

He also criticized Zwingli, who he said, "tried hard to protect and preserve the risen and ascended Christ but "forgot to define what is the presence of Christ in the supper in which one ought to believe. . . . So Luther thought that he intended nothing else but bare signs without any corresponding spiritual substance."[9]

> The others [Zwingli and followers] offended also by being so eager to decry the contrary opinion of the papists concerning the local presence of the body of Jesus Christ . . . that they labored more to destroy the evil than to build up the good; . . . they took no care to make the

reservation that the bread and wine are such signs that the reality is joined to them.[10]

Calvin concludes his efforts to seek a middle way by saying:

> On the one hand we must, to shut out all carnal fancies, raise our hearts on high to heaven, not thinking that our Lord Jesus Christ is so abased as to be enclosed under any corruptible elements. On the other hand, not to diminish the efficacy of this sacred mystery, we must hold that it is accomplished by the secret and miraculous virtue of God, and that the Spirit of God is the bond of participation, for which reason it is called spiritual. . . . We all confess then, with one mouth that, in receiving the sacrament in faith, according to the ordinance of the Lord, we are truly made partakers of the real substance of the body and blood of Jesus Christ.[11]

Calvin's theology of the Eucharist reflects his appreciation of the importance of signs. No one, he argued, can fully understand the mystery of how Christ is united with human beings. That mystical union is, by its very nature, beyond our understanding. But, out of divine graciousness, God provides us with visible signs as a way of accommodating our weakness and limited capacity. The sacramental elements are signs that provide visible means of God's love whereby "God imparts spiritual things under visible ones." Calvin sought to guard against two potential faults:

> First, we should not, by too little regard for the signs, divorce them from their mysteries, to which they are so to speak attached. Second, we should not, by extolling them immoderately seem to obscure somewhat the mysteries themselves. (*Institutes* IV.xvii.5)

For clarification, Calvin referred to the Words of Institution as a *metonymy*, "a figure of speech commonly used in scripture when mysteries are under discussion" (IV.xvii.21). In that sense, he could say that circumcision is a covenant, the lamb is the Passover, the sacrifices of the law are expiations. "Not only is the name transferred from something higher to something lower, but, on the other hand, the name of the visible sign is also given to the thing signified, as when God is said to have appeared to Moses in the bush" (IV.xvii.21). He sums up this meaning: "Our souls are fed by the flesh and blood of Christ in the same way that bread and wine keep and sustain physical life, for the analogy of the sign applies only if souls find their nourishment in Christ—which cannot happen unless Christ truly grows into one with us, and refreshes us by the eating of his flesh and the drinking of his blood" (IV.xvii.10).

The mystery is made possible, not by human words or actions, but by the power of the Holy Spirit "until our minds are intent upon the Spirit. Christ is in a manner unemployed, because we view him coldly without us and at a distance from us. . . . [I]t is by the Spirit alone that he unites himself to us" (III.i.3). He wishes to respect the ascension of Christ into heaven and affirms the words of the "Reformed *Sursum Corda*" by saying that we must be lifted up to heaven with our eyes and minds, to seek Christ there in the glory of his kingdom. Even though Christ has ascended, his heavenly kingdom is bounded by location or space. "Thus Christ is not prevented from exerting his power wherever he pleases, in heaven and on earth. He shows his presence in power and strength, is always among his own people, and breathes his life upon them, and lives in them, sustaining them, strengthening, quickening, keeping them unharmed, as if he were present in the body. In short, he feeds his people with his own body, the communion of which he bestows upon them by the power of his Spirit" (IV.xvii.18). This emphasis upon the Spirit's work avoids the tendency in the Western church to place a literal emphasis upon the words of institution and borrows from the Eastern church the emphasis upon the Spirit as central to the action.

To Calvin, it is not so much that Christ is present *on* the table as with us *at* the table. The Spirit makes Christ present by sanctifying us, by raising us up to where Christ is. In the sacrament, our hearts are lifted up (*Sursum Corda*) and we come into the presence of Christ.

Calvin's theology of the Lord's Supper is unique. It stands between Luther's and Zwingli's but is closer to Luther's because of the emphasis upon the mystery of what happens for believers as they take part. In the Reformed tradition, however, the Zwinglian position most often prevailed, and the sense of holy mystery was lost to a rational explanation that went far beyond Zwingli.

In summary, the *differences between Calvin and Zwingli* regarding worship are as follows:

1. Zwingli had two different services: one for regular weekly preaching and another for occasional (quarterly) Communion. Calvin designed one basic service that terminated at a certain point when the sacrament was not served (a so-called "dry" Communion because Communion was not actually served).
2. Zwingli had no music, while Calvin encouraged the writing and singing of music.
3. Zwingli did away with the historic structure of the Mass. Calvin kept that structure but modified it.
4. Zwingli believed that eating and drinking meant believing that Christ died for us and was a memorial act of faith. Calvin believed that eating and drinking mystically united us to Christ through the power of the Holy Spirit, so that Christ actually becomes one with us, a real presence.

The Development
of the Liturgy in English

For most American Protestants, the British Isles were the crucial place where the faith, as we have come to know it, was shaped. Most American Protestant denominations, with the exception of the Lutherans and Continental Reformed denominations such as the Dutch Reformed, trace their origins to Great Britain.

Henry VIII of England was not particularly interested in religion, and he was not at all sympathetic to the Protestant Reformation. In fact, he had proudly claimed the title "Defender of the Faith," given to him by the Pope for his opposition to Protestantism. Yet, Henry was a crucial figure in the development of British Protestantism. He intended only a political reformation, to take upon himself the authority that he wanted to exercise over the church and to replace the Pope as head of the church. In this, he was part of the rising nationalism throughout Europe. But whatever his motives, he set in motion a movement that could not be stopped.

In 1533, Henry appointed Thomas Cranmer as Archbishop of Canterbury, little imagining what the impact would be. He sent Cranmer as his ambassador to the court of Charles V of the Holy Roman Empire, where Cranmer observed the Lutheran Reformation in practice, especially in Nuremberg. Cranmer married Margaret Osiander, the niece of Andreas Osiander, who was Luther's theologian in residence. Cranmer brought her back to England, and he also brought the influence of the Reformation home with him.

Upon Henry's death in 1547, his son Edward VI became ruler of England. Because of his youth, political authority in England devolved to prominent Lords who exercised the power of the throne and who were strongly Protestant in their sentiments. During the reign of Edward (1547–1553) the work of Cranmer became most important. By 1547, Cranmer had already come to the conviction that the church needed a reformation of worship, and in 1549 he produced the first *Book of Common Prayer,* which was to replace the Latin Mass of the Roman Catholic Church. In writing this first English prayer book, he used the so-called "Great Bible" as the standard. This Great Bible, an English translation, had been authorized by Henry in 1538.

With his first *Book of Common Prayer,* Cranmer wanted a liturgy that could be understood by all believers. He attempted to provide an English Protestantized version of the Mass, preserving the essentials of the Mass while translating them into English, even as he made clear his acceptance of the key Protestant principle of the necessity for understanding the liturgy. In the preface to the first edition, he set forth four mandates:

1. The whole Bible should be read in continuity.
2. The Bible should be read in English (the language of the people).

3. Rules and ceremonials were to be reduced and simplified, especially those ceremonies that Cranmer believed were out of keeping with scripture, such as the elevation of the host and prayers to the saints and the blessed Virgin.
4. Uniformity in worship was to be established and one single liturgy used throughout the country. (This was, after all, to be a national church that supported the monarchy.)

Cranmer's "purified" Mass did away with holy water, the veneration of images, the doctrine of purgatory, and the invocation of the saints, and it reintroduced Communion in both kinds (giving both the bread and cup to the people—also a Reformation principle). One other important innovation, which remains to this day a unique feature of Anglican worship, is the daily office of morning and evening prayer, which involved the recitation of the Psalter and the reading of the rest of the Bible according to a greatly simplified church calendar. The central act of public worship was to be the sacrament of Holy Communion, which was to be celebrated on Sundays and festival days and perhaps even more often (also a Reformation principle).

The *Book of Common Prayer* was more strongly influenced by the Calvinist Reformation than the Lutheran. The progress of the Reformation in England benefited from a setback for the Reformation on the continent. The Roman Catholic Emperor Charles won control of some parts of Germany where Protestantism had been secure, and Protestant refugees poured into England, bringing their faith with them. Among those refugees who fled to England and exercised considerable influence were Martin Bucer, Valeran Poullain (Calvin's successor in Strasbourg), and John A'Lasco, a Polish nobleman and a Zwinglian. Cranmer's first edition of the prayer book retained some ceremonials with which Calvin would not have been comfortable. Almost as soon as the prayer book was printed, Cranmer, concerned about Roman Catholic interpretations, began to work on a more strongly Protestant version. Yet even in this first edition, the prayer of consecration departed from the Latin Mass in one important way: Instead of asking that the bread and wine *become* the body and blood of Christ, it asked that the bread and wine *become for us* the body and blood of Christ.

In 1550 and 1551, Calvin's two French services, those of Strasbourg and Geneva, were translated into English, aiding the Reformed influence upon Anglican worship. In 1552, Cranmer issued his second edition of the *Book of Common Prayer*, which was to become the substantive liturgy of Anglicans for many years. In it, Cranmer introduced Bucer's long exhortation before Communion and changed the rubrics so that the word "altar" became "table." The influence of the Scot John Knox, who had been the royal chaplain and who had opposed kneeling at the Lord's Supper, was felt in this second edition, in the introduction of the so-called "Black Rubric," which stated that, although kneeling was required for the sake of reverence and humility, kneeling to receive the elements implied no adoration of the elements nor transubstantiation.

Only one year later, in 1553, Mary Tudor (1516–1558) came to the throne and took immediate action to suppress the use of this new *Book of Common Prayer*. She removed Cranmer from office and had him imprisoned. In 1556 he was burned at the stake. In the purge that followed, Knox and other Reformers fled England and returned to the continent, most to Zurich, Geneva, or Frankfurt. Knox went to Geneva to minister to the English refugee congregation there, and in 1556 he produced his *Form of Prayers*, a version of Calvin's liturgy that became the basis for English Puritan worship.

Mary's reign was mercifully brief, though bloody. In 1558 she died, and her half-sister Elizabeth became queen. Knox returned to Scotland, not welcome in England because he had published a tract, "The Blast of the Trumpet against the Monstrous Reign of Women." Although it had been directed at Queen Mary, Elizabeth took offense and did not want him back.

In 1562 the Scottish Church adopted Knox's *Book of Common Order*, which grew out of his *Form of Prayers*. Despite his suggestion that Communion be monthly, the shortage of ministers soon made it necessary to reduce the requirement to four times each year. The church discarded the liturgical calendar and set the times for Communion for the first Sundays of March, June, September, and December. Two readings of scripture were to be read, the Old Testament and the New. Most of the service was to be conducted from the pulpit, probably to ensure that the minister could be heard.

When the people gathered for Communion, they sat at long tables set in either a 'T' shape or a 'U,' in either the chancel or the nave, but without any Zwinglian interpretation of the event. The Scots Confession made that clear: "And so, we utterly condemn the vanity of those who affirm the sacraments to be nothing else than naked and bare signs."[12] A positive view was stated: "Thus we confess and believe without doubt that the faithful, in the right use of the Lord's Table, do so eat the body and drink the blood of the Lord Jesus that he remains in them and they in him."[13]

Worship in Scotland always reflected the struggle of the Scottish people for independence from English domination. In 1603, when James VI of Scotland became James I of England, he hoped that the Scottish people would join with England in a single nation with a single church that used the same order of worship, the *Book of Common Prayer*. The Scots, though, were always reluctant to accept the *Book of Common Prayer*, which they saw as a sign of English domination. In 1633 Charles I had himself crowned in Scotland, in St. Giles Cathedral using the full Anglican service, including every permissible ritual and ceremonial.

In 1637 Charles tried to force the *Book of Common Prayer* upon the Scots and installed English bishops over the Scottish Presbyteries. Scottish rebellion broke out in St. Giles when Jenny Geddes flung her famous, perhaps fictitious, stool at the dean of the cathedral with the words, "Thou foul thief! Wilt thou say Mass at my ear?" The ensuing revolution brought about the National Covenant of 1638, which was both a political and ecclesiastical declaration. Bishops were deposed and Presbyterianism became the official religion of Scotland. Because Charles was having problems at home with a Puritan-dominated Parliament, he could not resist the Scots, and Knox's *Book of Common Order* was restored as normative for the Scottish church. Ironically, many congregations did not use it because by this time a new influence, English Puritanism, had come on the scene.

Puritanism

Puritanism had begun during the reign of Elizabeth I. Puritans were opposed to medieval ceremony—shrines, images, vestments—that reminded them of Rome. In a time of religious wars, the fear of invasion from Catholic Spain was very real in England. Puritanism was both a form of English nationalism and a protest against the lack of preaching, which Elizabeth had forcefully curtailed. She was, appropriately for a monarch, suspicious of the power of preaching and limited the number of sermons that could be preached to four a year. On a Sunday in 1567 a group of Londoners who had gathered in a hall to worship God according to the Genevan rite were imprisoned for refusing to join in the worship of the Church of England. Archbishop Grindal—who was, like them, a Calvinist—refused to obey Elizabeth's demands to prosecute them and was removed from office. His successor, Archbishop Hooker, justified the policy of limiting preaching by arguing that simple reading of the Word of God was as effective as a preached sermon. In response, many Puritans left the Church of England to become independents of various traditions: Baptists, Quakers, Presbyterians, and Congregationalists.

Puritans were loyal to England and fearful of the Counter-Reformation; they rejected the Anglican ritual because it was too "catholic," even though they were not necessarily opposed to the *Prayer Book*. Above all, Puritans insisted on the centrality of preaching. The antiliturgical bias of Puritanism was influenced by the Separatists, who had given up on the Church of England and were no longer interested in trying to reform it. Separatists Robert Browne and Henry Barrow began small groups who opposed all set forms, all ceremonials, and, especially, read prayers in worship.

The opposition to read or set prayers became a major Puritan emphasis. Preachers were judged by their ability to pray extemporaneously. Among the

Reformed churches, those influenced by Puritanism took up the cry against read prayers. They feared that a reliance upon written words would deprive the people, especially ministers, of the capacity to pray in their own thoughts and words. Puritans believed that set forms could not meet the varied needs of differing congregations and different kinds of world events. They also felt that worshiping God with a set liturgy was a form of idolatry that might equate the right words with the words of Holy Scripture and imply that human words were of equal value with God's Word. Finally, Puritans also believed that the use of the same prayers over and over would lead to such a familiarity that the prayers might become rote matters that people would recite with little attention to content. Written prayers might come between people and their personal relationship with God. Some extreme Puritans went even further in their opposition to anything written or read, opposing even the reading of the Bible. A worshiper was simply to speak from the heart. The Quakers were the direct heirs of this branch of Puritanism.

The Reformed churches on the continent followed very similar practices and also resisted set prayers. One unique form of prayer that persisted among the Dutch and German Reformed was the reading of the Decalogue on Communion Sundays, followed by a prayer of confession recited either by the people or by the pastor as part of the pastoral prayer. Continental Reformed Churches were not strongly influenced by Puritanism until their adherents came to America, at which time the all-pervading influence affected even these German and Dutch Calvinists in varying ways.

Although Puritanism was a democratic movement, worship devolved from congregational participation and centered the service around the minister. Worship became almost completely dependent upon the minister's views, calling for deep feeling and exalting a sense of intimacy and immediacy in human relationship with God. Puritan worship had the merit of flexibility, spontaneity, and warmth. The Puritan meeting house was a place for community experience of the whole family. Puritanism in England reached its political zenith with the overthrow of the crown, the beheading of Charles I, and the period of rule by Parliament in the interregnum in which Oliver Cromwell served as Lord Protector from 1653 to 1658. During that period, Puritanism became the official government of England. The Scots were fascinated at the possibility of the establishment of a common Presbyterianism in both England and Scotland, and they joined the Puritans in an alliance ratified by the Solemn League and Covenant.

When, in 1643, the English Parliament set up a commission to develop a form of government and a confession of faith and forms of worship for the new Church of England (Puritan/Reformed), Scottish representatives were invited to Westminster Abbey and attended as nonvoting delegates. Although the resulting Westminster documents (the Westminster Confession of Faith, the Longer and Shorter Catechisms, and the Directory of Public Worship) were only partially and temporarily accepted in England, they were enthusiastically adopted by the Church of Scotland.

To examine the Westminster Directory of Public Worship is to note its debt to Puritanism. Neither a prayer book nor a liturgy, the manual is for the discretionary use of ministers. The Westminster Directory has been described as the only liturgy in the world that consists of nothing but the rubrics; it simply states the rules and limitations but does not set out the words of prayers. This approach pleased Puritans who did not want anything like a Prayer Book to be imposed upon them and who valued their congregational right to worship as they chose.

Nonvoting Scottish delegates strongly influenced the Westminster Assembly. The Directory put a strong emphasis upon the reading and preaching of scripture. Following Knox and in contrast with Cranmer's advocacy of readings according to the church year, the Directory called for a full chapter from both the Old and New Testaments to be read in continuous order. Bucer and Calvin wanted only a single reading of scripture. After the reading and exposition of scripture, the sacraments were to be celebrated. The Directory suggested frequent celebrations of Communion and required preparatory services for those who wished to receive Communion, unless the Supper was held weekly. The manner of receiving the sacrament was left open so that English Puritans could continue their tradition of sitting in their pews and the Scots could continue to come to the Table. (The Puritan practice of sitting was adopted so that everyone could receive at the same time and each person could serve another.) The structure of worship was essentially that of Calvin and Knox. One peculiar change involved placing the prayers of confession and intercession between scripture and sermon. The Scottish Assembly objected and urged that these prayers be made after the sermon. Note also that the Creed was not included in the order of worship. The Directory had explicit directions for the prayer of consecration in Communion. The invocation of the Holy Spirit (*Epiclesis*), which Cranmer had omitted, was included, as ministers were instructed to pray in this way:

> to vouchsafe his (God's) gracious presence and the effectual working of his Spirit in us, and so to sanctify these Elements, both of Bread and Wine, and to blesse his own ordinance that we may receive by faith the Body and Blood of Jesus Christ, crucified for us, and so to feed on him, that he may be made one with us and we with him.[14]

This invocation is one of the very few places in which the Directory is so explicit about the words for a prayer.

The great irony of the work of the Westminster Assembly is that the English Parliament called for this massive undertaking, yet the English nation never accepted it, although the Scots did. The Assembly had tried to establish a more Calvinist point of view with more shape and form to worship. In the end, however, the Scottish church became Puritanized, rejecting its liturgical heritage, from Calvin through Knox. The Puritan insistence upon spontaneity in prayer, the rejection of an ordered liturgy, and the quality of teaching in prayer and sermon alike all became normative for the Congregationalists, Presbyterians, Baptists, and—by way of the Church of England—Methodists also. Thus American Protestantism is essentially a product of Puritanism.

The Reformed Tradition in America

The restoration of the monarchy in 1660 ended Puritanism in England, but it survived in America and strongly influenced all forms of American Protestantism. In the United States, Puritanism itself was influenced by Pietism. Pietism came from the continent and was like Puritanism in many ways. Both insisted upon the immediacy of experience; both had a high view of scripture and preaching. Pietism, like Puritanism, aimed at formal orthodoxy. Pietism put much emphasis upon the assurance of salvation as well as upon conversion, which was a prerequisite for church membership. In the United States, the practice of Pietism became highly emotional as a result of the great revivals.

Preaching in most Protestant churches today reflects the influence of both Puritanism and Pietism in the value of spontaneous prayer versus "read" prayer, the hesitation regarding all forms of pomp and ceremonial, and the rejection of much expenditure on the objects of worship except the organ. The simplicity of many Reformed church buildings is a continuing debt to Puritanism. So also is the insistence upon an educated clergy.

The Frontier

Another important influence upon American Protestantism was the belief that with enough effort, energy, and talent, the wilderness could be tamed and most human problems could be solved. The frontier revivals were an expression of this pragmatic spirit, hopeful that the lawlessness of the people could be tamed along with the wilderness.

These revivals were basic to the development of American Protestantism. Conversion became a primary purpose of worship. Because worship was often held outdoors in order to accommodate the crowds, there was no place for any symbol but the Bible and no liturgical tradition as such. Music was used to encourage people to make a decision for Christ, and the sermon was moved to the end of the service so that everything could build up to it, and the sermon would reach its climax with the invitation or altar call.

In the churches themselves, the pattern of revival was replicated as the furniture was minimized and the preacher was maximized. Thus, replacing the pulpit was a small lectern on a large platform on which the preacher could move about. A small Communion table on the floor level became a kind of simple worship center with offering plates and perhaps some flowers on it. The baptismal font nearly disappeared, often reduced to a bowl that was brought in for baptisms.

The basic order of worship was music, prayers by the preacher (especially the so-called pastoral prayer), scripture, the offering, and then the sermon and altar call with a final hymn as the accompaniment for those who would "hit the sawdust trail" and come forward to profess their faith.

Respectability

As American Protestants became upwardly mobile during the second half of the nineteenth century and the first part of the twentieth century, they sought more respectability, especially in worship. Slowly, they replaced the ecstatic with sobriety and the boisterous with restraint. These newly respectable Protestants had a hard time conveying the religious passion of the revivals when they believed that they had "made it" and frontier worship was beneath them. Respectable people did not want to be told that they were sinners needing to be saved. Conversion was for others, the great unwashed, but not for these folks, who lived decent lives. The emphasis upon respectability led to emotional restraint. Nothing boisterous must remind people of their more primitive past. Emotions were to be left at the door of the church because respectable people did not show their feelings in public. Good choirs and fine organs became the mark of having arrived. Preachers donned special garments, and churches became more architecturally detailed, with stained glass windows and carved woodwork. Great pipe organs became the supreme symbol of status about which parishioners could boast.

The worship service itself developed with more attention to tradition. A recovery of the common prayer of confession, the saying of the Creed, and the use of formal orders of worship took place. The mimeograph machine made possible the Sunday bulletin, which took the place of a prayer book for most Protestants.

In some places, especially after World War II, the revived interest in liturgy led to the divided chancel, candles, robed choirs, and processions, sometimes even when these were not particularly well suited to the practice of worship or the theology behind it. This trend had to do with a recovery of a sense of history and a new appreciation for denominationalism. Nearly every denomination published its own liturgical materials. Whereas previously a hymnody had been mutually shared, a new emphasis focused upon the distinctiveness of the hymnody of each denomination.

Ecumenism

After centuries in which Protestants knew what to expect from Rome, the Second Vatican Council (1962–1965) changed everything. Vatican II transformed Roman Catholic worship. Mass was celebrated in the vernacular, public confession came to replace the private confessional, a new emphasis was put upon preaching, the singing of hymns and folk songs by the people was revived, and many of the rules about fasting were removed. People were invited to share in the bread and in many places the cup as well. Much of the agenda of the Protestant Reformers was accepted in this radical move.

Protestants, who had previously determined much of what they would or could do in response to what Catholics did, were now somewhat confused. They could no longer easily caricature Roman practices. One of the results of this move on the part of Rome has been a new willingness on the part of many Protestants to reconsider practices they once frowned upon. The use of the common lectionary, the introduction of the liturgical year, use of the cross as a central symbol, and more colorful clerical gowns have become common. Communion is now celebrated far more frequently, often monthly instead of quarterly, and in some places weekly.

Black worship also influenced Reformed practices, far beyond what the numbers of African Americans within these denominations might lead one to expect. Through participation in the civil rights struggle, pastors and laypeople alike experienced the spiritual power of black preaching, gospel music, hand clapping, and even the spoken "Hallelujah" or "Amen," and these practices are now part of Protestant worship.

Today, we are at a major point of transition in worship. Much that was taken for granted has been questioned, and much that was shunned is now common. Reformed Christians now feel free to draw from any number of resources to make informed decisions for new excitement in worship leadership. Sometimes this flexibility has led to confusion about denominational loyalty, but it has also brought together American Christians of all traditions in a common mutual appreciation of each other's traditions and the gifts that can be used to strengthen all worship.

4

The Sacrament of Baptism

Church members regularly witness baptisms. In most churches, the baptisms are likely to be of infants and are happy occasions for celebrating the gift of a new life. Congregations are intrigued by the various unpredictable responses of babies—"Will they cry or not?"—and delight in watching the parents holding them or even in the pastor's somewhat awkward efforts to handle a child who is stiff with rage. Often, this very delight obscures the language so that it is either not heard at all or is completely misunderstood. There is often little sense that the child is going through an important initiation which marks that child for life, that a decision has been made about the child's future life and its meaning, or that the child has entered into the death and resurrection of Christ. The event of baptism is rarely understood as life-transforming. Much more likely, the members of the congregation enjoy the event and make promises to assist the parents to raise the child in the Christian faith (usually this promise means providing a Sunday church school), and the whole thing is over in a matter of minutes. Even the date is forgotten by the parents and certainly by the one being baptized.

If baptism is to communicate the powerful meanings that it has promised for Christians throughout history, the ceremony must be experienced as an event of importance: the beginning of a lifelong process for which the whole congregation takes responsibility.

The response of the Heidelberg Catechism to the question, "Since, then, faith alone makes us share in Christ and all his benefits, where does such faith originate?" is: "The Holy Spirit creates it in our hearts by the preaching of the gospel, and confirms it by the use of the holy sacraments."[1] Our baptism signifies this affirmation of faith. Calvin puts it this way: "The sacraments have their effectiveness among us in proportion as we are helped by their ministry sometimes to foster, confirm, and increase the true knowledge of Christ in ourselves; at other times, to possess him more fully and enjoy his riches. But that happens when we receive in true faith what is offered there" (IV.xiv.16). The letter to the Ephesians includes baptism in its sevenfold description of Christian truth: "There is one *body* and one *Spirit*, just as you were called to the one *hope* of your calling, one *Lord*, one *faith*, one *baptism*, one *God* and Father of all . . ." (Eph. 4:4–6, emphasis added). Baptism is central to the Christian life and not simply some nice ritual.

The Earliest Roots of Baptism

Sometime during the Exile, Judaism began the practice of baptizing proselytes coming to Judaism from other religions. In proselyte baptism, parents and children were baptized together, but children born after the parents' conversion were *not* baptized, for they were considered Jews, just as much as any other children born into a Jewish family. Male children were circumcised shortly after birth in fulfillment of Jewish law, whether born in a regular Jewish home or to a proselyte family. Both baptism and circumcision were signs of belonging to the covenant people of God.

John the Baptist adopted the practice of proselyte baptism and applied it to all Jews who, he said, needed to be baptized as confession of sin, as washing for forgiveness, and in anticipation of the coming of the Messiah. For John, the immersion symbol clearly dramatized the washing for forgiveness. The Greek word *baptizo* originally meant "to immerse," but had also come to mean "wash" in the popular Greek of John's time.

John baptized in the wilderness of the Jordan. The wilderness was a place of preparation, of beginning anew, as it had been for the Israelites coming out of Egypt. In the wilderness, God prepared the people for entrance into the Land of Promise. Then, after their preparation, Joshua led them across the Jordan into the land. John's baptism suggests a new entry into a promised land, a reconstituting of Israel and the establishment of the long-promised reign of God through God's Messiah, who is called *Jesus* or *Joshua*. This new "Joshua" will lead his people across the Jordan into a new land, a realm not of this world.

John's baptism was for both repentance and forgiveness. Mark tells us, "John the baptizer appeared in the wilderness, proclaiming a baptism of repentance for the forgiveness of sins" (Mark 1:4ff). Luke makes it clear that John demanded fruits of this repentance: "Bear fruits worthy of repentance . . . Whoever has two coats must share with anyone who has none; and whoever has food must do likewise" (Luke 3:8, 11).

John also predicted that this baptism was the foretelling of a new baptism that the Messiah would bring: "The one who is more powerful than I is coming after me; I am not worthy to stoop down and untie the thong of his sandals. I have baptized you with water; but he will baptize you with the Holy

Spirit" (Mark 1:7–8). The Fourth Gospel draws the distinction between John and Jesus, but not in terms of power: "After me comes a man who ranks ahead of me because he was before me. . . . [B]ut I came baptizing with water for this reason, that he might be revealed to Israel" (John 1:30–31).

All four Gospels agree that Jesus came to John to be baptized, although the Fourth Gospel does not explicitly refer to Jesus' baptism. In Matthew's account, the drama of Jesus and John is made clear. Unknown and unnoticed, Jesus came with other penitents to be baptized. People came to John, "confessing their sins" (Matt. 3:6). Why should Jesus come to be baptized for repentance? "John would have prevented him, saying, 'I need to be baptized by you, and do you come to me?'" (Matt. 3:14). Jesus answered, "Let it be so now; for it is proper for us in this way to fulfill all righteousness" (Matt. 3:15). Jesus' intention is not open to argument, for he knows what he is doing. He does not go it alone. God's righteousness becomes reality among us as the Righteous One makes common cause with us. That is the meaning of Emmanuel, "God with us." Jesus steps forward to join us all, to become needy with us. When Jesus was baptized, Matthew tells us that the Spirit of God descended upon him, and the voice of God was heard to say, "This is my Son, the Beloved, with whom I am well pleased" (Matt. 3:17). The evangelist is recalling the Servant of the Lord in Isaiah 42:1. The mighty one who comes to be baptized at the Jordan comes as the humble servant whose rule is expressed in servitude and suffering. At the Jordan, Jesus was "numbered with the transgressors" (Isa. 53:12). In his baptism, Jesus began his own costly ministry of love that finally led him to a baptism of blood on the cross. That is how we may read the saying, "I have a baptism with which to be baptized, and what stress I am under until it is completed!" (Luke 12:50). On the other occasion in which Jesus speaks of his baptism, he also connects it with his death: "Are you able to . . . be baptized with the baptism that I am baptized with?" (Mark 10:38).

Our baptism is based on God's pledge and promise expressed in Jesus Christ. God claims us and welcomes us into the household of faith. Too often we have sought the meaning of baptism in our own action, our decision and promises. Christian baptism declares that God's own righteousness has come to us in one who in his baptism made our lot his own. In the Fourth Gospel, John the Baptist makes this point especially clear when he says: "Here is the Lamb of God who takes away the sin of the world!" (John 1:29). Jesus' baptism takes place not for his sin, but for the sin of the whole world. Jesus was baptized on behalf of all humanity.

Jesus' baptism finds its fulfillment in his mission, which includes his suffering and death. He receives his commission to undertake the role of the Suffering Servant of God, taking onto himself the sin of his people. His baptism points toward the end of his life, its climax upon the cross. His death is the accomplishment of the general baptism of all, offered for all, quite independent of their decision of faith and understanding. Baptismal grace is rooted here, offered on behalf of people who have no understanding of its meaning for them.

Since our baptism is rooted in Jesus' own baptism, a dominant scriptural image for baptism is participation with Christ. Paul speaks of baptism as a dying and rising with Christ. The classic passage is Romans 6, especially verse 4: "Therefore we have been buried with him by baptism into death, so that, just as Christ was raised from the dead by the glory of the Father, so we too might walk in newness of life." The same imagery appears in Colossians 2:12, except that here the rising with Christ and dying with Christ are put into the past tense: "When you were buried with him in baptism, you were also raised with him through faith in the power of God, who raised him from the dead." The change in tense demonstrates the way memory and hope connect in biblical faith. For Calvin, our baptism is an engrafting with Christ, and in this union his Spirit strengthens us and transfers his power to us.

Christian baptism really does not begin until Pentecost and is accompanied by the Holy Spirit. John's baptism of Jesus prefigured this gift. In Peter's sermon at Pentecost, the climactic statement concerns baptism: "[B]e baptized every one of you in the name of Jesus Christ so that your sins may be forgiven; and you shall receive the gift of the Holy Spirit" (Acts 2:38).

One could argue that washing with water is no longer necessary, that it is superseded by the gift of the Holy Spirit, because the forgiveness of sins has been already accomplished on the cross. The early church apparently did not make this assumption. Christians still needed forgiveness, the church believed. Offering the gift of the Holy Spirit was not enough; it must be received.

For Paul, the parallelism between dying with Christ and being baptized means that baptism is rooted in the cross. Such a view prevents us from seeing baptism as something *we do* on our own for ourselves. In 1 Corinthians 1:13, baptism is clearly pictured as participation in the cross: "Was Paul crucified for you? Or were you baptized in the name of Paul?" In baptism, Christ does the work, and the believer is a passive recipient of the crucial deed. The central meaning of baptism was accomplished, without any cooperation on anyone's part, at Golgotha on Good Friday and on Easter at the empty tomb.

The necessity of baptism is grounded in the meaning of the body of Christ. We are baptized into the resurrected body of Christ as we are baptized into the church. Paul says in Galatians 3:27–28, "As many of you as were baptized into Christ have clothed yourselves with Christ . . . all of you are one in Christ." To be baptized is to be incorporated into the context in which one can be most likely delivered from the powers of evil, and that context is the body of Christ or the church. Faith is that which follows as an answer to divine action. Throughout the New Testament there is, on the one side, a humanity redeemed by Christ, and on the other, a community that knows this reality and celebrates it with joy. The church is the special locus of the Holy Spirit and, although people who are baptized are not preferred in matters of salvation, they are set upon a new course of life. The difference between the old and new life is portrayed in the New Testament as putting on a garment, "for . . . [a]s many of you as were baptized into Christ have clothed yourself with Christ" (Gal. 3:27).

There was probably an early catechetical baptismal teaching that included renunciations (putting off) and vows (putting on) of the new life in Christ, enacted physically in the removal of the old clothes and putting on new, white robes at baptism.

> But now you must get rid of all such things—anger, wrath, malice, slander, and abusive language from your mouth. Do not lie to one another, seeing that you have stripped off the old self with its practices and have clothed yourselves with the new self, which is being renewed in knowledge according to the image of its creator. . . . as God's chosen ones, holy and beloved, clothe yourselves with compassion, kindness, humility, meekness, and patience. . . . Above all, clothe yourselves with love, which binds everything together in perfect harmony. (Col. 3:8–10, 12, 14)

Washing with Water

In Jewish purification rituals, ritual bathing was associated with putting on a clean and fresh garment. In terms of the imagery of washing, the water itself is very important throughout the New Testament: "Get up, be baptized, and have your sins washed away, calling on his name" (Acts 22:16). "[Y]ou were washed, you were sanctified, you were justified in the name of the Lord Jesus Christ and in the Spirit of our God" (1 Cor. 6:11). The water of baptism represents the water of chaos, which in creation was brought under God's order. The flood story can also be seen to portray the work of Christ:

> For Christ also suffered for sins once for all, the righteous for the unrighteous, in order to bring you to God. He was put to death in the flesh, but made alive in the spirit, in which also he went and made a proclamation to the spirits in prison, who in former times did not obey, when God waited patiently in the days of Noah, during the building of the ark, in which a few, that is, eight persons, were saved through water. And baptism, which this prefigured, now saves you—not as a removal of dirt from the body, but as an appeal to God for a good conscience, through the resurrection of Jesus Christ. . . . (1 Peter 3:18–21)

Noah was saved *through* water from a world enslaved to demonic powers. In the same way, Israel's great salvation event was the Exodus through the waters of the Red Sea, and Paul links baptism to this event: "I do not want you to be unaware . . . that our ancestors were all under the cloud, and all passed through the sea, and all were baptized into Moses in the cloud and in the sea" (1 Cor. 10:1ff).

Water is also connected to the miracle of birth and the mystery of new life. Jesus says to Nicodemus, "Very truly, I tell you, no one can enter the kingdom of God without being born of water and Spirit" (John 3:5). Titus 3:4–7 shows traces of an early baptismal hymn:

> But when the goodness and loving kindness of God our Savior appeared, he saved us, not because of any works of righteousness that we had done, but according to his mercy, through the water of rebirth and renewal by the Holy Spirit. This Spirit he poured out on us richly through Jesus Christ our Savior, so that, having been justified by his grace, we might become heirs according to the hope of eternal life.

Baptism has a number of meanings, which can be summarized as follows:

1. Baptism expresses our participation in Christ's death and resurrection.
2. Baptism expresses the primacy of God's grace and initiative, which always precedes our response in faith and obedience.
3. Baptism vividly expresses cleansing and forgiveness, which apply to the whole of life, not just that which has already been done. Baptism looks forward to forgiveness in the future, not just forgiveness of what is past.
4. Baptism incorporates us into the body of Christ, the church.
5. Baptism conveys an understanding of mutual responsibility for supporting each other in faith.
6. Baptism expresses the need for our dependence upon the gift of the Holy Spirit.
7. Baptism points toward the culmination of baptism in the reign of God.

Baptism in Early Christianity

In the Christian community the mandate for baptism is as ancient as the words of Jesus in the Great Commission in Matthew 28:19, "Go . . . make disciples of all nations, baptizing. . . ."

The source of the question of the baptism of infants born to Christian parents and how important an issue it was remain unclear. Perhaps the accounts in the Synoptic Gospels in which Jesus calls the children to himself were meant to provide a rationale for the practice of baptizing infants. We do know that the practice of baptizing infants was not common until the fifth century.

The *Didache* and *The Apology of Justin*, both second-century documents, indicate that a change from New Testament practice was taking place in the baptism of believers. Those coming to the faith were no longer primarily Jews but Gentiles of every social background. To become a member of the Christian Church, they had to find a sponsor who would oversee their moral and spiritual formation for two or three years, after which the candidates were presented for baptism. Prostitutes, actors, money lenders, gladiators, or soldiers had to find a new profession in order to be considered for baptism.

The candidates were called *catechumens*, and the period of induction was called the *catechumenate*, from the Greek word meaning "instruction." Until the fourth century, when Christianity could be practiced openly, catechumens were told little of the mysteries of the faith or even the locations of the larger meetings. The sponsors were the guardians of their reliability, charged with the task of ensuring that they would not betray the community of Christians. In the case of children, parents were usually their sponsors. Masters presented their own slaves.

Originally, baptism occurred immediately after conversion. Later it was moved to any Sunday before the celebration of Communion. Then it was moved to the night before Easter, the Easter Vigil.

Since the early church expected the change in lifestyle to be immediate and radical for new Christians, the three-year catechumenate became a time to "try out" the new life, a time for the catechumens to see if they could live with it. If, after this period, they wanted to proceed, they entered a several-week period of intense preparation immediately prior to Easter. During this time, they were presented to the bishop, who examined them on such matters as whether they honored widows, visited the sick, and fulfilled other good works. People who passed the examination were presented as candidates. Each Sunday they were exorcised and prayed over, anointed, and signed with the cross on different parts of their bodies.

Then came Easter Eve. The Easter Vigil included scripture readings that told the great story of redemption and salvation. These readings were the stories of Israel's liberation and the journey, by faith, into the new land. Then, in the early morning hours, as the sun of Easter was about to rise, the candidates were led to the place of baptism, either a baptismal room or a river. Again, they were asked to renounce evil and were anointed with the oil of exorcism. As the candidates were called by name, they removed their clothes, symbolizing the casting off of the old life; men were baptized separately from the women. In the case of the women, women deacons shielded the nakedness of the women candidates from the sight of both the male candidates and also the celebrant.

The water symbolized not only cleansing but also the watery grave of death to the old life. After a final exorcism and renunciation of evil, the candidates were plunged beneath the water three times with the words: "I baptize you in the name of the Father, and of the Son, and of the Holy Spirit." The candidates were then raised to new life out of the water of death, anointed with oil, this time as a sign of thanksgiving, and clothed in new white garments.

Next, the newly clothed Christians were led into the assembly. They were given the "secret" of the Christian church, which they had not yet heard, the Lord's Prayer. Salt was poured into their hands and a candle was presented to them with the words: "Be salt! Be light!" (see Matt. 5:13–16). For the first time, they were invited to witness and participate in what had previously been kept secret from them, the sacrament of the Lord's Supper.

During the persecution, martyrdom was considered a form of baptism—a baptism by blood—which brought comfort to those who had not been baptized by the church.

Baptism at the Time of Constantine and Beyond

After the time of Constantine, when baptism could be publicly administered, the sacrament came to be seen as the means of God's forgiveness of sins. People who were baptized were exhorted to live exemplary lives, for they had now been washed clean. The church offered no provision for a second baptism, from earliest times. Some converts, like Constantine, chose to remain catechumens throughout their life and be baptized on their deathbeds, so that they would enter eternity sinless. However, Augustine (Bishop of Hippo, 396–430) and John Chrysostom (Bishop of Constantinople, 398–407), both of whom had been baptized as adults, began to urge Christians not to delay their baptism. Augustine argued that as a sacrament of grace, baptism should be received at the beginning of the Christian life; the baptism of infants demonstrated that salvation was the gracious and unmerited gift of God. He said that people who were baptized received a seal of the Spirit, and this seal marked them as belonging to Christ.

By the end of the fifth century, infant baptism had become normative in southern Europe and the Near East. At first, infants were baptized with everyone else at the yearly paschal feast, but eventually the baptizing of infants brought about some changes. Since babies could not be instructed, the catechumenate disappeared. Exorcisms and anointings were retained, since it was believed that they were effective even without the child's understanding or consent. Brief instruction was introduced, but for the parents and sponsors rather than for the baby.

But how was the child to make a confession of faith? Parents and sponsors, who would be raising the children, were asked what they believed.

Sponsors became those who, rather than prepare the candidate for baptism, watched over the newly baptized, raising them in the "nurture and admonition of the Lord."

The ritual also changed. The need for secrecy had not allowed the construction of places deep enough to immerse the baptized, so candidates stood in a pool with water poured over them. Infants were easier to immerse in water and immersion became the norm, eventually replacing pouring completely and remaining the common practice in Eastern Orthodoxy. In both the East and the West, the Trinitarian formula, "I baptize you in the name of the Father, and the Son, and the Holy Spirit," became normative rather than the more primitive formula that baptized in the name of Jesus alone (Acts 8:15–16).

By the Middle Ages, baptism was believed to be necessary for salvation, which led to the practice of baptizing infants immediately after their birth. The practice of baptizing infants quickly after birth began as an emergency measure to protect against their death without being baptized. By the fourteenth century, this practice acquired the force of law, and infants were required to be baptized no later than one week from birth. A liturgical consequence of considering every baptism an emergency was the replacement of immersion by pouring. Also, the baptism's personnel changed. In emergency situations, the state of a soul was at stake, and thus a priest was not necessary. The Council of Florence in 1439 declared that because of the urgency of baptizing to ensure that the child is able to enter heaven, anyone, male or female, might baptize, even a heretic or pagan, provided that the one baptizing observes the form of the church and intends to do what the church intends in the baptismal act.

The Protestant Reformation

The Protestant Reformers did little to challenge baptismal theology. The Reformers appealed to Augustine for an understanding of baptismal grace, and they purged the sacrament of some elements of superstition. Calvin sought to strip the sacrament of actions inappropriate to children. The Reformed sacrament involved three parties: the infant, the parents, and the congregation that acted as sponsor. Water alone was used, and no other symbol that might take away from the centrality of water was added; thus there was no salt on the tongue, no oil for anointing, and no candle. These symbols had made sense when adults were being baptized but had little meaning when the candidate was a baby. For the same reasons, Calvin eliminated words that did not apply to children, such as the renunciations of evil and a profession of faith. The child was baptized into the faith of the whole church, not the faith of the child or its parents. The parents were required to promise to raise their child in the church with the help of the whole congregation. Although Calvin did not object to godparents, the principal sponsor was the whole congregation.

For Calvin, baptism was not a cause of salvation but a *sign* of salvation. He wrote, "Nowhere do we find that he (Jesus) condemned anyone as unbaptized" (IV.xvi.26). As a sign of salvation, baptism is a reminder as people recall their own baptism and recall that they too have been washed clean.

For Calvin, the center of baptism is "prevenient grace." God's initiative always precedes our faith. The grace of God is revealed most clearly in the baptism of infants who cannot believe, yet are included in the covenant of grace. For Calvin and for the Reformed understanding of baptism, covenant is a central idea. The Westminster Shorter Catechism defines baptism: "Baptism is a sacrament, wherein the washing with water, in the name of the Father, and of the Son, and of the Holy Spirit, doth signify and seal our ingrafting into Christ, and partaking of the benefits of the covenant of grace, and our engagement to be the Lord's."[2] The understanding of baptism as a sign of the covenant is the reason that baptism was always placed in the context of public worship and followed the reading and preaching of the Word. The Reformed tradition has never looked favorably upon private baptisms, believing that the corporate nature of baptism must be preserved so that the one being baptized is baptized into a community of faith in fact as well as theory.

The phrase "engrafting into Christ" was also crucially important. The baptism of each individual is the sharing of a common baptism. People who profess their faith and their children are members of the visible church. Each person is engrafted into the body of Christ as a branch is grafted onto a vine. The individual participates in the life of the whole community, receives nourishment from the community, and becomes one with that community.

Calvin developed no form for the baptism of believers since everyone in Geneva was already baptized, except the newborn. Calvin struggled against the rebaptizers and insisted that the sacrament was not to be repeated, lest we make a mockery of God's promise. Not until 1604 did the Dutch Reformed Church develop a ritual for the baptism of believers and only because of the missionary movement into lands in which people had not been baptized.

The Baptism of Infants

The sacrament of Baptism has caused its share of disagreements through the centuries, and infant baptism even today continues as a source of controversy. The practice of baptizing infants is not found in the New Testament, and though references are made to whole households being baptized (Acts 11:14 and 16:15), one may or may not assume the presence of infants in these households. John Calvin acknowledged that the New Testament does not provide evidence of baptisms of infants but responded, "Even if this is not expressly related by the Evangelists, still, because infants are not excluded when mention is made of a family's being baptized, who in his senses can reason from this that they were not baptized?" (IV.xvi.8).

As a missionary faith, Christianity did not, at its beginning, have the opportunity to baptize infants. Infant baptism could only happen (1) when a whole household in which there were young children converted to Christianity, or (2) when children were born after the conversion of the parents. No evidence exists that the baptism of children was forbidden either in the New Testament or in the early church. In Peter's sermon at Pentecost, the implication is clear: "For the promise is for you, for your children, and for all who are far away, everyone whom the Lord our God calls . . . " (Acts 2:39).

Parallels exist between baptism as the sign of the new covenant and circumcision as the sign of inclusion in the old covenant with Israel. In both, the ritual had to do with incorporating a child into the covenant community. Paul writes of this in Colossians 2:11–12,

> In him also you were circumcised with a spiritual circumcision, by putting off the body of the flesh in the circumcision of Christ; when you were buried with him in baptism, you were also raised with him through faith in the power of God, who raised him from the dead.

Circumcision meant reception into the covenant community that God had established on the basis of the promise to Abraham and Sarah and their children's children. Similarly, for Christians, baptism meant reception into the body of Christ. Again Paul says, we "are children of the promise, like Isaac" (Gal. 4:28). Outsiders who converted to Judaism could be circumcised after their baptism, as could children born into the community of faith by their birth to Jewish parents. Calvin made a great deal of the similarity between the two ordinances:

> The promise is the same in both, namely, that of God's fatherly favor, of forgiveness of sins, and of eternal life. Then the thing represented is the same, namely regeneration. In both, there is one foundation upon which the fulfillment of these things rests. Therefore, there is no difference in the inner mystery, by which the whole force and character of the sacraments are to be weighed. What dissimilarity remains lies in the outward ceremony, which is a very slight factor, since the most weighty part depends upon the promise and the thing signified. We therefore conclude that, apart from the difference in the visible ceremony, whatever belongs to circumcision pertains likewise to baptism (IV.xvi.4).

For Christian baptism, the forgiveness of sins through Christ is expressed in and through reception into the community of Christ (the locus for growth in Christ). One becomes holy by participation in the fellowship of the saints, whether that is the people of Israel or the body of Christ. The crucial difference between baptism and circumcision is that in baptism, the distinction between men and women is erased. Proselyte baptism included both men and women, and both were incorporated in the community. Christian baptism, by its inclusiveness, erases gender distinction, so that Paul can declare that "there is no longer male and female . . . in Christ Jesus" (Gal. 3:28). This radical inclusiveness is the reason that Paul argues so vigorously against the continuation of the practice of circumcision among Christians. Baptism is "circumcision in Christ," yet it is without distinction between male and female. Baptism symbolizes the equal welcome into the household of faith to both women and men.

Several accounts of baptism in Acts use a strange phrase that may be from an ancient baptismal ritual formula. In Acts 8:37, in the story of the baptism of the Ethiopian eunuch, the eunuch says, "Look, here is water! What is to prevent me from being baptized?" In Acts 10:47, Peter says, "Can anyone withhold the water for baptizing these people who have received the Holy Spirit just as we have?" The question, "What prevents or forbids me from being baptized?" can only be understood as a ritual question. The issue apparently was that of a possible hindrance to baptism. When a person came to be baptized, inquiry was made as to whether any hindrance existed. The word translated as either "forbid" or "stop" is crucial when we look at the accounts of Jesus and the children, in Matthew 19, Mark 10, and Luke 18. In each case, Jesus says, "Let the little children come to me, and do not stop them." In Luke it is not merely children who are brought to Jesus, but *infants*. Of course Jesus did not actually baptize these infants (as he did not apparently baptize anyone), but the formula given in these accounts establishes a connection between these stories and baptism. Jesus lays his hands upon them and blesses them. All that is missing is the water!

The baptism of infants and the baptism of believers is one and the same sacrament, which is one reason that it should not be referred to as "infant baptism" or "believer's baptism." The two practices are alike in all necessary respects: The person is baptized into the church and incorporated into the body of Christ, the fellowship of the body of Christ. Whether administered to infants or new believers, baptism has the following basic meaning:

1. Baptism is something that is done to a person; no one baptizes himself or herself.
2. Baptism is always a sign of God's grace, and no one earns or deserves baptism.
3. People are baptized into the faith of the Church, not simply their own belief. For that reason, the Apostles' Creed is recited by the people, rather than some local or denominational confession of faith.

4. Baptism is the beginning of a life of faith, and the whole of life is lived in response to the grace manifested in baptism.

The baptism of the children of believers and the baptism of believers each have different strengths and different dangers. To emphasize one form of baptism, as has been done frequently, may make the most of the strengths but also risks some of the dangers of any single form when used exclusively:

Dangers and Strengths of Both Forms of Baptism

Baptism of infants has the following advantages:

1. The baptism of infants reflects a theology of grace. The child has done nothing to merit inclusion in the covenant community.
2. The baptism of infants takes the corporate nature of the community seriously. The child is not baptized by virtue of his or her own faith but very obviously by and in the faith of the community, which nurtures the individual toward faith.
3. Baptism of infants emphasizes the initiative of God, whose grace accepts and loves us all before we do anything in response.
4. The baptism of infants makes clear that baptism is the beginning of a process of growth in Christ.

The exclusive baptism of infants can also cause problems:

1. It can lead to an automatic or even superstitious relationship between the act of baptism and acceptance by God, so that it becomes necessary for salvation, to assure the safety of the soul. Baptism thereby becomes a cheap insurance policy.
2. It can minimize the fact that our life as Christians demands personal trust in Christ's promises and a conscious acknowledgement of our relationship with Christ as savior. We who do not remember our own baptism may find it difficult even to think about a time when we made a personal commitment.
3. It can lead to smug complacency and a kind of dead faith that lacks depth and a sense or urgency. Faith can seem to be an inheritance from one's parents and not something with which one has to come to personal terms.

The baptism of believers, it is argued, is purer and has its own advantages:

1. The baptism of believers symbolizes what baptism originally intended: the change from unbelief to belief. People who remember their own baptism often have a clarity about their faith that others lack. When put together with immersion, the baptism of believers acts out the death and rising with Christ about which Paul so dramatically speaks.
2. Baptism of believers can connect baptism with Communion; the newly baptized candidates can, as their first act after baptism, receive Communion.

Baptism of believers can also prove susceptible to weaknesses:

1. The exclusive practice of baptism of believers can minimize the corporate character of faith and thus encourage individualism.
2. It may lead to pride in one's own accomplishment. Faith becomes a work achieved ("I have done this") so that faith becomes a personal sign of one's own goodness or purity and becomes a work for salvation rather than a sign of grace.
3. Scriptural arguments for baptism of believers alone tend to separate the Old from the New Testament, producing a kind of New Testament fundamentalism.
4. Exclusive baptism of believers may lead to a demeaning of the presence of children as members of the community of faith or even as little pagans who must be converted.

The Practice of Baptism

All too often, baptism is treated as a minor event. Even its place in the service of worship is minimized. An abbreviated sacrament that takes place before the sermon so the parents may slip out afterwards is not an event for the whole congregation. In many instances, baptism feels like a private ceremony that is merely conducted in front of an audience.

Even the baptismal font is often hidden away, out of sight except for baptismal occasions when it is moved out where it can be seen. Such treatment of the font suggests a secondary role for this sacrament, especially in churches where the Lord's Table is a permanent fixture and never moved.

Baptism needs to be reasserted to its deserving place as a sacrament of the church. Baptism should take place as part of the response to the sermon just as the Lord's Supper does. The font, large enough to suggest a bath, should be so located that people are reminded of their own baptism when they see it. Under no circumstances should the sacrament be abbreviated in such a way as to appear rushed, even when the baptismal candidate is expressing strong disapproval with shrieks or tears. The congregation should be involved in such a way as to make it clear that all the people are more than observers.

Some educational work needs to precede a person's celebrating the sacrament of Baptism. Those who are to be baptized, or their parents, should be instructed as to its meaning.

When a child is to be baptized, ordinarily the parents or those exercising parental authority are members of the congregation. People who are presenting the child promise to provide nurture and guidance within the community of faith until the child is ready to make a personal profession of faith at confirmation. Because of the mobility of our culture, most families will not live in one community for the duration of their children's growing years and a move to another congregation is very likely. Thus the role of sponsors selected by the church governing board and the parents together is to follow the child and provide guidance and encouragement to the child and the parents, no matter where they may live.

Baptism is an important event in the life of the one to be baptized as well as in the life of the congregation, and should be prominently featured in the service. It is a sacrament of the whole church and is not to be administered privately unless for extraordinary reasons; if the whole congregation cannot be present, elders representing the congregation shall be present. Baptism requires the prior approval of the governing board and is to be administered by a minister of the Word and Sacrament.

The sacrament of Baptism should be accompanied by the reading and proclamation of the Word, and on occasion, the pastor might preach on the meaning of baptism. The administration of the sacrament should also include statements concerning the biblical meaning of baptism as well as the responsibility assumed at baptism by those being baptized, those who present children for baptism, and the congregation.

The Baptismal Rite in Reformed Churches Today

The structure of the baptismal rite generally follows the ecumenical order very closely. The parallels with other denominational traditions ensure that people from other traditions will be at home with the words and actions. The services include the following elements:

1. *Welcome and presentation of the candidate:* For most Reformed denominations, this action is performed by an elder who represents the congregation. This portion of the baptismal ceremony includes the renunciation of evil (an ecumenical importation into Reformed liturgies), the question of one's desire to be baptized or to have the child baptized, and the question to parents or sponsors about the willingness to raise the child as a Christian. The sponsors and family members are also asked to support the parents, and then the whole congregation accepts its role to uphold and support the parents.

2. *The profession of faith:* Baptism has always involved some kind of confession of the faith of the church into which the person is being baptized. John Calvin did not believe that the confession should be made by any single individual but by the whole church, since it was the faith of the church into which the person was being baptized. In the *Book of Worship of the United Church of Christ*, an abbreviated form of the Apostles' Creed is used in question-and-answer form. In most other Reformed liturgies, the Apostles' Creed is recited in full. The profession of faith is that of the whole church and not just that of a single denomination. Although people often speak

about being baptized as a Lutheran or a Methodist, in reality all Christians are baptized as Christians.

3. *Thanksgiving over water:* This prayer has three movements: first, it is thanksgiving for God's faithfulness; second, it praises God for God's reconciling acts; and third, it asks that the Holy Spirit empower this particular baptism and sanctify the water. As developed by ecumenical consensus, the prayer over the water has become fairly standard, and differences among denominations are only slight.

4. *The act of baptism:* Following long tradition, the provision is given in most Reformed liturgies for baptism in any of three possible forms: pouring, sprinkling, and immersion. Calvin was open about the mode, "whether the person being baptized should be wholly immersed, and whether thrice or once, whether he should only be sprinkled with poured water—these details are of no importance, but ought to be optional to churches according to the diversity of countries. Yet the word 'baptize' means to immerse, and it is clear that the rite of immersion was observed in the ancient church" (IV.xvi.19). Whichever form is used, water should be used in sufficient quantity to symbolize the washing, which is an essential part of the sacrament. The damp finger is an inadequate sign that reduces the sacrament to a sterile form.

The baptismal formula is generally given and, in some variation, calls for baptism in the name of the triune God. Some people have difficulty with the use of the word "Father" in this formula. Depending upon the branch of the Reformed tradition in which one labors, some variation may be possible, but for most, the word "Father" is required.

The laying on of hands follows the act of baptism. The minister, on behalf of the congregation, prays a blessing upon the newly baptized. The sign of the cross may be made on the forehead and oil may also be used here.

5. *The welcome:* An elder or pastor announces that the newly baptized has been received into the one holy, catholic, and apostolic church. The people respond with either a unison statement of welcome or a unison prayer. Sometimes the newly baptized is brought down the aisle into the midst of the people who offer words of personal welcome, touches, hugs, or handshakes. Though congregations may have special elements they want to add, this baptism is into the whole church of Jesus Christ.

6. *The peace:* The service ends quickly with the peace.

The strengths of this order are many. As a service of substance, it cannot be concluded in five minutes, and it demands the attention that each newly baptized person deserves.

Most Protestant churches today also offer services for the reaffirmation of baptism, which may mark occasions of growth in faith or return to faith. Such services may help to quell the demand for rebaptism that most Reformed pastors have to deal with regularly.

Every baptism is an occasion for renewing our own baptism and for taking heart from the remembrance of how much God's favor is extended to us without any strings attached. "Therefore as often as we fall away, we ought to recall the memory of our own baptism and fortify our mind with it, that we may always be sure and confident of the forgiveness of sins" (IV.xvi.3).

Some Practical Considerations

1. Water may be brought to the font in a pitcher. As it is poured in the sight of the congregation, everyone is aware of the centrality of water in this sacrament.

2. The minister asks the name of the one to be baptized (first and middle, but not surname), then uses the ancient formula: "I baptize you in the name of the Father and of the Son and of the Holy Spirit."

3. When water is being poured, the one being baptized may lean over the font so as to minimize spillage; or a kneeling bench may be used at the font. People presenting infants may hold the head of the infant over the font.

4. Other actions may follow baptism, such as the laying on of hands in blessing; praying for the anointing of the Holy Spirit; anointing with oil (the minister may make the sign of the cross on the forehead and say, "You are Christ's, sealed as his own forever"); and presenting the newly baptized to the congregation. These actions should not, however, overshadow the act of baptism itself.

5. If the minister uses oil for anointing, having a towel nearby to wipe oil from the hands is helpful. Having a supply of towels available to protect clothing or mop up spilled water may also be wise. Sometimes a baptismal napkin or towel is used and, following the baptism, given to the family as a memento.

6. A letter may be written to the candidate afterwards by the pastor, personalizing the service and serving as a reminder of what happened, especially for the infant who will have no memory of the event. A parent or sponsor could read that letter on the baptism anniversary.

Sometimes people who think they may have been baptized but have no record or memory of it ask to be baptized again. With the permission of the appropriate governing body, ministers may explain the situation to the congregation and then baptize with the following formula: "(Name), in the event you have not been baptized, I baptize you in the name of the Father, and of the Son, and of the Holy Spirit." This procedure should be used only when the baptism is in doubt, not because one who has been baptized as an infant wants to be baptized again as a believer. When adults want to renew the vows of their baptism, a service of renewal of baptismal vows is appropriate, and instead of rebaptizing them, the minister may admonish them to "remember your baptism," and then anoint them with oil as an act of rededication. The minister may say something like: "You have been baptized in the name of the Father, and of the Son, and of the Holy Spirit. You have been called by God, and sealed as Christ's own, forever. Now commit yourself anew to live as a full citizen of the household of faith."

In a typical congregation the sacrament of Baptism takes place frequently enough to serve as a source for everyone's renewal of faith. People who bring their children, who come to be baptized themselves, and all who witness baptisms benefit from this sacrament. We are all claimed by God in Jesus Christ in divine grace, which is not dependent upon anything we say or do. God's love for us is too wonderful for words, but the sign of washing with water captures its wonder and power.

5

The Sacrament
of the Lord's Supper

People of other traditions quite likely—but mistakenly—associate Calvinism with one central doctrine, predestination. For some reason, predestination seems to many people the distinctive doctrine of Reformed theology, even though Luther, Cranmer, and even Rome did not differ substantially from Calvin on this.

In reality, the doctrine of Calvin's theology that is responsible for Calvinism's separate existence is sacramental theology, and especially the distinctively Calvinist interpretation of the central mystery of Christ's presence in the Lord's Supper. Some maintain that his doctrine of the Lord's Supper shapes Calvin's entire theology. Were it not for this distinctive doctrine, Lutherans and Calvinists would have come to agreement and mutual recognition long before the very recent understanding.

Yet most members of Reformed churches are likely to be unaware of the importance or uniqueness of the doctrine of the Lord's Supper in their tradition. If one were to suggest, for example, that the Reformed tradition insists upon the real presence of Christ in the sacrament, most church members and even many ministers might be surprised or even alarmed. They might protest that such a notion is too "catholic" for their taste.

Throughout the ages, Calvin and Calvinists have often been seen as Zwinglian by Lutherans and Anglicans, as well as by a great many Calvinists. Both Zwingli and Calvin used figurative language to explain that the bread and wine are tokens or reminders of the presence of Christ. Both were concerned about idolatry and thus about the confusion of the presence of Christ with the bread and wine.

Calvin himself insisted that Zwingli was wrong, especially about the principal agent in the sacraments, which, Calvin argued, was God rather than humanity or the church. The sacrament is an act of God, a sign by which God strengthens faith. Zwingli insisted that the Lord's Supper was an act of faith on the part of the communicant and thus argued that to eat was the same as to believe. For Calvin this would make the sacraments far too subjective and dependent upon human power; when people create their own meaning for the sacraments—getting baptized to celebrate one's own conversion, believing and thus experiencing Christ's presence, for example—the sacraments are not true signs.

Calvin drew upon scripture to understand the meaning of the Lord's Supper. As a Hebrew scholar, he was familiar with the meaning of the Passover festival and understood the Last Supper of Jesus in that light. Just as the Jews understood that the bread of the seder meal did not actually transport them back to Egypt at the time of the exodus, so Calvin sought to explain that the bread and wine did not enable participants to actually relive the Last Supper. Yet, as the Passover bread becomes the sign of the continuing reality of exodus and the people who partake are made one with their ancestors, so the bread of Communion unites the believers with Christ. Thus, to maintain that Christ is present in the sacrament follows from Calvin's understanding of Passover.

The Real Presence of Christ

The doctrine of the real presence of Christ in the sacrament is a consistent theme of Reformed confessions, as the Scots Confession makes very clear:

> We must assuredly believe that the bread which we break is the communion of Christ's body and the cup which we bless the communion of his blood. Thus we confess and believe without doubt that the faithful, in the right use of the Lord's Table, do so eat the body and drink the blood of the Lord Jesus that he remains in them and they in him; they are so made flesh of his flesh and bone of his bone.[1]

Calvin's own Geneva Catechism poses the question, "Do we then eat the body and blood of our Lord?" and the answer is:

> I understand so. For since all our confidence of salvation is placed in him, so that the obedience he offered to the Father may be accepted for us just as if it were our own, it is necessary that he be possessed by us. For he communicates his benefits to us in no other way than in making himself ours.[2]

Although this presence is often identified as a spiritual presence, the presence is nevertheless real and cannot be divorced from the elements of bread and wine. How this presence is realized, what causes it to take place, and other questions of that nature cannot ever really be answered but remain in the realm of mystery, as do most of the really important questions of faith and life.

The sacrifice of Christ upon the cross was a once-for-all-time event that is not repeated in our celebrations. Thus it can be said, "we do not re-enact God's grace or God's saving action or the story of salvation when we celebrate the Lord's Supper. We neither go back in time to sit with Christ and the disciples nor do we make Christ present in this particular celebration."[3] What happens in the holy meal is that Jesus Christ is given to us in the flesh and blood of our very souls. We are sealed by the presence of the Holy Spirit and made one with Christ.

Calvin had a flexible and constantly evolving view of the nature of the sacrament. In each edition of the *Institutes*, he made small changes in which he carefully worked to express the inexpressible; Calvin was trying to walk the difficult middle way between what he saw as overidentification of sign and what it symbolized, on the one hand, and too great a divorce between them, on the other. Holding the balance between these two extreme positions has been difficult for Reformed Protestants. We tend to slip into memorialism without even realizing that our tradition teaches otherwise. Inscribed upon countless Communion tables are the words, "in memory of me," in testimony to the mistaken importance placed upon the Supper as "nothing but a memorial." As if in response to our tendency toward emphasis upon symbol as disconnected from what it symbolizes, the Scots Confession declares, "Therefore if anyone slanders us by saying that we affirm or believe the Sacraments to be symbols and nothing more, they are libelous and speak against the plain facts."[4] Eating brings us into relationship with the crucified and risen Christ himself and includes more than our understanding; this relationship includes all that we are and thus our feelings as well.

Calvin insisted upon the reality of Christ's resurrected body and was concerned that Roman Catholic teaching had reduced that body to an idea or a concept. Quoting Paul, "Our citizenship is in heaven, and it is from there that we are expecting a Savior, the Lord Jesus Christ. He will transform the body of our humiliation that it may be conformed to the body of his glory . . . " (Phil. 3:20–21).

To Calvin, Christ meant something more noble and elevated than literally his eating his flesh. In Calvin's teaching about John in 6:56, he says that by eating his flesh, we mean our union with him, our partaking in his very life. Just as eating bread and not merely looking at bread nourishes our bodies, so it is with Christ: merely looking at him from afar accomplishes nothing for our salvation. Calvin believed that Zwingli completely missed this profound mystery.

Although Calvin agreed with Luther on the necessity to hold on to both a clear view of Christ's presence in the sacrament and the mystery of that presence, he could disagree with Luther over the issue of Christ's ubiquity. In order to assert that Christ is present at all times and places in the bread, Luther had to teach that the risen body of Christ can be everywhere at once, without limitations. Calvin insisted that Christ's resurrected body is connected to his human body, which ascended into heaven; otherwise, what kind of body is it? The doctrine of the ascension is necessary, for it informs us that Christ dwells at the right hand of God and, as Calvin puts it, "It is not in all places, but when it passes into one, it leaves the previous one" (IV.xvii.30). Christ, at the right hand of God, carries his humanity into heaven where he intercedes for us. Calvin was concerned about blurring the distinction between God and human nature and, thus, he was concerned about the nature of Christ's body: "If Christ's body is so multiform and varied that it shows itself in one place but is invisible in another, where is the very nature of a body? Which exists in its own dimensions, and where its unity?" (IV.xvii.19).

Christ cannot be brought down to us by any sacramental words or actions. About this, Calvin agreed with Zwingli. But he went beyond Zwingli to insist upon "the secret working of the spirit, which unites Christ himself to us" (IV.xvii.31). The Western church had for centuries identified the words of institution as the center of the sacred action, bringing to pass the miracle which the words speak so that when the words, "This is my body" and "This is the blood of the new covenant," are spoken, they are able to bring about what they proclaim. The Eastern Orthodox churches had, however, located the center of the eucharistic action in the invocation of the Holy Spirit, and the Reformed tradition borrows this approach from the East. The invocation of the Spirit was central to Calvin's eucharistic theology, because he argued the Spirit raises us to Christ's presence:

> This is the wonderful exchange which, out of his measureless benevolence, he has made with us; that, becoming Son of Man with us, he has made us sons of God with him; that, by his descent to earth, he has prepared an ascent to heaven for us; that, by taking on our mortality, he has conferred immortality upon us. (IV.xvii.2)

To eat the bread and drink of the cup is to participate mysteriously in the very being of the Christ, to become bone of his bone and flesh of his flesh, and to allow him to dwell in us fully. Before this powerful mystical experience, Calvin can only bow in homage. He knows he cannot fully understand it.

> Now if anyone should ask me how this takes place, I shall not be ashamed to confess that it is a secret too lofty for either my mind to comprehend or my words to declare. And, to speak more plainly, I rather experience it than understand it. Therefore, I here embrace without controversy the truth of God in which I may safely rest. He declares his flesh the food of my soul, his blood its drink. I offer my soul to him to be fed with such bread. (IV.xvii.32)

The spirit of divine mystery that Calvin understood so clearly has been dimmed by our tendency toward explanation of miracle rather than adoration of it. We are so much the product of the eighteenth-century Enlightenment that we have a hard time with anything we cannot understand. A recovery of Calvin's appreciation of mystery might well go a long way toward reviving the spirituality of Reformed Protestants. The sense of mystery shatters our rational desire to know and explain everything and puts us on our knees before the ultimate mystery of God's grace.

Over the centuries, "spiritual presence" has been the phrase most often used in the Reformed tradition to describe the mystery of the Lord's Supper. The Westminster Confession emphatically states that worthy receivers who partake of the visible elements "do then also inwardly by faith, really and indeed, yet not carnally and corporally, but spiritually, receive and feed upon Christ crucified, and all the benefits of his death."[5]

Christ's presence cannot be found in the bread, yet it cannot be divorced from it either. Christ's presence is the work of the Holy Spirit, which lifts us up to where Christ is and unites us in a mystical union to him. Some people have called this joining the "transubstantiation of the people." The mystical union is accomplished, not by bringing Christ down to the Table, but by raising us to heaven where Christ dwells with God.

Uses of the Sacrament

Calvin identified three particular "uses" of the sacrament that the Reformed tradition emphasizes: to confirm faith, to awaken thankfulness, and to encourage mutual love.[6]

Confirming Faith

The sacrament has a teaching role: to make clear the promise that Christ's body, which was once sacrificed on the cross, is now and will always be ours. God, out of love for us, invites us to partake so that we may have courage and strength for our lives. This invitation is the truth of the gospel itself. Yet, we need more concrete assurance of the basic promise that Christ is for us. The truth is too good to believe; our minds cannot understand it. We must be addressed in a language that we can comprehend.

The sacrament in dramatic form acts out this meaning so that we can grasp it. The sacrament is a powerful form of instruction for believers, and Calvin uses the language of instruction to describe the sacrament: *attests, confirms, shows, signifies, teaches*. Although he sounds like Zwingli, he speaks about more than memorialism, since Calvin consistently insisted that believers have a continuing relationship with Christ's bodily existence. The first function of the sacrament is to confirm this mystery in the hearts and minds of believers. This confirmation is always more than intellectual, although it includes the mind. The sacrament is a matter of our whole being, which needs that confirmation. The Heidelberg Catechism asks, "How are you reminded and assured in the Holy Supper that you participate in the one sacrifice of Christ on the cross and in all his benefits?" The answer is:

> In this way, Christ has commanded me and all believers to eat of this broken bread and to drink of this cup in remembrance of him. He has thereby promised that his body was offered and broken on the cross for me, and his blood was shed for me, as surely as I see with my eyes that the bread of the Lord is broken for me, and that the cup is shared with me.[7]

Awakening Thankfulness

As we understand the truth that Christ is mystically made one with us, our only possible response is thankfulness. Gratitude is the principal function of being human; our creation enables us to relate to God with grateful hearts. We are distinguished from the rest of the created order because we alone can respond to the majesty of God's goodness toward us by a conscious response of gratitude. In a sense, Calvin's whole theology is eucharistic: everything he wrote was for the purpose of developing thankfulness.

Without gratitude, there is no real piety. At the very beginning of the *Institutes*, Calvin shows that knowledge of God is for the purpose of piety, which he defines as, "that reverence joined with love of God which the knowledge of his benefits induces" (I.ii.1). Unless we recognize that we owe everything to God, we will never give our lives to God. All of life is really nothing more than a thankful response to our knowledge of God's love for us. Theologian Brian Gerrish says, "Gratitude or lack of it, is not only the theme of the Lord's Supper but a fundamental theme, perhaps the most fundamental theme, of an entire system of theology."[8]

As a loving and faithful parent, God wants to nourish us throughout the whole of our lives but also wishes to assure us of that persisting love. Thus God has given us the sacrament, "a spiritual banquet, wherein Christ attests himself to be the life-giving bread, upon which our souls feed unto true and blessed immortality" (IV.xvii.1).

Our most authentic nature as human beings is realized by the act of giving thanks to God, and nowhere is that more clear than at the Table of the Lord, where God's goodness is graphic. God feeds us. The Westminster Shorter Catechism explains in detail what is required of all who receive the sacrament, ending with the following: "in earnest hungering and thirsting after Christ, feeding on him by faith, receiving of his fullness, trusting in his merits, rejoicing in his love, giving thanks for his grace."[9]

If we were really to grasp the meaning of gratitude, our worship might be more enthusiastic. We would gather to praise and thank God with more passion than is usually true among us. We seem so calm and controlled, so lacking in deep feeling. If gratitude were the norm for the Christian life, then we would need fewer "shoulds" and "oughts" because we would be eager to do God's will out of love and thankfulness. If Eucharist as giving thanks were central in our celebration of the Lord's Supper, we might find ourselves dancing in the aisles, clapping our hands, and becoming carried away in the exuberance of the moment. Perhaps one of the reasons Reformed Protestants are often characterized as "God's frozen chosen" is that we do not celebrate Eucharist frequently enough to be formed as a grateful people. Without Eucharist, we put too much emphasis upon what we accomplish, upon our duty and responsibility. When we do celebrate the sacrament of Holy Communion, we often do so with a funereal attitude that focuses upon the death of Christ and forgets that the sacrament is also a resurrection meal. One sign of hope is that many of the newer Communion hymns are joyful. The sad and grim focus of so many Communion services may be one reason that we want to limit their frequency. Who wants those doleful services any more often than absolutely necessary?

To Encourage Mutual Love

Quite late in chapter 17 of the *Institutes*, Calvin begins a section,

> Thirdly, the Lord also intended the Supper to be a kind of exhortation for us which can more forcefully than any other means quicken and inspire us both to purity and holiness of life, and to love, peace and concord. (IV.xvii.38)

Calvin's eucharistic theology and thus his spirituality in general (for they cannot be separated) are corporate: "Now since he has only one body, of which he makes us all partakers, it is necessary that all of us also be made one body by such participation" (IV.xvii.38). Because we share in the one body, we are made one with all who join us in that sharing. The Lord's Supper is thus the ground for Christian community. Calvin uses the analogy common in the early church about the bread being made of many grains, mixed together so that they are no longer distinguishable, "so it is fitting that in the same way we should be joined and bound together by such great agreement of minds that no sort of disagreement or division may intrude" (IV.xvii.38). Quoting from

Paul (1 Cor. 10:16–17), "The cup of blessing that we bless, is it not a sharing in the blood of Christ? The bread that we break, is it not a sharing in the body of Christ? Because there is one bread, we who are many are one body, for we all partake of the one bread. . . ." Calvin uses Paul to bolster his argument that unity of the church is rooted in unity in Christ. To be bound together with Christ is to be bound together with all those who share in Christ.

The real presence of Christ connects all that has been scattered and broken. Because of his mystical vision of union with Christ, Calvin sees the necessity of treating each other with tender care. In one of his most poetic and eloquent statements in the *Institutes*, he writes,

> None of the brethren can be injured, despised, rejected, abused, or in any way offended by us, without at the same time, injuring, despising, and abusing Christ by the wrongs we do; that we cannot disagree with our brethren without at the same time disagreeing with Christ: that we cannot love Christ without loving him in the brethren. (IV.xvii.38)

The very word "communion" implies both a vertical connection with the risen Christ and a horizontal connection with each other. The Confession of 1967 makes those connections very clear: "The Lord's Supper is a celebration of the reconciliation of men with God and with one another in which they joyfully eat and drink together at the table of their Savior."[10] We belong to each other because we are one with Christ. We should show the same care for others that we show for ourselves because we are united to what Calvin, quoting Augustine, calls "the bond of love." As Christ makes us one with himself, he makes us, therefore, one with each other. The Belgic Confession summarizes the meaning of the sacrament in these words: "In short, by the use of this holy sacrament we are moved to a fervent love of God and our neighbor."[11]

The mystery of Christ's presence in the sacrament holds us together in community; his presence is the real source of a union with each other that goes beyond anything really rational. A healthy sacramental understanding can help us to avoid vagueness, hard logical rationality, otherworldliness, the antihuman bias common in much spirituality today, and also the individualistic privatism that is everywhere in our culture. The social dimension of Christianity is at the very heart of a sacramental spirituality so that the whole of humanity is present at the Lord's Table, including the poor, the sick, and the oppressed.

The different names for the sacrament point to the various meanings among us. We call it the *Lord's Supper* to remind ourselves of its connection to the last supper that Jesus ate with the disciples and also to demonstrate that we believe that we eat the meal together as a community of faith. We call it *Holy Communion* to signify our belief that in this meal we are made one with each other and with the risen Christ who is present with us. We commune with him and with one another. We call it *Eucharist* because it is a meal of thanksgiving. We may also refer to it as the *breaking of bread* to point to the connection of what we do to what was done in the New Testament church. Each of these meanings holds up one particular facet of the many-faceted meanings of this sacrament.

The Shape and Order of the Lord's Supper

As one reads various denominational worship resources, an ecumenical consensus becomes obvious; the similarities are much more apparent than the differences. Nowhere is this consensus more obvious than in the ordering of the sacrament. The various Reformed liturgies share with the liturgies of traditions as varied as Lutheran, Episcopalian, Roman Catholic, and Methodist, a structure that points to the result of decades of dialogue and mutual study. All these orders for the Lord's Supper place the sacrament after the sermon as a response to the preaching of the Word. Called, variously, the response to the Word, the visible Word, or the enacted Word, the sacrament follows after and is validated by the reading and preaching of the Word written. The basic order is as follows:

1. *The invitation to the Lord's Table:* The invitation is nearly universal although it takes many different forms, from reading the constitutional requirements for reception to an open invitation using scripture such as, "Come to me, all you that are weary and are carrying heavy burdens, and I will give you rest. Take my yoke upon you, and learn from me" (Matt. 11:28–29a). Often the invitation includes words from Luke's Gospel telling of the disciples on the road to Emmaus and their encounter with the risen Jesus. Such a reading or telling of this story helps to anchor the sacred meal in the resurrection as an opportunity to discover Christ's risen presence now in the breaking of the bread. Making the connection between Communion and the resurrection might free our celebrations to become more celebrative and less the funereal, mournful memorial to "poor dead Jesus" that they so often become.

2. *The words of institution:*

> For I received from the Lord what I also handed on to you, that the Lord Jesus on the night when he was betrayed took a loaf of bread, and when he had given thanks, he broke it and said, 'This is my body that is for you. Do this in remembrance of me.' In the same way he took the cup also, after supper, saying, 'This cup is the new covenant in my blood. Do this, as often as you drink it, in remembrance of me.' For as often as you eat this bread and drink the cup, you proclaim the Lord's death until he comes. (1 Cor. 11:23–26)

In the Reformed tradition, these words come at this place in the service as a scriptural warrant for the sacrament, which is observed in obedience to Christ's command to his followers to "do this."

Since the words of institution (almost always from Paul's letter to the Corinthians) are not really in prayer form and because the action of the one presiding is important to see as well as hear, not including these words in the prayer is probably preferable. The minister takes a loaf of bread and breaks it in full view of the people, a dramatic and powerful act. Then the pastor takes a pitcher and pours from it into a chalice to emphasize the "poured out" sacrifice of Christ for us.

3. *The greeting:* The ancient greeting has become common to nearly all liturgies as a way of establishing the connection between the celebrant and the people:

The Lord be with you.
✠ **And with your spirit.**[12]

4. *The Sursum Corda:* Reformed Protestants have also adopted, with amazing ease, forms rejected by our ancestors, so that the "Reformed *Sursum Corda*"[13] has given way to the more ancient form as the beginning of the Great Prayer of Thanksgiving that follows the greeting. This ecumenical *Sursum Corda* establishes the celebration as grounded in gratitude, which is basic to the meaning of the sacrament:

Lift up your hearts.
✠ **We lift them to the Lord.**

Let us give thanks to the Lord, our God.
✠ **It is right to give our thanks and praise.**

5. *The Great Prayer of Thanksgiving:* This three-part prayer follows a Trinitarian pattern. The whole of this prayer and its hymnic conclusion offer praise and thanksgiving to God on behalf of the whole world. Many new and upbeat musical settings of these ancient hymns help to establish a tone of praise for the sacrament. Part one is devoted to thanksgiving to God for creation, salvation, and the blessings of this life. This part, which is *eucharist* proper (the word *eucharist* means "thanksgiving"), concludes with the saying or singing of the *Sanctus*, an ancient song of praise to God:

Holy, Holy, Holy Lord, God of power and might. Heaven and earth are full of your glory.

Very often, the words of the *Benedictus* are added, which in contemporary form are:

Hosanna in the highest! Blessed is the one who comes in the name of the Lord. Hosanna in the highest!

Part two is remembrance, or *anamnesis*, of what Jesus has done, and recites elements of his birth, life, teachings, death, and resurrection. Here we also offer our sacrifice of praise and thanksgiving, and conclude with the great memorial acclamation (spoken or sung), "Christ has died, Christ is risen, Christ will come again."

Part three of the prayer is the invocation (*epiclesis*) of the Holy Spirit, in which the action of the Spirit is sought for the recognition of Christ's risen presence in the bread and wine. Reformed prayers may emphasize the "transubstantiation" of the people at this point, praying for our unity as Christ's body in this place as the action of the Spirit. This section of the prayer often concludes with the commemoration of the faithful departed. Occasionally a Reformed prayer might include the words of institution at this point, but more often, following long custom, those words are offered either right after the invitation and before the prayer or after the Great Prayer has concluded with the Lord's Prayer.

6. *The distribution:* With the words "The gifts of God for the people of God," the time for distribution has come. In Reformed congregations, the elders along with the pastors typically serve the people either by taking the elements to the people in their pews or by standing at the head of the aisles as the people come forward.

7. *The conclusion:* The service concludes with a prayer of thanks for the gift of the sacrament and the singing of a hymn.

Contemporary Issues

Many congregations are struggling with particular issues having to do with understanding and celebrating the Lord's Supper. These issues may be a source of conflict in particular congregations, and they point to the need for education about the meaning of the sacrament in our Reformed tradition:

1. *Recovery of mystery:* One of the tragedies of Reformed churches today is that we have largely forgotten our heritage. Most Reformed churches have adopted Zwinglian memorialism, which far outdoes Zwingli by reducing the sacrament to something rational, and insisting that the bread and wine are *only* symbols, as if symbols were not very important. We tend to reduce the sacrament to a kind of visual aid to remember what Jesus did long ago without much sense of the holy mystery of his presence.

2. *Frequency of celebration:* Our infrequent celebration of the Lord's Supper suggests that we do not believe it is essential for the Christian life and is, perhaps, an "add-on" to worship. The integrity of the relationship between Word and sacrament has dissolved into an emphasis upon the Word over against the sacrament. This emphasis upon the Word alone has produced an overly intellectual form of worship that lacks heart. The sermon, without the balance of the sacrament, has often become a kind of lecture on things religious, and the people, instead of being participants in the divine drama, think of themselves as spectators whose role is to be resident critics of what takes place. Fortunately, a present trend is to increase the frequency of celebrations so that many congregations now have monthly rather than quarterly Communion, and some congregations have moved to weekly Communion. Regular and frequent celebrations make clear that the sacrament is a normal part of Christian worship, and that it balances the sermon with something for the eye to see, the hands to touch, and the mouth to taste. In other words, Communion provides substance for the senses. We take part in a meal that announces who we are and binds us together with each other and with our risen Lord.

3. *The presider:* No New Testament guidance on this matter is available because who presided probably varied from congregation to congregation in the early church. Presiding may have been a shared responsibility among many leaders, but gradually it came to be the right and privilege of those set apart by ordination as clergy. The Reformers did not challenge this approach, and for most Reformed Protestants the pastor is the only celebrant. Some exceptions permit elders to preside as long as this person clearly does so under the authority of a proper governing body. In the Christian Church (Disciples of Christ), elders preside at the Lord's Table.

4. *The elements:* The minimal material objects often used in the sacrament—tiny precut cubes of bread and thimble-sized glasses of grape juice—bear little resemblance to actual bread and wine. They certainly do not represent the wholeness of the body of Christ broken for us nor the fact that together we make up that body as we take from the one loaf; breaking a cube of bread with any dramatic action is difficult indeed. In many congregations, no chalice is present and wine is not poured at all. While good reasons for using grape juice rather than real wine may be present, the symbolism is more difficult to maintain. The chief argument for not using wine is the concern about causing difficulty for alcoholics. Nonalcoholic forms of wine are available so that people with an alcohol problem are not caused temptation, and in this manner everyone would have some sense of the ancient symbol. Whether wine or grape juice is used, the presider can pour the wine (grape juice) from a pitcher into

a chalice while saying the words of institution. In the same way, a large loaf of bread (or large piece of unleavened bread) should be on the table so that the minister can break it at the appropriate moment. If that same bread is used for the distribution among the people, then the unity of the congregation as the body of Christ is made clear. To have the server actually tear off a piece of the bread and place it in the outstretched palm of the communicant is a further sign of being served by the host.

5. *The method of serving:* The Reformed tradition has recognized at least three different methods of serving: (1) having the people come forward to receive while standing, as Calvin did in Geneva; (2) serving the people seated in their pews, as Zwingli did in Zurich; or (3) serving the people as they sit at long tables placed down the aisles, which became the custom in the Netherlands. The method that became normative for most American Reformed congregations was likely the most efficient and least time-consuming: serving the people in their pews. This method permitted the elders to demonstrate their role as spiritual leaders of the congregation and enabled the people to serve one another, but also further encouraged a sense of the people as spectators. Because the congregation does not have to respond to the invitation, the people become passive recipients of the sacrament. Coming forward is a sign of one's acceptance of Christ's invitation and of one's willingness to take on the task of being a disciple. In the coming and going that are necessary for receiving the sacrament at the table, people meet each other, acknowledge each other's presence, and become more of a community of faith than they can possibly do sitting in their pews.

6. *The furniture:* The table, which is the center of the action, should look like a table and be treated like a table. The sacrament is a meal, and everything should indicate its character as a meal. Even traditions that have historically tended to place the table against the wall and have named it "the altar" have recently shifted their emphasis to a table and have either added another table, positioned so that the people can gather around it, or moved the altar itself away from the wall. Reformed Christians have always insisted upon a table, although some churches have been built to imitate cathedrals. The table should not only be placed so that the presider can stand behind it and be seen and heard; the table should have on it symbols that point to its use. The chalice and a plate should be on the table whatever the occasion. Candles may also adorn the table just as they would a dining table in one's home. If clutter can be avoided, a small bouquet of flowers may also be appropriate. The offering plates should not be placed upon the table, for this suggests that the offering is a sacrifice offered at an altar. Other than these essentials, the table should be kept as clear as possible.

The Lord's Supper
as a Source of Renewal

Restoring regular sacramental observance in which the people are involved in
the action and the symbols are magnified rather than minimized would be a
major component in the renewal of worship among Reformed Protestants.

Recovering a sense of the sacrament as a prefiguring of the messianic banquet is a central way that sacramental renewal can take place. Not only does
the sacrament point back to Jesus' saving death for us and to the present in
which we are gathered to be fed with spiritual food for our journey, the sacrament also points to the future. It is a meal between the ages, in anticipation of
the heavenly meal to which Jesus looked forward as he shared his last meal with
his disciples. The church always looks forward to this grand climax of history
as the source of hope in the present. Eucharist brings out the tensions between
the "already" and the "not yet" of our lives. Here, at the Lord's Table, we are
one; we leave aside petty differences to proclaim our unity in Christ. At this
table there is enough for everyone; all will be fed equally, and those matters
that mark some people as more important than others are left aside. Coming
to the table, we announce our common need to be fed by Christ.

By sharing in this feast of anticipation, we become bearers of hope in a
world that has little hope. The future dimension of the Eucharist is what gives
the sacrament a sense of joy and celebration. As those who bear witness to
God's coming future, we share and we are a joyful people. To be fed at this
table is to be sustained for the duties and hazards of discipleship . . . to be
enabled to see all things from the perspective of hope in the God of the
resurrection.

6

The Service
for the Lord's Day

Worship is the acknowledgment and response to a sense of the presence of the divine. Human beings worship to express the divine-human relationship; to communicate that relationship with each other; to express awe, wonder, and amazement because of who God is; and to communicate with God in some way by expressions of appreciation, confession, and petition. Worship is as natural as breathing: "To withhold acknowledgment, to avoid celebration, to stifle gratitude, may prove as unnatural as holding one's breath."[1] People who have given up on worship in churches often find a substitute of some sort, whether it be a twelve-step program, a meditation group, or even a book study group to try to meet at least some of the needs they surrender by avoiding worship.

The service of worship for the Lord's Day is the central service of worship for Christians in nearly all traditions. The Lord's Day has been understood to be the day of resurrection, and every Sunday is a little Easter and has the quality of celebration, even when Sundays fall within a penitential season such as Lent. Sunday is not the Sabbath day, which is Saturday, but it is the *first day*, the beginning of something new, the sign of the new creation.

The concerns of different historical periods have dictated the order and elements of a service of worship, but most of them—like a good drama—have a logical flow. The place, ritual, season or occasion, and leadership all make their impact.

One early order of service can be found in the great call of Isaiah, found in Isaiah 6. We can imagine Isaiah approaching the Holy of Holies in the Temple in fear and trepidation, for no one was allowed to look upon God and live. Smoke from the sacrifices and censers fill the holy place so that his eyes can barely discern the great figures of the cherubim and seraphim. The sense of the holiness of God is so overpowering that even the cherubim use two of their six wings to cover their faces, and a great song is lifted: "Holy, holy, holy is the LORD of hosts; the whole earth is full of his glory!"

79

Before the presence of the great God of heaven and earth, Isaiah is suddenly struck with a sense of his own unworthiness: "Woe is me! I am lost, for I am a man of unclean lips." But Isaiah is ritually purified by the touch of a live coal from the altar. At that moment Isaiah hears God's call to service: "Whom shall I send, and who will go for us?" Isaiah, in utter commitment and dedication, responds, "Send me!"

This simple account contains an important and natural four-part order for worship:

1. Entering the place of worship with a sense of awe in the presence of the holy.
2. Realizing and acknowledging one's unworthiness, then receiving absolution.
3. Hearing the Word of God.
4. Responding by giving of oneself and going out to serve.

Both eucharistic and noneucharistic services contain this basic pattern, which flows with the honest emotions of the worshiper. Worship that touches the spirit is not just a lot of elements thrown together; by this means, the worshipper is led into the presence of God, confronted with the Word of God, encouraged to make a commitment, and sent forth to serve.

From Jerusalem Temple to Reformed Sanctuary

The ancient Jerusalem Temple service centered on the sacrifice conducted by a priest at the altar. During the exile and later, well established by the time of Jesus, a new option had developed: a service of reading of and commentary on the Torah, led by a rabbi rather than a priest. With the destruction of the Temple in A.D. 70, the pattern of sacrificial worship disappeared from Judaism, and the service of the Word became the norm. Synagogues spread throughout the world as Jews dispersed to virtually every nation in Europe and to parts of Asia and Africa.

We can observe some parallels here with the Protestant Reformation. Though Luther retained the weekly Eucharist—which had been standard procedure since the time of the early church—people in many Protestant cities, especially Geneva, feared that the Mass had become too mechanical and too filled with superstition. Too many people believed that they could go into a church, eat the bread and wine, and be assured of their salvation—all without being exposed to the Word of God.

When Zwingli replaced the weekly celebration of the Lord's Supper with a quarterly celebration, the service of preaching and prayer became the accepted form of worship for the Lord's Day. His ideas caught on with Protestants, both

Lutheran and Reformed. The result was that Protestant worship evolved into what became essentially a preaching service. Rather than the garments of priests, ministers wore the black academic gown worn every day by scholars in the universities; they were ministers or "teaching elders" rather than priests who offered a sacrifice at an altar. The service centered upon reading and preaching the Bible, with singing hymns and prayers. The emphasis moved from reflection on the presence of Christ in the bread and wine to the task of mission and ministry, from contemplation to action.

John Calvin would have retained weekly Communion, but his town council would not allow it more often than four times a year, so his service also became a preaching service, much to his annoyance. Luther had a similar experience and was likewise disappointed. Many Protestants were glad to be free of the medieval Mass. They had been taught to fear eating unworthily to their damnation and were not eager for regular Communion. Also, the celebration of Communion in the West was so focused upon the death and sacrifice of Jesus that Communion had an almost funereal quality. The Reformers were unable to change that solemnity into a mood of joy. The spread of learning and the newfound ability to read also led to an emphasis upon logical thinking and a demeaning of the mystical.

The Reformation in England had to do more with ecclesiastical structure than with theology and worship, and this approach affected the American service. Archbishop Thomas Cranmer's *Book of Common Prayer* sought to provide an English Protestantized version of the Mass, but also included morning prayer and evening prayer, which were noneucharistic. Over the centuries, these noneucharistic patterns became preferred, and a liturgical renewal movement—the Anglo-Catholic Revival of the late nineteenth century—was required to again make the Eucharist the norm.

The medieval and renaissance church had neglected preaching so much that it was virtually not practiced. As the Reformers pulled back from the centrality of the Eucharist, preaching was elevated almost to sacramental status. The right exposition of the Word of God became the means by which the people had an experience of the living God or came into the presence of God. The people had been kept from reading and studying the Bible for so long that an almost insatiable hunger had developed among them. Sermons that lasted for as long as an hour were praised, and preachers were expected to preach both morning and evening six days of the week. The emotional impact that had previously come through the reception of the "body and blood of Christ" was transferred to the hearing of the sermon.

Certainly this form of worship predominated among the American revival services and camp meetings of the eighteenth century onwards. The service began with a great deal of enthusiastic singing and fervent prayers, climaxing with powerful preaching that included the invitation to accept the Lordship of Jesus Christ (known as the "altar call"), then a dedication and sending forth. Many churches in America still follow this format, although the worship materials issued by the various Reformed churches seek to make Communion more frequent and put the sermon at the center rather than the climax of worship.

Today, though most denominations encourage more frequent Communion, the typical Protestant service is noneucharistic. But even a preaching service can remind us that the sacrament still stands at the center of our worship. If the same structure is used for the Lord's Day service, whether or not the sacrament is being observed, the point is implicitly made. The noneucharistic service may thus be a preparation to receive the Lord's Supper. A prayer of thanksgiving can occupy the same position in the service that the Great Thanksgiving has in a eucharistic service and serve as a reminder of the normative quality of the sacrament.

Structure for Worship

The design of the service frequently includes a dynamic tension between freedom and structure. At least three types of order have emerged among Protestants: the variety service—sometimes called the "hymn sandwich service"—the thematic service, and the stimulus/response service. Each worship structure has its own rationale.

The variety service is made up of interchangeable parts but follows the same order week after week. The three hymns, praise, and reflection and commitment determine the order and set the themes, which is the origin of the nickname "hymn sandwich." The anthem always follows the sermon, and the service alternates between music and speech, standing and sitting, speaking and responding. The strength of this form of ordering worship is that people know what to expect. The pattern does not vary from week to week. Each piece of music fits into its context and has a rationale. The real center of the service is the sermon, to which all the other elements build. The weakness of this service is its resistance to change. Its logic is its predictability, and woe to the pastor who seeks to make even minor changes.

The thematic service, which is organized around a central theme such as ecology, family, or gratitude, is easiest to construct for special days, such as Easter, Thanksgiving Day, or Stewardship Sunday. The service has a clear rationale, since all of its parts are related to the overall subject. The hymns and other music are chosen in relation to that theme. The worshiper can immediately see how the parts fit together. The problem is that on a regular week-by-week basis, such thematic construction is difficult to achieve.

The stimulus/response or alternation service is built around forms of divine address, followed by a response of the people. The call to worship in scriptural words is followed by a hymn or a prayer of invocation. The invitation to confession is followed by a unison prayer of confession. The service thus moves back and forth. Each part has a clear reason for being just where it is. In this ordering of worship, the sermon as address to the people is followed by the response of prayer and offering. This form makes great sense and gives flow to the service, but persuading a congregation to try it may be difficult and resistance may be its chief weakness.

Whatever order is used, worship should not be so formulaic that it leaves no room for the work of the Holy Spirit. A word of caution is necessary, however, because some free forms exhibit a carelessness or disorder that may become an impediment to worship.

People who are responsible for worship should be guided by the Holy Spirit speaking through scripture; the historic experience of the church universal; the Reformed tradition; the creeds, confessions, and constitutional directives of the church; and the needs and traditions of the particular congregation.

The Ordering of the Service (Noneucharistic)

The fourfold division we noted earlier that comes from Isaiah is a valuable way to order the service, although the divisions are not necessarily balanced in terms of time requirements.

1. Gathering

Worship begins with God. God takes the initiative and calls us into being as a community during the gathering of the people. Ritually this part of the service is more than just having people come in and sit down. One issue to address immediately is: Do we gather in silent prayer and meditation or in community? No simple answer is necessarily forthcoming, as various communities adopt individual styles. In some, quiet music plays or silence is maintained as people come in and pray. In others, the musician strives to be heard over the joyous buzz of conversation as people greet and inquire after one another. Some argue that "we need time to prepare ourselves for worship." Others suggest a difference between corporate worship and private devotions, and that the greeting of the "body of Christ" is its own kind of music. The solution to the dilemma is probably a matter of congregational preference, for the skilled worship leader can work with either style.

Once the people have gathered, certain "business" may need to be conducted. Spoken announcements can be made here, so as not to disrupt the flow of worship. (An alternative is to make them at the end of the service, but in this position announcements can squelch the emotional high point achieved during the service.) This opening time is also good for "practice," to make sure that the people are prepared for their parts in the liturgy—whether it be the teaching of new music or comments about how the service will proceed.

Visitors must be made to feel welcome early in the service. Welcoming necessarily takes different forms depending upon the size of the congregation, but a warm and genuine greeting should be extended to visitors along with an invitation to participate in other activities of the congregation. If Communion is celebrated that day, visitors should be informed about who may participate in the sacrament (called "fencing the table") and be invited to partake, if they are eligible. This aspect of the service is part of the ancient rite of hospitality. In our culture, many people wish to be anonymous, and singling them out for too much attention may drive them away. Strike a balance between welcome and intrusive gushing over them. Placing the passing of the peace at this point in the service is useful, because it establishes the community that can then proceed to worship together. In some congregations, the subculture limits the greeting to a verbal exchange; in others, the subculture permits handshakes or even hugs. However warmly people welcome each other, encouraging them to say the words, "The peace of the Lord be with you," or something similar, eliminates confusion and awkwardness. If the people wear nametags, they may call each other by name.

Having performed the necessary business, the people are ready to begin the service itself.

The people are now called to worship, symbolically and literally (perhaps preceded by an introit from the choir). The call to worship invites the people to put away their other concerns and focus on the many ways God cares for the people—and will continue to do so. The Psalm of the day may be adapted responsively for this purpose.

Many calls to worship are responsive between leader and people. The following example involves these two parties and a third voice as well:

Call to Worship

Liturgist: In silence and in wonder, in order and disorder, Christ Jesus enters our world to make home in us.
People: **And God spoke: I am for you!**

Liturgist: In Christ there is neither Hebrew nor Christian, neither skeptic nor convert.
People: **In Christ there is neither African nor European, neither Central American nor Indonesian.**

Liturgist: And God spoke: I am for you!
People: **Christ is Light for the world.**

Voice One: Christ is unity for the world.
Liturgist: In Christ there is neither feminine nor masculine,
People: **Neither slave nor free.**

Liturgist: In Christ there is neither privilege nor poverty,
Voice Two: Neither learned nor ignorant:
Unison: And God spoke: I am for you!

Liturgist: Christ is our Light; our Life:
Voice Three: Christ is our confidence; our future,
Voice Four: Christ is the Hope of the World.

Liturgist: Christ calls a new church into being:
Unison: And God speaks: I am for you.[2]

Then comes a great opening hymn of praise to God. In those churches where it is possible, a procession of leaders may symbolize the entrance of the people of God. At this moment in the service is one of the few places where dramatic movement can happen regularly, easily, and naturally.

The procession may begin with a crucifer (cross bearer) carrying a cross, followed by worship leaders and choir. On festival Sundays, banners and processional torches may be processed. Churches that light candles can do so in this segment, possibly during the processional hymn.

2. Confession of Sin and Assurance of Pardon

As in Isaiah's experience, our coming into the presence of God gives us a sense of our own unworthiness. Honesty requires that the community be grounded in God, which can be done only by recognizing our brokenness. For this reason a prayer of confession occurs now, possibly followed by the response, *Kyrie Eleison* ("Lord, have mercy"). Then comes the joyous assurance of forgiveness, followed by the *Gloria Patri* or the *Gloria in Excelsis*. Another possible response is the *Te Deum Laudamus* ("You Are God, We Adore You"), or singing a hymn verse.

In the following section, we provide examples of prayers of confession and assurances of pardon. In the prayers, note whether or not these are "transgressions" that are applicable to the whole congregation. Nothing is worse for an individual or congregation than having to confess to something they didn't do!

Prayer of Confession

✠ *Merciful God, we are always wanting our due.
It is easy to see what we should receive,
but somehow we are blind to our responsibility.
We work to save what we do not even want
and value objects over people.
Help us to know your mind, O Christ,
and learn your way.
Commit us to building the place where all are welcome,
where all will be cared for. Amen.[3]

Assurance of Pardon

Our God is a loving God, but also one of expectations.
We are forgiven, but we must forgive;
and we must strive to live as though that forgiveness is important to us.
Live in the promise that we are God's people,
forgiven in Christ and empowered to serve.
✠ Thanks be to God. Amen.

Prayer of Confession

✠ As we come to your great table, Lord,
we realize how small we have made our own.
We carefully plan what we will eat,
not thinking of the many who will go hungry.
We hoard what we have while others starve.
We could open our purses and our hearts to the needy, but we don't.
Judge us harshly enough, Lord, so that we will be changed
to live—and give—as you would have us. Amen.[4]

*Words spoken by the congregation are set in boldface and follow a Greek cross.

Assurance of Pardon

Our Lord spoke of the Kingdom of Heaven,
comparing it to a great feast where all are invited.
Those who were unworthy were invited in;
those who prided themselves on being worthy
were asked to sit near the back.
We are invited to know God's love,
the most gracious part of which is divine forgiveness.
For in Jesus Christ, we are forgiven and saved.
✠ **Thanks be to God. Amen.**

Prayer of Confession

✠ **Almighty God,**
  You come to me to release me from feelings that are difficult for me,
  like sadness or grief, loss or disappointment, fear or anger,
  feelings in which I am caught because they are so difficult for me.
  To my mind, release means that I will no longer have these feelings.
  To your mind, release means that I will be able to have them,
  and to allow them to come and go as necessary.
  I confess that I hold on to my understanding of release,
  even though I know from experience that my way makes my life harder.
  Amen.[5]

3. The Service of the Word

One of John Calvin's greatest liturgical contributions was his insistence that the reading of the Word must be preceded by the prayer for the illumination of the Holy Spirit. Such a prayer is an open admission that the words of scripture only become the Word of God when they are received with prayer. Nothing automatic transmits the Word from the text to the people. People can hear the Bible read and keep a closed mind, unable to hear what God has to say. The Reformed tradition has, at its best, never been hospitable to a fundamentalism that assumes that simply by hearing the words of scripture the Word of God is automatically received. We pray that the light of God will shine upon our spirits and the Holy Spirit will be in the reading and hearing of the Word, bringing us out of darkness, thus changing the reading from a simple reading of words to an act of revelation. The Holy Spirit is invited to be present in the activity that is being undertaken, hearing the Word of God.

Prayer for Illumination

God of light, be our light.
Fill us with your Spirit
so that we may hear and understand and do
what is your will, through Jesus Christ.
✠ **Amen.**[6]

Prayer for Illumination

God who spoke to Moses in the burning bush,
speak through the words we read and hear this day.
God who spoke in the Word made flesh,
come and be incarnate in us.
God who spoke in many tongues at Pentecost,
remove our confusion and make us fit for service.
✠ **Amen.**

Most lectionaries provide three readings for each Sunday plus a Psalm: the First Reading or Old Testament, the Epistle, and the Gospel. However, in many congregations, reading all of these each Sunday may be too much scripture. Introducing each reading briefly helps prepare the listener for what is to be heard. The introductory comments should provide context or can suggest things to look for, or may even contain a very brief word study. They are not, however, intended to be miniature sermons or a paraphrase of what is to be read. Before beginning the reading, the lector may say something like, "Listen for the Word of God." Though the readings follow in order, they may be interspersed by appropriate hymns or songs, poetry, or music from the choir or soloists.

Whoever does the reading should prepare carefully; sloppy or thoughtless reading suggests that scripture is unimportant. The use of pew Bibles enables people to follow the reading and better comprehend the read passages; further, seeing the full scripture gives a better context for the reading.

Following the final reading, most contemporary orders suggest that the reader may say, "The Word of the Lord," and the congregation may respond, "Thanks be to God." Another ascription by the reader is, "The grass withers, the flower fades, but the word of our God endures forever" (Isa. 40:8).

(A word of warning about an issue of serious concern: A practice coming into vogue in some areas is for pastors not to read scripture but simply to paraphrase it using their own words. This practice defies every principle of the Reformation, for the Reformers felt it was essential for the people to have direct access to the Word and not have it mediated by a priest.)

Next comes the sermon, which is an exposition, interpretation, or weaving of one or a number of scripture passages. Pastors have no particular wisdom to give to the people beyond their training to interpret scripture, which sets pastors apart and provides their authority for preaching. Of course, sometimes pastors preach upon a particular subject or theme, but even then the sermon needs to be focused upon the biblical text. Most people who worship regularly are not readily conversant with scripture. They need help. Many of them are hungry for insight into the text.

The pastor stands with one foot (so to speak) in the biblical text and the other in the modern world in which people are struggling to live faithfully. Every sermon must speak directly to them and seek to shed light upon their lives, make faith more real for them, and provide guidance. A sermon that has no clear reference to the lives of the people becomes irrelevant and boring, no matter how well delivered. The pastor who is in daily touch with the people—praying for them, dealing with their problems, and struggling to be faithful to Christ with them—typically does not find difficult the application.

A good preacher takes biblical scholarship into account, although a sermon is not a Bible study. Part of pastoral integrity is treating people with respect for their minds and trusting that they can handle the truth, even when challenging their cherished fantasies. A sermon should not pretend that the biblical passage has miraculously descended from the mouth of God but rather acknowledge that it has gone through human minds and often endured a process of oral transmission. Not all scripture is equally inspirational. Some passages need to be seen as sub-Christian, such as those that cry out for vengeance, and the pastor needs to say so and give people permission to have their own internal debate with scripture.

The familiar definition of preaching as "truth through personality" is still relevant. The preacher's task is to be so personally present that the people can see the connection between the words that are spoken and the person doing the speaking. Of course, no preacher should ever pretend to incarnate the gospel, but honesty is the key. If the preacher does not believe something, either admitting doubt, which is likely to be shared by others, or speaking about something that does ring true is the best approach. People have a remarkable ability to distinguish the phony from the real, and younger people are especially suspicious; they long for authenticity. Not every sermon will require self-revelation on the part of the pastor, but many preachers err on the side of keeping the sermon at arm's length from their person by avoiding all personal illustrations—a tragic mistake. A canned illustration has nothing like the power of one that is drawn from real life.

Most sermons today are probably too long, although cultural differences are a factor here. A ten- to fifteen-minute sermon holds the attention of most congregations, because they are used to television segments of that duration. Sermons exceeding twenty minutes cause most minds to wander. Wandering minds can produce profound spiritual insights, but they are more prone to be planning activities for the rest of the day.

4. The Commitment of the People and Sending Forth

Having heard God's Word, the time has come to respond in appropriate ways. One immediate response to hearing the Word proclaimed might be a time of silence in which people are given opportunity to reflect upon what they have heard and consider the message. An affirmation of faith can also be used at this point. Every denomination produces wonderful new affirmations that add to the older ecumenical creeds and affirm the life of Jesus by applying his life to ours.

An Affirmation of Faith

✠ **We believe in God:**
    who welcomes our laughter
    and moves us to wonder . . .
We believe in Christ:
    who welcomes our questions
    and loves us to trust . . .
We believe in Spirit:
    who welcomes our doubts
    and loves us to faith.
This we believe! Amen![7]

Realizing God's goodness, we may want to bring an offering at this time. The offering is of ourselves and of what we have. Though money is collected, an offering is not a "collection," because the purpose is to offer what we have to God, not have our dues collected. Following the offering may be a sung response such as the commonly used Doxology, which now appears in a variety of texts in modern hymnals for congregations that prefer to avoid the masculine language of the traditional version. Hymn verses can be used for this purpose, e.g., "We Give Thee But Thine Own." Also appropriate at this time is a unison prayer of dedication as the ushers present the offerings. The following is one such prayer:

Prayer of Dedication

✠ God of abundance, Creator of all that is,
   we bring these offerings to you with thanksgiving
   for the multitude of blessings that we receive each day.
   We bring our monetary gifts
   as well as our gifts of time, talent, and creativity.
   Bless them to your service. Amen.[8]

Then the concerns of the people are lifted to God in prayer. The person leading the prayer can suggest concerns of the congregation, naming people who are ill, people who have died, a new birth, or people who celebrate another year of life or marriage. Including the concerns for the wider world is a way of extending the life of the congregation beyond the four walls. Various forms of prayer may be used—a single form or a number of forms, generally followed by our Lord's Prayer.

The service often concludes with a hymn, which speaks of the work or life of the Christian, a charge to service, and a benediction, and joyous music as the people depart.

Planning for Worship

Sometimes congregations expend little or no effort to plan worship. The pastor simply changes the hymns, scripture reading, and sermon title, and, of course, some of the announcements. The organist or choir director fills in the places reserved for their particular musical selections, and the bulletin is sent off to be put together by the secretary.

Unplanned worship has the advantage of not taking much time. The only deadline is the printing schedule of the church secretary, and simply putting in the words "Prelude" or "Anthem" or even "Sermon" avoids even that pressure.

Unplanned worship simply is, unfortunately, just that: not thought out. Hymns are dropped into place without much thought as to why or how they follow what went before or lead to what follows. The appropriate placement of other service music is even less planned. In the unplanned service, the anthem is placed regularly at the same point in the order to provide relief or change of pace. The anthem becomes a time for appreciative listening but has nothing to do with the rest of the service. Ideally, the tone and text of the anthem should determine its placement in the order of service. An anthem of thanksgiving should follow some action that calls for such a response, while a meditative anthem might follow a time of prayer.

Planning worship takes time, which is one reason that we see so little planning. Another aid to proper worship planning is a genuinely cooperative effort on the part of quite different people, which may not come easily. Church musicians and pastors are not always comfortable with each other, may resent suggestions made by the other, and may not want to meet together to plan. Unplanned worship avoids conflicts. Pastors and musicians go their separate ways and have little to do with each other. In these unfortunate situations, the service is divided up and each party takes its own piece of the whole, neither aware of nor concerned about what the other party is doing.

The Planning Team

What should worship planning involve? The pastor, as the principal leader of worship, is the one person most responsible for building a planning team. Ideally, the team should be made up of the pastor or pastors, the organist, the choir directors, other instrumentalists, drama group representatives, artists and dancers if there are any, and members of the worship committee. By its makeup, this group represents varied interests, different points of view, and possible competing or conflicting attitudes. In a small church, planning may involve only two people who have a variety of responsibilities.

Anyone who is interested in the planning process needs to recognize—before starting—some of the difficulties so as not to be surprised when things do not go as smoothly as expected. Any planning process requires give-and-take on the part of many different people. Above all, the pastor must occasionally step off center stage. Although the pastor has a great deal to say about the final product, for the pastor to convene such a group and then ignore the group's advice or suggestions is not conducive to good order or morale. People will not continue to participate in this process if they discover that they are being ignored, and the result will be pastor-dominated worship or disorganization.

Long-Range Planning

Planning needs to include both long- and short-range goals. Long-range planning should be done well ahead of a particular season. Advent planning, for example, should probably take place in the late spring or summer, at least six weeks before Advent begins. Such planning should include making a general outline of major themes, reviewing the principal texts to be used, and compiling some ideas as to how themes based upon the texts could be developed with music and the other arts. Some ordered way must be in place to decide well in advance what scripture texts will be central, either by using a lectionary or through some other method, such as studying a book of the Bible chapter by chapter.

Bible study should be part of the planning process so that the people who are making decisions about worship have some understanding of the significance of the text, how it can be used, what its implications may be, and so on. Such study also enables participants to identify major biblical images. The choir director can then begin to identify and order appropriate music.

Liturgical artists may wish to make new vestments or banners or other appendia for the season that present the major themes. These artists need a good amount of advance time. They will have to begin to design the liturgical environment and order materials months in advance.

The team may need to secure permission from the congregational governing body for special services, for the celebration of Communion or Baptism, or for expenses beyond the ordinary. If new hymns are used that are not in the congregational hymnal, permission to use those hymns may be necessary, so copyright permission must be secured and the necessary fees paid. In particular, obtaining permission can be a lengthy process.

Short-Range Planning

Short-range planning is also essential. Here the participants themselves actually construct the service, deciding what elements to put where and why. This team may be smaller than the one engaged in the long-range process. This short-range team needs to decide what hymns should be used, determine if they are easily singable, and if the choir is needed to introduce them, noting the date of last use. (Generally, no service should include more than one new hymn.) Worship planners should ask themselves: How do these hymns fit into the service? Do all verses need to be sung by everyone? How can the choir be included in the hymn (e.g., singing selected verses or a descant)? Having the choir introduce a new hymn is a good practice.

The team should also consider how hymns function in worship. Some hymns are prayers and should be used as such. A hymn can be a prayer of confession, or a single verse can serve this purpose. Not all confessions should be in the form of a unison prayer. The Creed can be sung as well as spoken; even the scripture can be sung, especially the psalm. The choral anthem can be a response to confession, the assurance of pardon, a creed, a response to a scripture lesson, a response to the sermon, or in relation to the prayers of offering.

Suppose the anthem for the coming week is one of praise. The choir has already practiced it. Now the question is, "For what does this anthem prepare people?" What hymns or readings might be a good response to that anthem? The question is not, "What comes after the anthem?" so much as "What comes after *this* anthem?"

Spoken parts must also be considered. The scripture lesson may lend itself to a dramatic reading by more than one person. A dramatic reading by several persons may be a better way to present a lesson that has dramatic content. Litanies may be chosen or written as prayer forms to include the congregation as participants.

Finally, those persons who are being asked to participate in the leading of worship need to be informed well in advance (more than a week) what part they are asked to lead so that they have plenty of time to prepare if they are to write a prayer or read a lesson.

This planning effort is inclusive. Undertaking this effort involves the creativity of all, provides opportunity to think through the service, avoids endless repetition of the same format, and encourages participation by a wide number of people who have a sense of responsibility. The time investment, especially by the pastor, is great. Therefore, the pastor must consider worship important enough to warrant this expenditure of time.

What takes place Sunday after Sunday shapes the life of the congregation. To worship in ways that are meaningful, appropriate to the needs of the people, congruent with the history of the congregation, and faithful to our theology as Reformed Christians is not easy. Because we do not have a mandatory ritual, each congregation is free to design its own worship within the limitations of the denominational polity. A great deal of responsibility thus falls upon the pastor and worship leaders. They are called to a ministry of artistic sensitivity and pastoral care, to theological integrity and contemporary relevance, all at the same time.

7

Music

No single issue creates more conflict in congregations today than music. Congregations argue, people complain, and they even leave the church over the choice of hymns and the style of music used in worship. Every pastor walks a tightrope trying to please those who want only the "good old" hymns and those who are bored with the usual fare and want something more contemporary and lively, such as "praise choruses." Making a choice is difficult and painful, no matter how the decision goes. Some congregations resolve the conflict by having a "contemporary" and a "traditional" service, thereby running the risk of creating two different and rival congregations. Many other congregations choose to blend both styles and end up pleasing no one and angering everyone.

Generally, music in the church fits into one or more general categories, depending upon who provides it:

> Music sung by the people
> Music sung by a leader, e.g., a priest, pastor, or cantor
> Music sung by a choir, duet, or soloist—that is, by professionals or people who are specially trained
> Instrumental music (music not intended for accompaniment or singing) before the service, during the service (sometimes as a bridge, to heighten a special liturgical moment, or as an accompaniment for meditation), or following the service (postlude)

Augustine defined a hymn in his "Comment on Psalm 148":

> Know ye what a hymn is? It is a song with praise of God. If thou praisest God and singest not, thou utterest no hymn. If thou singest and praisest not God, thou utterest no hymn. A hymn then containeth these three things: song (canticum), and praise (laudem) and that of God. Praise then of God in song is called a hymn.[1]

Augustine noted three elements of a hymn: (1) music (2) in the form of praise (3) directed to the divinity. This definition for a hymn isn't altogether startling, since the Greek word *hymnos* indicates songs in praise of gods or heroes.

Note, however, that hymns are a form of folk song in that they are meant to be songs of the people. Singing by the people became an important Reformation assertion that is occasionally contested in worship today. The issue involves both the difficulty and singability of the music as well as who sings it. Some hymns are so complex that only trained voices can sing them; some tunes are too complex to be learned easily, and the people resist singing them. Are these difficult pieces truly hymns? Or are they hymn forms that are not really hymns? The debate rages whenever a new hymnal is produced.

The Protestant Reformers took music in the liturgy very seriously, although little consensus existed among them. John Calvin's decision to make Psalms the music of the Reformed Church became definitive for the Reformed style of worship for at least three centuries. To understand the tenets that guided Calvin and the other reformers, we need to understand the process by which music in worship developed during the fifteen centuries preceding Calvin, noting the elements that Calvin sought to restore and those that he felt had to be discarded as abuses.

A History of Music in Worship

Music in Scripture

In the ancient world, music was an organic part of daily life. Biblical references to music must be understood from this perspective. The kinds of music found in scripture include:

> Music at family parties (Gen. 31:27; Luke 15:25)
> Music as acclamation of heroes (Judg. 11:34; 1 Sam. 18:6)
> Music upon a king's enthronement and martial music (Judg. 7:18–20; 1 Kings 1:39–40; 2 Kings 11:14; 2 Chron. 13:14, 20:28)
> Harem and court music (2 Sam. 19:35; Eccl. 2:8)
> Banquet and feast music (Isa. 5:12; 24:8–9)
> Occupational songs (Num. 21:17; Isa. 16:10; Jer. 31:4–5, 7; 48:33)
> Dirges and laments (2 Sam. 1:17–18; 2 Chron. 35:25; Matt. 9:23; and the customary wailing of women)
> Magic and incantations (Exod. 28:34; Josh. 6:4–20; 1 Sam., 16:16ff; 2 Kings 3:15)[2]

Music appears everywhere, but the real songbook of the Bible for both the Old and New Testaments is the book of Psalms. In the New Testament, Paul addresses the Ephesians, telling them to greet each other as you sing psalms and hymns and spiritual songs among yourselves, singing and making melody to the Lord in your hearts, giving thanks to God the Father at all times and for everything in the name of our Lord Jesus Christ (Eph. 5:19–20).

The Psalms were the hymnbook of ancient Israel, and they clearly were written to be sung in the Temple.

Early on, the Christian Church used in worship distinctly Christian musical compositions that were based upon the Gospels in addition to the Psalms. Among them were:

1. *The Magnificat:* Mary's Song of Praise (Luke 1:46–55), sung by Mary to Elizabeth when she greeted Mary as the mother of the Lord. The name comes from the opening word of the Latin text, "*Magnificat anima mea Dominum*" ("My soul magnifies the Lord").

2. *Benedictus:* Zechariah's Song of Thanksgiving at the birth of his son, John the Baptist (Luke 1:68–79): "Blessed be the Lord God of Israel, for he has looked favorably on his people and redeemed them. He has raised up a mighty savior for us."

3. *Gloria in Excelsis:* The Song of the Angels to the shepherds, proclaiming the birth of Christ in Bethlehem (Luke 2:14): "Glory to God in the highest, and on earth peace among those with whom God is pleased."

4. *Nunc Dimittis:* The Song of Simeon (Luke 2:29–32), proclaimed when the old man finally saw the Christ child and knew that the prophecy to him had been fulfilled: "Lord, now lettest thou thy servant depart in peace, according to thy word; for mine eyes have seen thy salvation."

5. *The Hallel:* "*Hallel*" means "praise." Although these songs are from the Old Testament (Psalms 113–118), they became connected with the Upper Room liturgy (Mark 14:26), where it is said that "When they had sung the hymn, they went out to the Mount of Olives." The Hallel was the hymn generally connected with the Passover: "Praise the LORD! Praise, O servants of the LORD; praise the name of the LORD. Blessed be the name of the LORD from this time on and forevermore. From the rising of the sun to its setting the name of the LORD is to be praised" (Ps. 113:1–3).

It is also significant that the book of Revelation, which closes the Christian canon, closes its own pages with the song of the faithful in heaven:

"Hallelujah! Salvation and glory and power to our God, for his judgments are true and just. . . . Hallelujah! Amen! . . . Praise our God, all you his servants . . . small and great . . . Hallelujah! For the Lord our God the Almighty reigns. Let us rejoice and exult and give him the glory." (Rev. 19:1–7, selections)

The Early Church

Music was an important means of worship in the early church, preparing on earth for what was to be the final song in eternity. The songs of the early church had a number of distinctive features: texts were from scripture; they were sung by all the people since there were no choirs; and the songs were probably unaccompanied or accompanied by a few simple instruments. They were sung from memory; there were no hymnbooks, so texts had to be relatively short and tunes easily learned. (The advent of the printing press would change this.)

From the fourth through the sixth centuries, the period of the monastic movement, the worship of the people changed radically. Now there were special places (monasteries) where worship was carried out around the clock, and there were special people (for the most part monks and nuns) to do this. Every three hours "the divine office" was celebrated—seven times a day, with prayers, songs, and scripture readings. Although the original intention of the divine office was to maintain a purity of worship in response to worship that some people thought was becoming contaminated (one of the principal concerns of the fourth century), the actual result was that worship lost much of its corporate nature. Now professionals conducted worship and also offered continuous prayers for those who did not have the time, inclination, or training to do so. In the desert, for the first time, the regular recitation of the whole Psalter "in course" became a practice of Christian devotion, and the Psalter began to take on the prominence it has held ever since in Christian corporate worship. As early as the sixth century, Benedict of Nursia in his Rule called for the singing of hymns at each office.

The music of this period, however, was in some shambles. Gregory I (the Great) (540–604) systematized music by standardizing the Gregorian chant as the official music of the church. After this initial systematization, in around 600, choirs virtually refused to use anything but the Gregorian chant for a century or more, thus inhibiting the writing of new music.[3] As a result of the complicated, memorized chants, worship lost much of its participative and even joyous character. The folk song was lost inside the church, but music was found outside the doors.

Even though music became the domain of professionals, the common people continued to sing. During this time, the carol emerged. The text for the carols could be secular or religious. When they were religious, they were often not so much biblical as narrative stories of faith, much as might be sung by a troubadour. The tunes were lively, intended to be danced to, and they gave rise to an interesting style that would later affect the hymn. When the "stanza" was sung, the dancers paused and stood to listen (*stanza* = to stand). They would resume dancing and singing with a chorus or refrain, which was often a short, repeated phrase.

No matter, though, whether the words were bawdy or religious, carols were very much unappreciated by the church. Many carols survived outside the church—joyously sung by the people—while the church maintained the chant to give worship a feeling of mystery and order. Martin Luther would turn to the music and style of the carol when he felt the necessity to create new forms for congregational worship.

Music and the Reformation of Luther and Zwingli

Although music seems to have been consigned to either the droning chants of the choirs or the merry carols of the common folk, the story does not, of course, end here. Music as a true expression of the soul was forever with the people, and when Martin Luther came on the scene, he did not "return music to the people," as some credit him with doing. Music had always been there, and had, in fact, played a significant role in the work of such preformers as John Hus. (Hus, called to the Council of Constance and condemned there in 1415, had died singing. The Council sent a stern warning to Hus's successors: "If laymen are forbidden to preach and interpret the Scriptures, much more are they forbidden to sing publicly in the churches."[4])

Martin Luther composed about thirty-seven hymns, based for the most part on scripture; his hymns were not precise scriptural paraphrases, in marked contrast to John Calvin's. Luther began to write hymns in 1523 on the occasion of the martyrdom of three new Lutherans. In the Augustinian cloister at Antwerp, the prior of the abbey and two youths were sentenced to death for their refusal to denounce their new faith. The prior was strangled in his cell, and the youths were led to the stake in Brussels on July 1, 1523. Asked to recant, they replied that they would rather die and be with Christ. Before the fire and smoke smothered their voices, they were heard singing the ancient Latin *Te Deum*, "Lord God, we praise Thee." Hearing of this, Luther wrote a hymn commemorating the death of the young martyrs.

Luther was an extraordinary musician; coupled with his deeply emotional nature, this talent gave Luther the ability to understand the need for music that the people could and would sing. He also had the ability to write great music, although his often-difficult music was simplified after his death. It had a majestic quality that lifted up the spirit.

In his *Discourse in Praise of Music*, Luther wrote, "I give music the highest and most honorable place; and everyone knows how David and all the saints put their divine thoughts into verse, rhyme, and song."[5] At another time he commented; "If any man despises music, as all fanatics do, for him I have no liking; for music is a gift and grace of God, not an invention of men. Thus it drives out the devil and makes people cheerful, then one forgets all wrath, impurity, sycophancy, and other vices."[6]

The foundation for Luther's liturgy was the Mass. For the most part, early reform efforts in worship meant adding hymns and psalms and subtracting anything considered superfluous or incompatible with the new Reformation teaching. Obviously a change in thinking was in the offing, because "the sacrifice of the Mass" was no longer the central part of each service. Luther's hymns became the "sung sermons" of the Reformation. So effective were these hymns of "the singing church" in spreading the Reformation that Luther's enemies often feared them more than his sermons.[7]

Ulrich Zwingli (1484–1531) was to be the most radical of the Reformers with regard to music. Though an accomplished musician, Zwingli felt that music had an entirely secular function and was without theological dimension. Aware, as a musician, of the power of music, he worried that music would dominate the service and undermine the centrality of scripture. In his largely original service, Zwingli justified the absence of music with three arguments:

1. Music in worship is not explicitly commanded by God in either the Old or New Testament.
2. Christ instructed his followers to pray to God individually and in private.
3. Saint Paul urged Christians, when together, to worship God and pray to him in their hearts.[8]

For Zwingli, worship was essentially instruction and prayer, and prayer was ideally silent prayer. Basing his argument on scripture, Zwingli contended that Paul said Christians are to praise God with their hearts, and the heart is entirely silent. Zwingli instead attempted to replace music with antiphonal recitations by the men and women of the congregation, but the authorities of Zurich forbade even this approach. Zwingli personally led the dismantling of the organs of Zurich and, until the end of the sixteenth century, no music was heard in the churches.

This was the stage onto which John Calvin would step.

Music and the Reformation of John Calvin

John Calvin, attempting to pass through Geneva, reluctantly acceded to William Farel's emphatic request to stay. Calvin found himself in a city where the newly reformed worship held no warmth of the Spirit. What he witnessed during his first months in Geneva clearly displeased him; his language on that score leaves no doubt whatsoever. "Certainly at present," he wrote, "the prayers of the faithful are so cold that we should be greatly ashamed and confused."[9]

But what would it take to change the nature of this worship? Within six months after his arrival, Calvin proposed changes to the city council, among which was the singing of psalms. In his plan he insisted, "It is very expedient for the edification of the church to sing some psalms in the form of public prayers, by which one offers petitions to God or sings his praise, in order that the hearts of all may be moved and incited to compose similar prayers and render similar praise and blessings to God with the same affection."[10]

Calvin recognized that although Roman Catholics used the Psalms in their services, they were obscured by the church's use of Latin, and their highly complicated forms could only be sung by professional musicians. Calvin wanted the whole congregation to sing in its own language.

Calvin and the city council disagreed on a number of issues, and he soon found himself no longer welcome in Geneva. He made his way to Strasbourg, where he was pleased to discover that the people were already singing psalms in the congregation where Martin Bucer was pastor.[11]

Calvin was not a musician, but he was a theologian, and before anything else he had to convince himself of the theological validity of music in worship. He found in scripture the certainty of the divine origin of music (in Genesis 4:21, which concerns Jubal and his lineal descent from Adam).

Bucer's appeal to history and the fact that the singing of the Psalms had been practiced in "the first and apostolic churches" struck in Calvin a responsive chord. But he was unsure how to accomplish the singing of psalms. He decided to break with the musical heritage and tradition and not employ the contemporary musical forms as Luther did. His genius was to create something entirely new with the Psalms.

But why psalms? For a number of reasons. The Psalms were the Bible's own hymnbook, inspired of God. Worship, humanity's highest praise to God, should involve only the holiest and best elements. Nothing less than what God had given in scripture and song would do. Further, the Psalms were a reflection of the soul. Calvin wrote in his preface to the *Commentary on the Psalms*: "Not without reason, it is my custom to call this book 'An Anatomy of All the Parts of the Soul,' since there is no emotion anyone will experience whose image is not reflected in this mirror."[12] David became for Calvin a model or example to imitate, and David's songs became Calvin's. If frequency of citation is a reliable criterion, the book of Psalms was for Calvin, as for Luther, the most important book of the Bible, next to Paul's epistle to the Romans.[13]

In the *Institutes*, what Calvin had to say about singing was brief but straightforward:

It is evident that the practice of singing in church . . . is not only a very ancient one but also was in use among the apostles . . . and surely, if the singing be tempered to that gravity which is fitting in the sight of God and the angels, it both lends dignity and grace to sacred actions and has the greatest value in kindling our hearts to a true zeal and eagerness to pray. Yet we should be very careful that our ears be not more attentive to the melody than our minds to the spiritual meaning of the words.[14]

On December 29, 1538, only four months after Calvin's arrival in Strasbourg, he wrote to Farel that he was preparing a French Psalter for his own congregation, that he would publish the Psalms shortly, and that he himself was composing poetic versions of Psalms 46 and 25.[15] The Strasbourg Psalter of 1539 contained nineteen psalms in French translation, all but one of which were rhymed; it also included Calvin's versions of the Song of Simeon, the Decalogue, and the Credo. The cantor of the Strasbourg Cathedral, Matthew Greiter, arranged some of the tunes. In the midst of Calvin's work, he unexpectedly came to know or become aware of Clement Marot, a poet in the court of Francis I. Music in the French court had always been of questionable taste, but in Marot's time had become indecent and unacceptable. For some unexplained reason, Marot began translating psalms into metrical French and distributing them to the ladies and friends of the court, where they became extremely popular. Calvin was also taken with the psalms and incorporated Marot's translations into the Strasbourg Psalter, replacing the texts he had translated with what he felt were the better texts of Marot. At last, Calvin realized he had the means to rid the church of the remote feel of worship and use the power of song to lift hearts and bring fervor.[16]

When Calvin returned to Geneva, he was able to institute the reforms in worship that he had called for earlier, and the metrical psalms became the instrument for some of this reform. In 1542 he issued the Genevan Psalter with thirty-nine psalms. Marot's contribution increased from thirteen to thirty-two psalm texts. That year, Marot came to live in Geneva where he could work with Calvin, although Calvin may have appreciated the translations more than he appreciated the man himself. In 1543 Calvin proposed to the city fathers that Marot be granted a subsidy to complete the Psalms, but the request was denied. Soon after, Marot came under ecclesiastical discipline for certain activities with some ladies in a local pub. To avoid the possible legal consequences, he left for Turin, where he died shortly afterwards, reputedly by poison, his work unfinished.[17]

It was Loys (or Louis) Bourgeois (born 1510–15, died 1560) who wrote so many of the great tunes for the Psalter and started the custom of hanging placards in the churches indicating the numbers of the psalms to be sung. The records of the city council of July 14, 1545, indicate that Bourgeois was hired as a singer to perform the psalms and to teach the choristers at St. Pierre; in December 1545 he began to receive an additional forty florins (now a total of one hundred florins) to fulfil the same functions at the church of St. Gervais. Bourgeois's work was brilliant, but not easy; in 1551 he was briefly imprisoned for having, without a license, changed the tunes of some printed psalms, an action troubling to those who had learned the old tunes that had already been printed.[18]

Bourgeois's job was to train choristers to lead the congregational singing, which was in unison and unaccompanied so as to focus upon the words and make sure that the human voice in praise of God remained central. The marvelous tunes that he composed lent themselves to harmonizations, however, which were allowed in arrangements for use in the home, but never in church, where they might distract worshipers from the text. (Instrumental music was so closely tied to dancing and secular entertainment that the religious authorities could see no way to make a sufficient separation.) In 1552 Bourgeois moved to Lyon for what was supposed to be a brief leave of absence; Lyon was a printing center, and he was having some of his music published there. He never returned to Geneva. In 1560 he moved to Paris, and his daughter, Suzanne, was baptized in the Catholic Church of St. Come. The final Genevan Psalter, of 1562, contained all 150 of the Psalms with 125 different tunes; 85 of these had been composed before Bourgeois's departure from Geneva and are either his own melodies or his adaptations of earlier melodies. The composers of the other 40 tunes have not been determined.[19] Claude Goudimel continued as musical editor after Bourgeois.

In his *Form of Prayers* (1542), Calvin called for only one psalm to be sung before the sermon. Later, he would order psalm singing at the beginning of the service, and before and after the sermon at certain services. Bourgeois's psalm tables were arranged so that in the three weekly main services, the entire Psalter would be sung twice a year. No connections with any liturgical seasons are apparent, but rather a gradual singing of the entire Psalter more or less in rotation.[20]

At first glance Calvin's service appears to have little music, but we must remember that some of the Psalms had as many as seventy-two verses, and each psalm was sung in its entirety; congregational singing, depending upon the length of the sermon, filled one-third to one-half of the service.[21]

What were the effects or impact of Calvin's psalm singing? A letter from a young man from Antwerp, who had sought refuge in Strasbourg during Easter week of 1545, indicates what it meant for some to hear the Psalms sung in their own language:

On Sundays . . . we sing a psalm of David or some other prayer taken
from the New Testament. The psalm or prayer is sung by everyone
together, men as well as women, with a beautiful unanimity, which is
something beautiful to behold. For you must understand that each one
has a music book in his hand; that is why they cannot lose touch with
one another. Never did I think that it could be as pleasing and delight-
ful as it is. For five or six days at first, as I looked upon this little company, exiled from countries everywhere for having upheld the honor
of God and His gospel, I would begin to weep, not at all from sadness,
but from joy at hearing them sing so heartily, and, as they sang, giving
thanks to the Lord that He had led them to a place where His name is
honored and glorified. No one could believe the joy which one experiences when one is singing the praises and wonders of the Lord in the
mother tongue as one sings them here.[22]

Calvin's Psalter so dominated the thinking of seventeenth-century Calvinists that in every major crisis and conflict, the psalmist's words seem to have
come almost automatically to their lips. The ordinary Calvinist soldier had
been trained in the Catechism and taught to worship with the Psalter.

The singing of the Psalter had a threefold effect: it provided identity and
unity, and it reminded people of their covenant relationship with God.

> *Identity:* The singers were provided with a sense of *identity*. They were the
> "psalm-singers," those fighting for a specific objective. "They sang
> psalms for the same reason that other revolutionary groups have sung
> their songs, to establish their identity and bear testimony to their moti-
> vation and their purpose."[23]
>
> *Unity:* This identity gave them *unity*. They sang as they went into battle,
> which gave them confidence, for they knew that they were on the win-
> ning side, the Lord's side. The singing of songs gave them strength to face
> persecution.
>
> *Reminder:* The singing of the Psalms reminded them that they were in
> *covenant relationship with God*, for the Psalms were the songs of the elect
> people of God. The singers let this be known in their endeavors without
> compromise or retraction.

The Psalms gave the Huguenot congregations the courage of martyrs, particularly as they faced the prospect of death at the stake. As one reads histories
of the time, one must be impressed with the fact that the Psalms were deeply
imbedded in the souls of these faithful witnesses. Calvin's view of the impact
of the metrical version of the Psalms had proven itself true as they sang

> Psalm 68, "Let God rise up, let his enemies be scattered"
> Psalm 118, "For the Lord is good, his mercy endureth forever," which was
> sung by the forces of Henry of Navarre before the Battle of Coutras in
> 1587 and on many other occasions

Psalm 124, most popular of all, "If it had not been the LORD who was on our side, now Israel may say . . ."

The Psalter made its way with John Knox to Scotland where the Psalms became battle tunes. Calderwood's *History of the Kirk of Scotland* (Edinburgh, 1848) recounts the return on September 4, 1582, of John Durie, a minister of Edinburgh exiled by James VI through the influence of Esme Stuart, Duke of Lennox, to his home.

> John Durie cometh to Leith at night the 3rd of September. Upon Tuesday the 4th of September, as he is coming to Edinburgh, there met him at the Gallowgreen 200, but ere he came to the Netherbow their number increased to 400; but they were no sooner entered but they increased to 600 or 700, and within short space the whole street was replenished even to Saint Geiles' Kirk: the number was esteemed 2000. At the Netherbow they took up the 124 Psalm, "Now Israel may say," etc., and sung in such a pleasant tune in four parts, known to the most part of the people, that coming up the street all bareheaded till they entered the Kirk with such a great sound and majestie, that it moved both themselves and all the huge multitude of the beholders, looking out at the shots and over stairs, with admiration and astonishment: the Duke himself beheld, and reave his beard for anger: he was more affrayed of this sight than anie thing that ever he had seen before in Scotland.[24]

Calvin recognized what was needed to remove the frigidity from the worship of his people and lift their hearts in such a way that they would sing the songs from Calvin's Psalter on the roads to their deaths. It was no accident that he recognized the best poet in the court of Francis I and collaborated with him on translations. The selection of Louis Bourgeois and the use of tunes by Matthew Greiter was not the work of one who had no artistic comprehension. Ford Lewis Battles even contends that Calvin's own metrical translations were better than either he or his contemporaries would admit.[25]

Calvin combined Zwingli's sternness with Luther's compassion. The result is theology and liturgy that is not arid but powerful. In the Catechism, the people learned that theology; in the Psalter, they sang it.

Today, few would agree with Calvin that the only songs to be sung should be the Psalms. But what a marvelous criterion this music provides when we compare the Genevan Psalter and the Psalters that grew out of it to some of the music that has been placed before congregations, particularly in the last one hundred years. The identity of the whole people of God, singing their praises, rooted and grounded in scripture, is certainly not an insignificant legacy. It is a touching experience, when leaving the Scottish War Memorial at Edinburgh Castle, to see the following words inscribed and remember the terrors of the nighttime bombing during the World Wars: "Our soul is escaped, even as a bird out of the snare of the fowler. The snare is broken and we are delivered" (The 1912 Psalter, Psalm 124).

The debate about music is long-lived. W. Sanford Reid has written:

> How then does all this affect us today? The answer to this question seems to lie perhaps in the fact that the Christian church needs to realize anew the importance of singing. It has committees, commissions, secretariats, and secretaries, but so often it seems to have lost the capacity to sing. Moreover, the answer may be that the church should turn back to the psalms, not in the meters and tunes of the sixteenth century, but in the idiom known and popular in our own day. If such a revolution should take place, we might well see both a renewal of vital Christianity and a resulting sense of unity that so many are seeking. This is the legacy of Calvin, Marot, Beza, and others which the church should revive in its defense of the walls of Zion.[26]

The Development of Modern Hymns

We might still be singing only Psalms today were it not for the pioneering work of Isaac Watts, who wrote "hymns of human composure," as he called them. Watts's hymns were usually Christian forms of the Psalms with a melody and meter more like a modern hymn than a psalm tune. With Watts, the hymn came into its own. His critics were shocked that anyone would want to replace the hymnal that God had given to the church. But we who follow him are left with a great legacy of hymnody that is still familiar to most: "Joy to the World," "Jesus Shall Reign," "Our God, Our Help in Ages Past," "When I Survey the Wondrous Cross," and "Alas, and Did My Savior Bleed." That output is a powerful heritage from one person.

Generations of hymn writers after Watts made their own contributions to the hymnody of the Reformed tradition. Over the years, the various traditions borrowed from one another so that a modern hymnal reflects many sources. Hymns by Luther and Wesley now find a comfortable place in Reformed hymnals.

Issues in Music Today

Given its importance to the Reformers, music not surprisingly was and continues to be one of the most controversial aspects of Reformed worship. Few aspects of worship are more powerful at defining the character of worship than music. Whether it be a capella psalm singing; the overwhelming power of the pipe organ and well-trained choirs; an old upright piano adroitly weaving its way through gospel tunes in a country church; capable guitarists or those who stick to three chords; "worship centers" where a full third of the area is committed to massive speakers, electronic instruments, and cables running everywhere; or elevator stages where choirs mysteriously appear from nowhere, the style of the music sets the tone of the service, and many worshipers, used to a particular style, feel they have not worshiped unless they have been accorded their favorite style. The tendency to defend a particular style of music has led to what some call "the worship wars." These battles over musical style are as divisive at the beginning of the twenty-first century as were the theological divisions early in the twentieth century.

Because music can express many emotions, congregations can benefit from exposure to a wide range of musical styles. This experiencing must be done, though, without compromising theological grounds for worship; moreover, we must present the music competently and follow procedures that allow the congregation to participate legally, without violating copyright laws. Most congregations feel comfortable with a surprisingly small number of hymns or songs; they like best those with which they are familiar. Moving congregations to explore new styles of music inevitably causes some discomfort. Neither the "old" nor the "new" is always better, but a familiarity with the great music of our tradition as well as a willingness to venture into the creativeness of the Spirit is a mandate for those who plan and lead worship.

Marva Dawn[27] has provided a lively critique of what goes on in worship, and she suggests some useful criteria for music in worship. Dawn is concerned with a number of problems, one of which is the tendency to offer a style of worship that has very little to do with God and concentrates primarily on the worshiper, who turns out to be more an audience spectator. She contends that people will not have a spiritual experience in worship if the Spirit is not the center of worship. Dawn suggests that worship leaders ask the following questions as they choose music:

1. Is God the subject and object in the music of worship? Do text and music give us greater understanding of the nature and working of God, or is the emphasis on how we feel and what we need?
2. Will the music play a role in the formation of the believer's character? Are text and music significant or trivial?
3. Will the music contribute to building a Christian community? Does the text focus on the individual believer to the exclusion of understanding that we are part of the "people of God"?
4. Is there a diversity of styles of music? As worship ought to include a rich diversity of people, are we presenting a wealth of styles—or does it all sound pretty much the same? Diversity does not mean, however, a mindless and artless conglomeration of styles. Some music may be so unique that it demands its own setting. But it is possible to combine numerous musical elements tastefully and have them fit together.

5. Is the music appropriate to the concerns of the service? To those who are singing? To the season? To the mood of major world events?
6. Does the music have worth? Though there is not always consensus among musicians as to what makes for "great music," one useful criterion is its staying power: is this a hymn that can be sung over and over again and still feed us spiritually, or does it quickly become banal? Even great music can be overused. Using a wide variety of hymns can help good hymns maintain their appeal.

The service of worship in many churches involves a number of kinds of music: music before and after the service (preludes, postludes—or "voluntaries" as many musicians prefer to call them in an attempt to see them as part of worship rather than musical contributions outside the service); responses by the choir (e.g., a benediction response); responses by the congregation (e.g., the Doxology, *Gloria Patri, Kyrie*); anthems; vocal or instrumental solos; offertories; music incorporated in the Lord's Supper (e.g., *Sanctus* and *Benedictus*); and hymns. The style and formality of the service as well as the musical capabilities of the congregations obviously determine the particular music used. With so many options available, we will speak to one major consideration: hymns from the denominational hymnal, which can serve as a common basis for theological and musical expression within the Reformed tradition. As our point of discussion, we will use *The Presbyterian Hymnal*.[28] (Most hymnals provide many of these same features.)

Exploring the Hymnal

At the beginning of nearly every hymnal appear "Aids to Worship," which include a brief outline of the order for worship suggested by the denomination. Following this are the Apostles' Creed, the Nicene Creed, and the Lord's Prayer. Next follow the hymns, the "Service Music," and then a series of indices.

The hymns are arranged in four categories:

1. Those that enrich the Christian year (e.g., Christmas, Easter);
2. Settings for the Psalms called for in the Common Lectionary; not all the Psalms are set to music here, and there are sometimes multiple settings for especially popular psalms (e.g., the Twenty-third Psalm);
3. Topical hymns, which have to do with God, Jesus Christ, Holy Spirit, Holy Scripture, Life in Christ, Church, Morning and Opening Hymns, Sacraments and Ordinances, Closing Hymns, Evening Hymns, Thanksgiving Hymns, and National Songs; and
4. "Service Music," which provides words and music for responses (by congregation and/or choir) called for in various services—e.g., the *Kyrie, Gloria in Excelsis, Gloria Patri, Nunc Dimittis, Sanctus*, the Lord's Prayer, etc. A

congregation's selection and use of short, favorite responses can provide musical continuity week by week, with the hymns providing the musical variety. Also, adding or deleting responses depending upon the season can be a subtle way of defining the liturgical season (for example, not singing the Doxology or *Gloria Patri* during Lent, adding the *Gloria in Excelsis* during Epiphany, omitting the *Kyrie* during Eastertide).

A number of indices enable worship planners to select music appropriate for the theme and mood of the service:

1. *Index of Authors, Translators, and Sources:* If you're looking for a hymn by John Calvin or Jimmy Owens, you can find it here. This is an index for literary texts.
2. *Index of Composers, Arrangers, and Sources* lists musical sources: If you're looking for the melodies of Louis Bourgeois, for example, you'd use this index. Infatuated with "Purcell's Trumpet Tune" by Jeremiah Clark and wonder if Clark wrote any hymn tunes? Look in this index.
3. *Index of Scriptural Allusions* suggests hymns that mention or accompany particular scriptural texts. If you want a hymn to go with a portion of the Sermon on the Mount, you would look to see if there are references to Matthew 5–7.
4. *Topical Index* provides suggestions for hymns on eternal life, grace, stewardship, etc.
5. *Metrical Index of Tunes* lists tunes by meter: If you're singing hymn 84—"In the Cross of Christ I Glory," tune: RATHBUN—and you decide you want to change the tune, you will notice that the meter for this hymn is 8.7.8.7. This mysterious code is the result of counting beats in each phrase:

   In the cross of Christ I glo-ry = 8 beats
   Tower-ring (tow'-ring) o'er the wrecks of time = 7 beats
   All the light of sa-cred sto-ry = 8 beats
   Ga-thers round its head sub-lime = 7 beats

   The Metrical Index lists eight other tunes that accommodate the 8.7.8.7. meter, any one of which might work *if the musical emphases come on the proper syllables.*
6. *Alphabetical Index of Tunes* tells you where to find a particular tune and how many times the tune is used in the Hymnal. Tunes are assigned a name; the name of the tune used for hymn 141, "A Hymn of Glory Let Us Sing," is DEO GRACIAS; it is used for three separate texts in the Hymnal. Do you like the Shaker tune, SIMPLE GIFTS? This index will tell you what hymn is set to this tune.
7. *Index of First Line and Common Titles:* Most hymns do not have names but are known by their first lines. This is the index that most people use because it lets you search by the familiar first lines. Remember, though, that many gospel songs are known by the first words in the chorus, so you may have to search around a bit.

Music can be one of the most powerful tools in involving a particular worship mood or theme. Thus, though there is always room for "old favorites," music should be chosen with particular theological concern, as this may be the element of worship that is most remembered.

It is naïve to think that denominational committees, making selections for a hymnal, can determine what congregations will sing. Even if that was true in the past, it is not true now. With new technologies available to congregations today, music is not limited to a few favorite hymns accompanied by piano or organ. Companies who license the reproduction of hymn texts offer an annual lease for thousands of hymns for congregations to use. Styles in congregations move from the chantlike music from Taizé to toe-tapping pop numbers accompanied by praise bands. The future seems to be more one of diversity than uniformity. Through this maze of options, worship planners—aware of their historical roots and responsibilty for the theological integrity of worship—will have to make some difficult choices. But one thing is sure: music, for centuries, has lifted the human soul to the greatest heights. Hymn texts have provided inspiration for the young, of course, but they are also held tightly by those preparing to die. Here is a resource that can be a rich treasure or a trite filler.

8

Prayer
_____

Prayer is a conscious relationship with God, no matter how we understand God. In prayer, we place all of ourselves before our fullest concept of God in an attitude of attention and reverent awe. But prayer is not a mindless task. It makes four demands of us:

1. We have to show up; that is we actually have to pray, by making time for the act of prayer. In our modern world of overactivity, showing up is very difficult and prayer gets easily neglected in the press of other activities.
2. We have to pay attention. Because prayer is two-way communication, noticing what is happening as a gift or response from God is as important as what we say. Paying attention is very difficult in a noisy world; we must cultivate this skill because we are easily distracted. We have to stop the flow of words and listen.
3. We have to tell the truth. Pretending in prayer makes a mockery of what we are trying to do; we fool no one. We have to let God know what our own deepest desires are. The honesty prayer requires is sometimes painful because it forces us to face our own deepest longings as well as our fears and feelings of failure.
4. We must look for the outcome. Often, because we do not get what we ask for, we give up on prayer, failing to see that our prayers were answered in surprising ways. It takes real effort to reflect upon our own situation and notice the sometimes hidden work of the Spirit in response to our prayers.

Because prayer is at the heart of the Christian life, prayer is naturally central to the corporate worship of a Christian congregation. The private prayers of individual Christians prepare them for public prayer, and the public prayers of the congregation enrich and expand the private prayers of individuals. Both public and private prayer are essential. Without public prayer, solitary prayers can easily become lazy, sporadic, self-centered, and limited in scope. Without the private prayers of the people, the public prayers of the congregation can become stale, rote, and without heart. Calvin is very clear about the need for this balance between private and public prayer:

> Whoever refused to pray in the holy assembly of the godly knows not what it is to pray individually, or in a secret spot, or at home. Again, he who neglects to pray alone and in private, however unremittingly he may frequent public assemblies, there contrives only windy prayers, for he defers more to the opinion of men than to the secret judgment of God.[1]

Private prayer does not need form; it can flow freely from the heart. Corporate prayer, however, requires some structure to enable the people to participate; this type of prayer must articulate a shared life in terms that are less inward, and it must be inclusive of all the hopes and needs of everyone present. Thus, corporate prayer must be more objective.

Prayer includes *thoughts* that are not expressed aloud but held in the silence of the human heart, as well as *words* uttered aloud in words or song, and *meditation* that is concentration upon God without words and sometimes without images at all. Prayers may be unspoken, made with the lighting of a candle or when a ribbon is tied on a prayer wreath. All of these forms of prayer have a place in the life of the individual Christian as well as in the worship of Christians in community.

The Protestant Reformers sought to replace the monastic hours of the Roman Catholic Church with a regular program of family prayer time; each Christian home was to be a kind of miniature monastery, that is, a place for the development of the souls of the family members.

In the modern world, most families have a difficult time gathering for prayer. At most, children may be encouraged to say prayers before bed, and perhaps shared prayers of thanksgiving are offered before the main meal; but the whole idea of the family as the center for prayer has largely disappeared. This circumstance has increased the importance of congregational prayer as the only balance for the private prayers of individuals.

Corporate prayer can take at least three forms: (1) extemporaneous, (2) read, and (3) learned or recited. A major task of the worship leader is to design prayers for the congregation that are truly prayers and that can serve to give voice to the real feelings of the people present. Further, one must be sensitive as to how to involve "individual" prayers within the corporate activity. Every written prayer must avoid the extremes of being so personal, on the one hand, that it leaves out many of the people present, and being so general, on the other, that it grasps no one.

A variety of prayers may be used in corporate worship:

1. *The collect* (pronounced kol'lekt—coming from the idea that the prayer may be a gathering or collection of ideas from the day's reading): This form of corporate prayer has a long tradition. A collect is a short, one- or two-sentence prayer that opens with a clause or phrase that describes a characteristic of God and then weaves that affirmation into a petition. Archbishop Thomas Cranmer in England was a master in the creation of collects, and his great prayer for purity is an excellent example:

A Prayer for Purity

Almighty God, unto whom all hearts are open, all desires known, and from whom no secrets are hid; cleanse the thoughts of our hearts by the inspiration of thy Holy Spirit, that we may perfectly love thee and worthily magnify thy holy name; through Christ our Lord. Amen.

A Contemporary Collect (Prayer for Illumination)

Lord God, giver of light,
as we hear your word,
may your truth shine in our hearts,
that we may be changed and equipped for service.
✠ **Amen.**[2]

2. *The litany* is a series of short petitions followed by a congregational response that is often repeated many times. A litany involves the whole congregation actively, yet does not require careful reading of the words. People, therefore, can pay attention to the petitions as they are voiced by the leader; their response is a way of affirming the petition and making it their own.

A Litany

Let us pray for those who are in sorrow and pain today.
✠ **You hear our prayer, O God.**

Let us pray for those in need: without food, clothes, a place of shelter or meaningful work.
✠ **You hear our prayer, O God.**

Let us pray for those who live without hope.
✠ **You hear our prayer, O God.**

For those who live as the objects of scorn or anger of others.
✠ **You hear our prayer, O God.**

Let us pray for those who suffer from loneliness.
✠ **You hear our prayer, O God.**

For those who live in the path of war.
✠ **You hear our prayer, O God.**

For those who hear only a distortion of the good news of the gospel.
✠ **You hear our prayer, O God.**

For those who need our attention to make their lives more full.
✠ **You hear our prayer, O God. Amen.**[3]

Other responses may be more theologically appropriate for some congregations, for example, "We thank you, gracious God," said after prayers of thanksgiving have been offered. Variety can be provided by having different parts of the congregation (other than simply "leader and people") read antiphonally: men and women, choir and congregation, children and adults. Further, the division need not always be twofold, but can be among three or more groups.

Assurance of Pardon for Easter Sunday

Minister: With the stone rolled away, came light;
Choir: A light to illumine our darkness, a light to dispel our fear, a light radiant with new hope.
Minister: With the stone rolled away came a new heaven and a new earth;
People: ✠ **The old things are passed away.**

Minister: The new things have come,
Choir: Jesus Christ is risen!
All: ✠ **And we are forgiven! Alleluia! Amen!**[4]

3. *The bidding prayer:* Bidding prayers may be either free (spontaneous) or read and prepared ahead of time. The leader or pastor invites the people to pray by suggesting subjects and perhaps offering an opening prayer on that subject. The people then pray in silence; at the end of this time, the leader says a cue line and the people respond in unison. For example, the leader might say, "Lord Jesus, you can do anything," to which the people respond, "Hear now the prayers we bring."

A Bidding Prayer

Lord God, we bring to you concerns from the four corners of the earth—and the small corners of our own lives. Only you can touch and heal. (Slight pause) Lord Jesus, you can do anything.
✠ **Hear now the prayers we bring.**

We pray for brothers and sisters who have no homes, no food, and who feel that they have no future. . . . (Silence) Lord Jesus, you can do anything.
✠ **Hear now the prayers we bring.**

We pray for the children of the world—and the children in our own community. . . . (silence) Lord Jesus, you can do anything.
✠ **Hear now the prayers we bring.**

At the end of the responsive prayer, there is usually a short, closing prayer given by the leader.

In another form of bidding prayer, the leader simply suggests subjects and then invites the people to pray in a time of silence.

4. *Free prayer:* Here, various people are encouraged to voice sentence prayers or offer names of those they wish the whole community to remember in prayer. A variation is when the leader asks individuals to name something for which they may be thankful. At the conclusion of the individual's statement, the group may respond by saying, "Thank you, God."

The chief advantage to this form of prayer is its freedom and spontaneity. Free prayers are the heartfelt, direct, and immediate expressions of God's people, and they offer a good way to teach people to pray. Among the dangers of free prayer are that some people may feel compelled or bullied into saying more than they are comfortable with, and others may use the opportunity to regale others with details of their private lives or causes or even their own self-righteousness. The risk is usually worth taking, however, especially in smaller congregations or small group settings.

5. *The pastoral prayer:* Here the pastor brings a broad perspective to bear on the concerns of the congregation and can express, on their behalf, matters that are on their hearts. This prayer may be offered freely (spontaneously) or read and prepared ahead of time by the leader or more typically by the pastor. The people pray by following and silently acknowledging what is spoken. The greatest danger of this form of prayer is that the pastor may be tempted to use it as another way of preaching. An appropriate pastoral prayer should speak on behalf of everyone present and truly become the prayer of the whole people.

6. The prayer for illumination: This prayer, which has a unique place in Reformed worship, occurs before the reading of scripture and asks that the Holy Spirit be present in the reading and hearing of the Word. In the medieval Roman Catholic service, the prayer of consecration of the Host was the holiest part of the service, wherein it was believed the elements were transformed into the body and blood of Christ. Since the Reformers did not hold to transubstantiation, they felt the primary place the believer encountered the risen Christ was in the reading and preaching of the Word. Thus this short prayer, placed before the reading of the lections (not before the sermon), is of particular historical significance. To pray before the reading of scripture is to act out the Calvinist idea that we do not automatically hear God speak to us in the reading of scripture. We must be led by the Holy Spirit to hear truly the particular message of God for us in that portion of scripture.

A Prayer for Illumination

God of light, be our light.
God of wonder, cause us to wonder.
God, the shepherd, lead us on your path.
As we hear these words of scripture,
send your angels to tell us again of peace on earth—and in our hearts. Amen.[5]

7. The offertory prayer: Although originally a prayer of thanksgiving for the elements as they were brought forward for the sacrament of the Lord's Supper, the offertory prayer is now a prayer of thanksgiving and dedication of the (usually monetary) gifts that are brought forward, as well as for those bringing their gifts. Rightly constructed, this prayer can provide a powerful moment during which Christians recommit their lives to the service of Jesus Christ. The following prayer of dedication is a good contemporary example.

A Prayer of Dedication

✠ **Lord, we are foolish if we do not count the cost.**
 We are poor stewards if we do not know what it will cost to follow you.
 So we dedicate who we are and all that we have to your service.
 We give away everything—and thereby gain everything. Amen.[6]

8. Our Lord's Prayer: In the early church, the Lord's Prayer was in the liturgy of the Eucharist. New communicants, after their baptism, were allowed to take Communion for the first time and were given one of the great treasures of the church: the Lord's Prayer. Found in both Matthew and Luke, this prayer was given by Jesus in response to the request of the disciples, "Lord, teach us to pray." The Lord's Prayer is appropriate at any number of places in the service and, in some ways, serves as the lynchpin for all prayers. In the eucharistic service, it is part of the Great Prayer. In other services, it should be placed where it is most appropriate. Though some people object that the Lord's Prayer is often repeated by rote, it is nevertheless a prayer held dear in times of greatest trial and despair, and it should be used regularly in the service. Using various translations may help to guard against thoughtless repetition.

9. *Guided meditation:* Guided imagery meditation is a form of prayer in which a leader, who is the only one who speaks aloud, guides the people through a process of meditation allowing time for quiet so that the people can form mental images at their own pace.

A Guided Imagery Meditation

Sometimes in worship we talk about God, we even think about God, but we do not take the time to experience God. Let's take a few moments to relax and let God come to us and give us a special word: a challenge or word of encouragement.

Relax now. Get in a comfortable position. Relax your feet and legs. Relax the tightness in your stomach and chest. Relax your arms. Most of all, relax your mind. You are safe, and you have come to this place to be in the presence of God. In the next few moments, God will come to you.

The Holy Spirit breathed over the chaos of creation and made life come to be. Surely the Holy Spirit can breathe over the chaos of your life, going in so many directions all at once, and bring order and reason.
The Holy Spirit is the wind.
The Holy Spirit is the breath.
Breathe deeply as an invitation for the Holy Spirit to come into you.
Invite the Spirit in deeply enough to seek out, find, and touch your Spirit.
(period of silence)
The breath of God lifts you,
lifts you right out of this room,
lifts you high into the sky;
and you can look down on the earth.
You've never seen it this way.
It is green and fresh and beautiful.
You see mountains, covered with snow as you glide by them.

You go into clouds that release rain on grassy hillsides and fields.
You see young animals, born in the spring, romping and playing.
You are overwhelmed with a sense of the goodness of all creation.
(period of silence)
But in this euphoric happiness, you sense a certain sorrow of the Spirit.
You go to see lakes that no longer can support life.
You see people who have so much while others have not enough to live.
You see senseless wastefulness.
You come to a quiet place and the Spirit says something to you.
The Spirit communicates something to you and no other.
(period of silence)
What does the Spirit say?
Now it is time to go back.
The Spirit gently returns you, safely, quickly,
and once again you are seated in this room:
Relaxed but still holding on to a word given to you by the Spirit.
You take a moment to remember all the Spirit has shown you. . . .
And then you slowly open your eyes.
Now you realize that each breath you take
will have for you that same Holy Spirit and the word the Spirit has given you.
You are not what you were moments ago:
You are more, because God has touched you.
And you know you belong to God
and nothing can ever take you from God.
And you have your work to do in God's name.
(silence)

When you are ready, quietly say "Amen," aloud or to yourself,
And join your friends in worship and service.[7]

Some leaders are naturally comfortable in leading this form of prayer, others feel awkward. Most people have had little experience with meditation and may need to begin with short prayers or practice before using a prayer as long as the above example. A leader may, for example, guide meditation in a prayer group before attempting it in Sunday morning worship so that at least some people present are comfortable with the experience.

The Fourfold Nature of Prayer

The Westminster Shorter Catechism defines prayer as follows: "Prayer is an offering up of our desires unto God, for things agreeable to his will, in the name of Christ, with confession of our sins, and thankful acknowledgment of his mercies."[8] This definition of prayer identifies four kinds of prayers that belong in every service of worship: adoration, confession, thanksgiving, and supplication, sometimes abbreviated with the acronym "A-C-T-S." In addition to the previously suggested forms of prayers, worship leaders can use these categories to provide a proper balance to pastoral prayers as well as the entirety of prayers used in the service of worship.

Adoration

Adoration is the celebration of the qualities of God as revealed in scripture and as experienced in the lives of the people. Adoration is the most difficult type of prayer for most people because it requires a vivid sense of God's presence. Of all the types of prayer, adoration is the least likely to be verbal; it may be best expressed in a gasp of awe at the wonder of a sunset or the magnificence of a Bach cantata or in the silent appreciation of an insight received through the hearing of scripture, as if for the first time.

The church has often been somewhat suspect of mystical adoration and has preferred more disciplined and verbal forms of praise. In this form of prayer, we do not ask anything of God, but rather we express our love for God.

A Prayer of Adoration

✠ **Lord our God: we adore you.**
  When we look at the heavens, the work of your hands,
  we wonder why we have been chosen to share such delights,
  and we join with all creation in praise
  to you and for what you have done.
  You reached down and made us from clay and breathed life into us.
  You gave us your Son so that we might have life anew.
  Help us this day to reconsecrate ourselves to you
  so that we might serve you forever. Amen.[9]

A Unison Prayer of Adoration for Easter

✠ **Glory to you, O God,**
  who on this day won victory over death,
  banishing the powers of darkness,
  and giving us light forever.
  You are light and truth,

and without you, there is no life.
So shine into our lives
that we may ever reflect your radiance
and thereby illumine those who walk in darkness.
For we pray in the name of the Lord of Easter,
even Jesus Christ, our Lord. Amen.[10]

Prayers of adoration are probably better sung than recited, and such sung forms of adoration include the *Gloria Patri*, the *Sanctus*, and the *Gloria in Excelsis*, which can be found in most hymnals.

Many great Christian hymns are sung prayers of adoration: "Come, Christians, Join to Sing," "Crown Him with Many Crowns," "Earth and All Stars," "Joyful, Joyful, We Adore Thee," "Praise Ye the Lord, the Almighty," "When Morning Gilds the Skies," and "How Great Thou Art."

Confession

Confession is the act of acknowledgment of sin by the believing community and it involves sorrow for past transgressions, petition for forgiveness, and an expression of our intention to make amends. All prayers of confession are, in a sense, modeled after Psalm 51. Confession may come after a time of self-examination and, in public worship, may take the form of a bidding prayer so that generalized subjects can be suggested and then the people can pray in silence for the specific failings that are on their hearts. Such a form of confession avoids the danger, often found in corporate prayers of confession, of seeming to put words into people's reluctant mouths, making them confess things that they do not feel guilty about at all.

A Bidding Prayer of Confession

Let us pray for forgiveness for the angry words we have spoken. . . . (silence)
Let us pray for forgiveness for the bitter thoughts we have harbored. . . . (silence)
Let us pray for forgiveness for our thoughtless neglect of the feelings of others. . . . (silence)[11]

Much of the time, the prayer of confession is a unison prayer either printed in the bulletin or another printed source. The unison prayer may be preceded or followed by a time of silence in which people can reflect upon their own lives in the light of God's love and dare to acknowledge their own failings. Such a time of silence needs to be long enough to encourage reflection, and fifteen seconds is not enough!

A Brief Prayer of Confession

✠ Almighty God, sometimes when I need to be kind, I am not.
Sometimes when I need to listen, I can't and don't.
There are times when I need to express my love and I do so ineffectively.
When I need to be loved, I often do not seek it.[12]

A Unison Prayer of Confession

✠ Merciful God, we are always wanting our due.
It is easy to see what we should receive,
but somehow we are blind to our responsibility.
We work to save what we do not even want
and value objects over people.
Help us to know your mind, O Christ,
and learn your way.
Commit us to building the place where all are welcome,
where all will be cared for. Amen.[13]

Prayers of confession should be familiar enough that the people do not have to stumble through them trying to read the words correctly and puzzling about the meaning. Using the same prayer over and over can help it truly become the prayer of the congregation. Here are more examples of prayers of confession.

A Prayer of Confession

✠ Gracious God, you place us in a world of wonder,
and far too often we miss it.
We see what we expect, what we want to see,
what fits in with our plans and visions.
We are slow of heart to believe the good news that is entrusted to us.
Forgive our shortsightedness and lack of faith.
Open our eyes and hearts that we may see your wonders,
share your vision, and live in your love.
In the name of the risen Christ. Amen.[14]

A Contemporary Prayer of Confession

✠ Lord of possibilities, forgive our clinging to impossibilities.
Your freedom causes us to tremble,

for you become unmanageable and unpredictable
by our deductions, definitions, and calculations.
When we seek to reduce you, you dance beyond our grasp.
When we attempt to define you, you delight in holy exceptions.
When we decide to make you head of our committee,
you don't attend the meetings.
Lord, help us to discover the wonder of your ways
and find our delight in your freedom. Amen.[15]

On some rare occasions, it may be possible to sing the confession using a version of Psalm 51 or Psalm 130 or a hymn such as "Lord Jesus, Think on Me" or "Just as I Am" or "O God of Earth and Altar." Another possibility is to invite people to silent confession and have no spoken prayer at all.

A pastor who constructs prayers of confession, as we have mentioned before, should avoid putting into the mouths of the people words that do not, in fact, reflect their own feelings. Avoid overstatements such as: "We have not loved our neighbors and have done nothing to help the needy." Putting words like this in the mouth of someone who has been trying all week to do good to others can be offensive and may produce a spirit of argument, which is hardly conducive to prayer.

The Psalms are also full of prayers that are really complaints against God. The following confession is a kind of complaint.

A Prayer of Complaint

Almighty God, I hurt.
It is unfair that I hurt, and I am angry.
I blame you. I blame the situation. I blame the people involved.
It is unfair.
As I wrestle with my pain
I discover that the pain I feel in the present
uncovers another hurt from my past,
a hurt to which I had grown numb,
a hurt around which I have much suffering,
suffering that I have carried without much awareness.
I am aware that the healing of the pain in the present brings with it
the healing of the pain from the past.
It is not fair, but it is just.
I am angry.
And I am beginning to be grateful, just slightly.[16]

The goal of the confession is to aid people in acknowledging and letting go of their guilt, not wallowing in it. Many people in our culture today are already overburdened by a sense of guilt and they do not need it increased. What they need is the sense of a gracious God who forgives.

The assurance of pardon is an essential component and response to the time of confession. In words that are spoken clearly and with vigor, the pastor or other leader announces God's forgiveness, if possible looking at the people as he or she speaks these words. Since the assurance of forgiveness is a pastoral act, pastors should be reluctant to give up this part of the service.

An Assurance of Pardon

Our God is a loving God, but also one of expectations.
We are forgiven, but we must forgive;
and we must live as though
that forgiveness were important to us.
Live in the promise that we are God's people,
forgiven in Christ and empowered to serve.
✠ **Thanks be to God. Amen.**[17]

Responsive assurances of pardon can also fit into a worship service.

A Responsive Assurance of Pardon

The Good News is this: Christ entered the world
✠ **to free us,**

to accept us,
✠ **to love us to be the women and men we were created to be.**

Friends, through the love of Christ, we are forgiven and welcomed home.
All: Alleluia! Amen![18]

A particular prayer of confession is sometimes not appropriate for an individual worshiper, in the same way some people do not like to sing certain hymns. Part of the leadership of worship is to instruct worshipers that they are to feel free to use those elements in worship that help them and not to feel burdened to pray prayers or participate in other activities to which they cannot relate.

Thanksgiving

Thanksgiving is the response we make to some experience of God's goodness to us. Unlike adorations, thanksgivings are rooted in specific experiences of God's graciousness and involve remembering occasions in which God has been particularly responsive to us in our need. By being thankful in prayer, we become more thankful in our living. Brian Gerrish concludes that, for Calvin, "authentic humanity is constituted by the act of thanksgiving to the Maker of heaven and earth, whose goodness has prepared a table before us; that is the truth of our being grounded in the creation."[19]

Our private prayers of thanksgiving need to be very specific and personal. They are composed as we count our daily blessings. In corporate prayer, however, thanksgiving, like confession, must be more general. Not all people are at the same place or share the same attitudes or experiences.

A Unison Prayer of Thanksgiving for Lent

✠ **God of the chosen people,**
  during this time of preparation,
  we remember with grateful hearts,
  the life and work of your Son, Jesus the Messiah.
  He came to teach us how to live life fully and faithfully.
  He showed us that obedience to your will
  does not always lead down painless paths,
  but does end in rewards beyond our imagining.
  Give us the courage to follow faithfully,
  knowing that your steadfast love will be with us forever. Amen.[20]

A Prayer of Thanksgiving for Advent

(Anyone can use this prayer during the Christmas season; it captures the sense of joy and wonder, and is broad and general enough to speak to the variety of moods and needs present in any given congregation on any Sunday.)

✠ **God of love, you come to us in the smile of a baby**
  who had only a manger for a bed.
  We see you in the joyful play of children.
  We hear you in the retelling of the stories
  of Mary, Joseph and the baby,
  and the community of believers who followed them.

We feel your awesome presence as we sing carols,
walk through the stillness of winter snow,
and experience the smells of love
in the baking of special Christmas confections.
Thank you, glorious God, for coming to us,
taking on our limitations and humanity,
so that we may learn more fully
about your wondrous love for us. Amen.[21]

A Prayer of Thanksgiving for Use on Any Occasion

✠ Almighty and merciful God,
from whom comes all that is good,
we praise you for your mercies,
for your goodness that has created us,
your grace that has sustained us,
your discipline that has corrected us,
and your love that has redeemed us.
Help us to love you,
and to be thankful for all your gifts
by serving you and delighting to do your will,
through Jesus Christ our Lord. Amen.[22]

Prayers of thanksgiving ought to occupy as important a place in public worship as do prayers of confession. Singing our thanks is also possible; the Psalms are very helpful because so many of them are songs of thanks. In particular, Psalms 65, 103, and 138 have been set to music in a variety of settings. The following hymns of thanksgiving are appropriate also: "For the Beauty of the Earth," "Come, Ye Thankful People, Come," "Let All Things Now Living," and "Now Thank We All Our God."

Supplication

Supplication involves our praying for something from God and, therefore, necessitates our belief that God hears and responds to our requests. Whether or not we theologize about this, supplication is the most basic and instinctual form of prayer. We ask God for that which we most dearly seek and desire. Prayers of supplication include both prayers of petition and prayers of intercession.

Petition. Prayers for ourselves raise many questions about what are proper subjects for prayer and how God actually answers these requests. To pray in the name of Jesus is to trust that even our least acceptable prayers are accepted by the God whose love for us is made known in Jesus.

A Prayer of Petition

You are Lord, even in the darkness.
You are God, even when our cries have no words.
You promise to send your Spirit to utter the prayers we cannot sound
and mend the broken spirits that can be whole only in you.
Lord of the darkness, Lord of the depths,
lift us to the light and life of your presence. Amen.[23]

Many hymns are petitions: "Jesus, Lover of My Soul," "Christ of the Upward Way," "Be Thou My Vision," "Breathe on Me, Breath of God," "Guide Me, O Thou Great Jehovah," and "Open My Eyes."

Intercession. Prayers of intercession are those prayers we pray on behalf of others, known or unknown to us. Such prayers prevent us from becoming self-centered as individuals and as a community of faith. The prayer of intercession might include some or all of the following concerns:

> The universal church, its members and obedience in mission
> The nation and all in authority
> The welfare of the whole world
> The concerns of the local community outside the church
> Those who suffer and are in trouble, especially those known to us

A Prayer of Intercession

Lord God of the nations,
you have promised that when two or three are gathered in your name,
you will be in the midst of them.
We pray for your presence and ask that you will be with your people
that we might be strengthened to serve you better.
Lord, the weight of government is a terrible burden.
Be with the men and women who have been elected to public office
that their choices will bring life and hope and justice for all people.
Be especially with our president, our governor. . . .
We pray for those who are ill; we pray for those who care for the ill.
And finally we pray for this people,
that we will serve you faithfully and well. Amen.[24]

Intercessions may come in the form of litanies or in opportunities for people to express their concerns for friends and relatives so that the leader can weave these into a spoken prayer. In some congregations, people are encouraged to put names of those whom they wish remembered in prayer in the offering plates and these are, in turn, passed on to the pastor and spoken aloud. To hear the name of someone prayed for aloud is a source of great comfort to those who bear the burden of worry and anxiety.

Prayers of petition and intercession are now commonly named "The Prayers of the People," but is this accurate? Are not the prayers of confession, adoration, and thanksgiving also the prayers of the people? To call them what they are is preferable: Prayers of petition and intercession.

Public prayer is a high point in the service of worship. To lead people in prayer is a great privilege. No matter what the particular human condition of each one who worships, some form of prayer will speak to that particular need. People may be burdened with a sense of unworthiness and need for release and sense of forgiveness of confession and pardon. They may be troubled by the loss of a loved one and need intercession, or they may be celebrating the joy of a new birth in the family and need to express thanks. To give full expression to the A-C-T-S of prayer is to meet the widest variety of human need.

9

The Setting of Worship

Art and Architecture in the Place of Worship

King David's dilemma as to whether he should continue to hold the worship of Israel in a moveable tent or build a temple is as timely today as it was three thousand years ago. Congregations sometimes attempt to exist without the burden of a building; they meet in rented space or in private homes. One reason for making this decision is to be able to use more money for mission beyond the congregation and to take more risks on behalf of the gospel by virtue of their freedom from debt. Most of the time such congregations are eventually forced to conclude, perhaps reluctantly, that they need to build for their own use in order to have a sense of identity, a space shared by all and owned by no one, and a sacred and special space that is set aside for the purpose of worship.

Judaism focused its worship life upon the Temple in Jerusalem. It was the center for the three great pilgrimage festivals: the Feast of Tabernacles in the fall, the Feast of Unleavened Bread in early spring, and the Feast of Weeks in late spring. Every Jew attempted to make the arduous journey to Jerusalem at least once in a lifetime. The Temple was a place of awe, pointing to the magnificence and transcendence of God. Temple worship was centered in sacrifice. Yet as Jews increasingly moved out into the Greek world, they began to worship in simple structures called synagogues, and their worship centered not upon sacrifice but upon instruction. The destruction of the Temple in Jerusalem in A.D. 70 completed the shift to worship in the local synagogue for Judaism and the primitive Christian community.

The synagogue was a far different place for worship from the pomp and magnificence of the Temple. The worshiper was not dwarfed by the immensity of the structure, and the center of worship became the rabbi's or teacher's reading and interpreting of scripture. Early Christians joined with Jews in synagogues; in his travels, Paul always seems to have begun his preaching in a new city in the synagogue. But soon Christians found they were not welcome in the synagogues any longer, and gradually they separated into their own communities of faith, which became largely Gentile by the end of the second century.

Christianity was born in persecution, and congregations could not build churches for centuries. As a result, worship was held in the homes of worshipers, or the "house church." These small gatherings fostered a sense of family and shared responsibility. Women and men shared in leadership, and offices were fluid. Over time, however, the sites of martyrdom became important places of worship and veneration, and the shift away from the intimacy of the home led to more leader-centered worship space.

The Emperor Constantine's Edict of Toleration, issued in A.D. 313, allowed Christians to worship publicly for the first time. With the Emperor now favoring Christianity, suddenly a need arose for large worship locations. At first the church used public buildings, adapting them to suit their unique purposes. Intimacy was lost as large numbers of people became Christians, and worship became much more centered upon the official leaders, who were now all male. Subsequently, churches were built in communities, shrines were erected at holy places, and, as ecclesiology developed, cathedrals were built as a seat for the bishop and as the coordinating hub of the area. Many of these great masterpieces of architecture still stand as witness to the genius of the time and to the enduring nature of the human spiritual vision. But why should worship require special places?

Holy Ground

When Moses approached the burning bush, he was told to take off his sandals, for he was standing on "holy ground" (Exod. 3:5; see also Acts 7:33). Many of the Psalms speak of the utter joy of entering the place where the presence of God is known (Psalm 122). Places like Iona, the Resurrection Garden in Jerusalem, Coventry Cathedral, Notre Dame in Paris, St. Giles in Edinburgh, St. Pierre in Geneva, and the National Cathedral in Washington are capable of stirring deep feelings and the conviction that "surely God is in this place."

The reason for such sentiment, of course, is that these are places of worship and consecrated as such; some, like Iona, are sites of worship that date back as far as anybody can remember. These ancient places still inform us as to the authenticity of consecrated worship spaces. As, over the years, people have offered their prayers, the very walls have become hallowed. A sensitive visitor can detect that these are "thin places," where the veil between the world of ordinary sense experience and the mystery of God's presence is nearly parted.

People tend to think about the building in which they have worshiped for years as "holy space," and they may resist efforts even to remodel it. Rational appeals are quite likely to have little impact, for the attachment is one that is felt more than it is thought. People associate the divine with the space in which they have consciously encountered God.

Escaping the notion of holy space is nearly impossible. Even the most secular people are likely to feel a sense of awe in a place such as Muir Woods, among the giant redwoods of California or on the rim of Grand Canyon. These places, by their sheer magnificence, dwarf the individual and cause an awareness of that which is bigger than any of us. People may also revere other spaces, not so much because of any inherent beauty but because of association: the place of one's birth, schooling, or marriage, graves of loved ones, or other such sites.

In his landmark book *The Idea of the Holy*, Rudolf Otto identified three universal and elemental aspects of all religion: the devotion to truth as so understood, the commitment to an ethical way of life, and the awareness of what he called *Mysterium Tremendum* (formidable mystery). All religions seek to deal with each of these issues, but the mystery itself is at the very heart of all religious practice. The unknowable, transcendent Other is perceived through intuition and experience, rather than through reason. Edward A. Sovik, a church architect, identified that feeling of transcendence and holy mystery with our experience of beauty: "not a particular beauty, not just the beauty of a 'dim religious light,' but all beauty. For beauty is also a mystery—ineffable, unknowable, but perceivable, remote but fascinating. We sense it, we do not deduce it."[1]

Sacred space and beautiful space are not the same thing, but all churches attempt to build buildings that elevate the human spirit, that speak of what cannot be fully understood, that are reminders of a holiness beyond all words. Some sacred spaces succeed well, and others do not. But, Sovik insists,

> If any architect wishes to make a particular environment a symbol of the holy, it is absolutely required that the place be one of beauty. People who have undertaken to build temples or shrines or church buildings have always held this to be true. If we assume that the symbol of the holy is not a particular beauty, but beauty of any sort, then it is not surprising that we can love equally places as diverse as Chartres and Vierzehnheiligen, the Old Ship Meeting House, and Christ Lutheran Church. It is not surprising that Christians could adopt the Parthenon and the Pantheon for use as places of worship, and that Muslims would turn the Church of Santa Sophia into a mosque. These buildings were not ideal for the uses of the religious groups that adopted them, and

they certainly had no acquired sacredness for these groups. But the beauty of the places was convincing.[2]

Success or failure in the building of a sacred space is also a matter of human experience and taste, but the effort to construct a sacred space is at the core of all church architecture and has always been so. In some way we sense what Jacob sensed when—following his dream at Haran in which he saw a ladder reaching to heaven, with angels ascending and descending on it—he woke and cried out, "Surely the LORD is in this place—and I did not know it!" Jacob was afraid, and he said, "This is none other than the house of God, and this is the gate of heaven" (Gen. 28:16–17).

Early Christians moved from informal spaces in homes, catacombs, and forests, or from borrowed public buildings, into their own spaces. By the second century, even before Christianity was tolerated by Constantine, Christian worship was not simply an informal affair but had begun to develop a "fixed liturgy." Though all worship was not likely the same at this early date, nevertheless as Christians became free to travel from church to church, that liturgy gradually became somewhat standardized, and it, in part, determined the kinds of spaces they sought.

With a fixed liturgy came a need for certain similarities in worship spaces and, eventually, special forms of architecture. The forms had to make the functions possible: the font was to be at the place of entrance to represent joining the community; a central, very visible table was necessary for the sacrament of the Lord's Supper; people needed room to approach the table and the deacons needed space to receive the elements to distribute to the poor; a reading stand (lectern) was required; a chair (*cathedra*) was necessary for the bishop and aisles for processions.

Christians already had these needs in mind by the time they were allowed to build public places of worship. Different patterns and styles would develop over the centuries with regional variations, but the tendency was toward increasing similarity in a basic architectural plan. Along with this came increasing ornateness, viewed as a gift to the Almighty—and sometimes as a way to recognize the generosity and piety of the donors.

Reformation Reactions to Architecture

Reformed Christians have always had some suspicion of holy places. Fear of idolatry has been a particularly strong theme among followers of Calvin and Zwingli. The cathedrals of the Middle Ages were centers of piety, but the Protestant Reformers were uneasy with what they saw as luxury and excess. Elaborate altars, statues of the saints, costly vestments for the clergy—as well as the competition, commerce, and commercialism of the localities—all seemed to them to cause the focus of worship to move from God to the place itself.

Martin Luther did not consider all art to be "graven images," but he found himself surrounded by iconoclasm in Wittenberg in 1533, after Karlstadt published *On the Abolishing of Images*. Luther's attitude reflected the dictum that what is not forbidden in scripture is acceptable in practice. Thus, he preserved much of the art in the churches of Germany. Surprisingly, the Swiss reformer Zwingli, himself a musician and art lover, urged abolishing art in the churches in Zurich. As the interiors of churches were whitewashed, Zwingli wrote to a friend: "We have churches which are positively luminous; the walls are beautifully white."[3]

John Calvin's response was more complex. He allowed carvings and paintings of what the eyes are capable of seeing; but he declared, "Let not the majesty of God, which is far above the perception of the eyes, be debased through unseemly representation."[4] Although there was no wholesale whitewashing of the churches in Geneva, Calvin's anxiety about graven images resulted in a cautious response by his followers to art.

New Emphases in Architecture

Protestants were never able to separate from the realization that places set apart for worship become holy places. Even the simple and severe worship places of the Amish invite and enhance worship. The stark simplicity of Puritan meetinghouses and Quaker meeting places have their own compelling beauty and sense of the holy.

The New England meetinghouse was probably the first truly Protestant architecture. Until then, Protestants had inherited the buildings of the Roman Catholics throughout Europe and had removed items they could not tolerate, moved altars out from the wall in many cases, put the pulpit where the preacher could best be heard, and "made do." The New England meetinghouse was clean space, with clear glass windows to let in maximum light so that the worshipers could read their Bibles and hymnals, the pews arranged to facilitate everyone's hearing and seeing the preacher, and a table placed close to the center of the worship space. New England meetinghouses often served as the meeting place for the local government as well and were symbols of the unity of the community, sitting on the edge of the town green. These plain buildings are masterpieces of simple beauty.

As the centuries passed, Protestants experimented with a variety of styles of architecture as they attempted to meet the needs of a changing world. They continued to copy medieval cathedrals wherever they could afford to do so as well as the New England meetinghouse. But they also evolved new styles such as the Akron Plan, a largely square building with the entrance in one corner, the pulpit/table area in the opposite corner, and the pews curved and often on a slanting floor. Sometimes a false wall enabled the space to be doubled for special occasions such as Christmas, Easter, Mother's Day, and large weddings or funerals.

In spite of the Reformers' nervousness about luxury, over time Protestant churches often became quite elaborate and expensive. The church building became one of the ways that churches of different denominations competed with each other, each trying to outdo the others in building bigger, better, and more comfortable buildings.

In the nineteenth century, the competition for worshipers led many city churches to construct magnificent buildings in order to display their massive pipe organs, robed choirs, and great preachers. The preachers were given lots of room to move about as they acted out their sermons. The pulpit almost disappeared as an unnecessary piece of furniture that stood in the way of the preacher. With some significant exceptions, the buildings of this period are often recognized for their enduring ugliness.

Partly in reaction to the excesses of the nineteenth century, congregations in the twentieth century demonstrated some ambivalence toward places of worship. Some people argued that "they can worship God anywhere" and have felt uncomfortable with building expensive sacred spaces of any kind. Arguments continued, especially in the last several decades, between people who wanted to point with pride to beautiful buildings and others who wanted simplicity and economy. Both groups recognized that some kind of building was needed, however. The question then became: what is this space to be like?

Three important issues need to be remembered about constructing a place of worship: First: Is the space humane—that is, does it give the worshiper a sense of belonging in that space? Or, on the contrary, does the space dwarf the individual and suggest insignificance? Second: Is the space accessible to all? Can a child fit in the pews; can a person with a physical disability be included in the congregation; do the elderly and infirm sense that they are important in the space? Third: Does the space assist in creating a community of worshipers so that a horizontal dimension is enhanced as well as a vertical one? Is community made more possible by how the space is used?

Certainly God can be worshiped in simple settings as well as in the large or ornate ones, but art and architecture should not distract from worship and can make strong statements that this place is for the worship of God—and all are welcome!

People designing a new place of worship can give careful attention to its construction. But most worship leaders inherit a space, which may be excellent or may require modification. Possibly the best situation is a convenient, adaptable space that provides for the basic needs of the worshiping community but has plenty of undedicated area that is convertible to various innovations. Fortunate is the congregation whose church has flexible seating that can be rearranged from time to time. Fixed pews can be very limiting.

Using Space Appropriately

The first question for worship leaders in considering their use of space is "what will be happening in worship?" Is it primarily a preaching service? Will Baptism or the Lord's Supper be observed? How important are these sacramental actions? Will any kind of movement or drama occur during the service? Are there special musical needs, such as places for choirs, soloists, instrumentalists? Each activity requires some kind of space.

Worshipers' needs must be considered. Will they be able to hear and see the worship activities? Is there room or access for them to participate in the service, e.g., coming forward to receive Communion? Where will hymnals or other worship materials be placed? Is there sufficient light to read text or music? Some of these questions seem elementary, but the answers make a difference as to whether worshipers see themselves as spectators or participants in worship.

Most modern church buildings are designed on the principle that form follows function. Instead of imposing a design upon the congregation's worship—whether that of a Gothic cathedral, a ship, or a simple A-frame—the idea became building from the inside out, on the basis of what the congregation actually did. The architecture did not shape the worship, but rather, the worship life of the congregation shaped the architecture.

For Reformed Christians, this idea means beginning with the three centers of worship—pulpit, font, and table—and designing the space to focus upon the action associated with these three centers. The pulpit needs to be situated for maximum visibility by all present. With elaborate sound systems possible in even the humblest of churches, we have more flexibility in situating the pulpit, but acoustics and line of sight of the worshipers are still important. The font should be placed so that it both symbolizes entrance into the congregation and is visible to the people. Quite often fonts seem to be afterthoughts added to an otherwise complete building, suggesting that baptism is not a very important activity. The table should look like a real table rather than a tomb, and should function like a table around which people can gather. An irony of the modern church is that just as Roman Catholic churches are pulling the altar/table out from the wall for the purpose of gathering around it, many Protestant churches have constructed altars that are fixed in place and inaccessible to all but the clergy. When the congregation's needs for seating are taken into account and provision has been made for musicians and their instruments, then the building can be constructed to accommodate the major furniture and actions that follow. Such a design may not "look like a church," but it will serve the needs of a real congregation and inspire, rather than inhibit worship.

Involving the Senses: Aesthetics

The Reformation's emphasis on "*sola scriptura*" and the reading and preaching of the Word tended to make worship primarily an intellectual activity. In theory, there was little deference to the senses, but in reality, the senses cannot be put aside. Even the Bibles coming off the presses of Gutenberg were objects of beauty. Aesthetics are always an issue when believers worship God by doing things as well as they can. Beauty, even stark beauty, is bound to emerge. To involve the whole person in worship means involving all the means by which that person participates in an experience, and that means the five senses as well as the intellect.

The primary art of Reformed congregations, aside from the architecture of the building, has always been music. Beyond that, any symbols that illuminated the biblical text came to be appreciated slowly over the years. Symbols were not allowed simply for decoration; they were to be instructive.

In many early churches, paintings, frescoes, and mosaics were important; as Gothic architecture (starting in the twelfth century), with its vaulted arches reaching for eternity, became the norm, wall space was given over to windows—and the most appropriate art for the window was thought to be stained glass. These windows, like the great rose windows, could speak nonverbally of the splendor of God's creation, or they could be filled with symbols and figures to tell the gospel story. In an age before literacy was common, church windows were the great teachers. Even the glow of the rich colors provided an uplifting experience.

Stained-glass windows, like all art, can be great or cliché. When great, they continue to give new insights and inspiration over the years. When cliché, they soon become tiresome with outmoded images. That these windows are not easily removable and may last for centuries should make their initial installation a matter for careful decision.

A Feast for the Worshiper

Stained-glass windows, mosaic floors, wall carvings, and often even the color of the sanctuary cannot be easily changed. But much art can be displayed and utilized throughout the year, coming and going with the seasons or worship emphases. Better to have a painting or banner that makes periodic appearances than one that is hung on the wall and stays there forever. The worst of all options is the sagging banner that remains in place year after year and becomes unintentionally permanent as it fades and gathers dust.

Worship planners who seek to bring the vitality of art into worship should keep a few general principles in mind:

1. *Embrace the temporary.* All art need not be permanent, or even great! There is a thrill when a congregation sets about creating art for a service (such as a huge mobile of origami cranes) that is used for that service alone.
2. *Don't reduce everything to words.* Art is the great means by which we add the nonverbal to our worship, thereby inviting entirely different kinds of responses in the worshipers. But Protestants don't really trust the nonverbal and do their best to convert everything to words. Some banners have nothing but words! Other than arts like poetry or music texts, try to limit or eliminate words from as much of your art as possible.
3. *Explain to involve.* In what may seem to be a contradiction of the above suggestion, be sure the congregation understands why the art is being used but not necessarily what it means. They may need the assurance that what is being used in that service of worship is experimental and is not intended to be the inauguration of a new style. People can put up with a lot if they think it won't last forever. If, for example, someone explains what will be happening in a very experimental piece of music, the worshipers will most likely enjoy listening, even if they don't particularly enjoy that style of music.
4. *Generally, bigger is better.* With banners and related art forms, size may determine the impact. A small banner in a big room doesn't do much.
5. *Good art is evocative.* Art that "says it all" makes for worship that doesn't go anywhere! Good art will suggest, then draw in the worshiper to ponder and bring forth new and individual insights. Good symbols are evocative; otherwise they are simply "signs." At an intersection, one seldom ponders the deeper meaning of a stop sign!

Ways to Enrich the Worship Setting

Many approaches are possible for enriching the worship setting.

Bulletin covers. Fresh art can be introduced weekly to the congregation by means of the most underused instrument in our worship: the church bulletin. Rather than purchasing commercially prepared covers, ask members of the congregation to design covers. With present technology, congregations can often print these in color on their office printers.

Paraments and stoles. Placed on the communion table, pulpit, and lectern, and worn by worship leaders, these textile creations are constantly in sight of the congregation. Rather than buying them from catalogs, ask people to design and make them.

Paintings, posters, and photography. These visual statements can be displayed on easels if there is no room to hang them. Make sure they can be seen; placing them at the entrance sometimes allows people to examine them as they enter or leave; they then can be moved into the worship area during the service, if necessary.

Banners, pennants, and flags. These items are highly effective in setting a particular mood in worship. Have ways to display them; weighted banner stands or removable brackets on the ends of pews do the job. They add drama to a procession when carried, with attached ribbons flying. Mounting them on a wall works, but is less effective. (Steel conduit pipes with wooden dowels as cross pieces, held by chains and pipe caps, are an effective means of displaying banners.)

Constructions. Multiple constructions can be carried in processions or simply be displayed throughout the sanctuary. For Pentecost, make a T-frame and hang from it wind chimes or Noah bells—or windsocks from weathervanes. For Communion, use bamboo poles as fishing poles, and hang from them paper fish and small loaves of bread. (See p. 198.) During Lent, hang grapevine wreathes from poles by means of ribbons. (See p. 200.) For Reformation Sunday, hang tartan pennants throughout the sanctuary.

Processional crosses. A cross purchased from a church supply house or one made by someone in the congregation is effective when it leads the procession. The person who carries a cross is called a "crucifer." The task of crucifer can be taken up by older children or young people, providing a way for them to assist in the leadership of worship.

Temporary hangings. Some church worship designers achieve remarkable effects with draped cloth, clear plastic sheets, huge paper constructions (such as angels), etc. (See the work done by Nancy Chinn, which is listed in the bibliography.)

Seasonal decorations. Most churches regularly use greens at Christmas and lilies at Easter. How about red geraniums for Pentecost or autumn leaves in the fall?

Light. Candles, lanterns, and luminarias are all portable and affordable sources of light, and they set a remarkable mood, particularly in places that are not too bright. Use a paschal candle during Lent and Easter; use seven-day bottle candles, continuously burning, throughout the four weeks of Advent.

Items for Communion. Multiple loaves of crusty bread in baskets; coarse napkins; and pottery goblets, pitchers, and plates for the elements (made or purchased by the congregation) all add visual interest to the sacrament. Rotate serving items from celebration to celebration to maintain interest.

Water. Just as bread and wine may be visually beautiful for the Lord's Supper, much can be done with water to remind us of Baptism. Worshipers may be greeted at the door with a bowl of water and encouraged to "Touch the water that will touch the child, touched by the Spirit." Some worship leaders go through the congregation, sprinkling water on the worshipers and asking them to "Remember your baptism." Simply having different colored glass bowls of water on the Communion table can be striking. And home building stores can provide materials to make temporary fountains and ponds.

Decorations from nature. Plants, branches, palms, blossoms, driftwood, and stones can speak to such themes as the temptation of Jesus in the wilderness, the wandering of the Israelites in the wilderness, Palm Sunday, etc.

Theatrical sets. On Easter morning, make the entranceway to the sanctuary appear to be the entrance to the empty tomb; or the stable with a manger might greet worshipers on Christmas Eve. Jonah's ship, the gates of Jerusalem, the catacombs, and other sets could be constructed to fire the imagination of those who worship.

Let it fly! Concluding worship outside with a balloon release may be effective. Where the service is available, a dove release is beautiful at Pentecost, or for a funeral.

A church can use these activities and others over the years to enrich the setting of worship and provide for evocative activities. But a word of warning: if your congregation has not had much variety in worship, don't introduce all these ideas at once!

Certainly our theology, words, and music are important in worship, but worship planners need to think about the whole person who comes to worship: a person with five senses. Environment affects all of us, perhaps more than we will ever realize. Don't overlook the many factors that may contribute to a person's feeling that "this indeed is a place where I will meet God."

10

The Church Year

Historical Background

The Service for the Lord's Day was the primary celebration of worship for the Reformers. A liturgical calendar had evolved that consisted mostly of saints' feast days, but the celebration of these occasions became a reason for revelry rather than worship. In response, the Reformers chose to retain from that calendar Christmas, Good Friday, Easter, Ascension, and Pentecost—what they called "evangelical feasts"—as days worthy of remembering the Lord. The Second Helvetic Confession noted

> If in Christian liberty the churches religiously celebrate the memory of the Lord's nativity, circumcision, passion, resurrection and his ascension into heaven, and the sending of the Holy Spirit upon his disciples, we approve it highly.[1]

The criterion for liturgical practice was faithfulness to the New Testament witness to the gospel.

One of John Calvin's innovations had lasting consequences for the church year, however: he followed Zwingli and Favel and abolished the medieval lectionary, choosing to preach through whole books of the Bible in sequence. Calvin was concerned because the lectionary of his day was made up of snippets of scripture taken out of context. He did not believe that reading texts in such a haphazard manner would educate the biblically illiterate people he sought to serve. He chose instead to read and preach on only one text at a time and to read and preach in sequence, developing texts from one book of scripture. The people would thus get acquainted with a given Gospel and hear each lesson in its proper context. By doing this, he bypassed the use of the liturgical year and, despite his inclusion of the five major feasts, the practice of observing them began to disappear among the Reformed. A significant difference between Lutheran and Reformed Protestants developed around this distinction: Lutherans retained the lectionary and, thus, the church year, and Reformed Protestants opted for preaching in sequence and dropped the church year.

As the Puritans joined with the Scottish separatists to maintain the type of worship that was meaningful to them, they found themselves opposed to the use of the English Prayer Book, not so much because of what it contained but because it was being imposed upon them by people in political power, thus removing the freedom to worship as they chose. The struggle in Great Britain by the Reformed churches was thus quite different from the struggle of Reformed Christians on the continent, who were not threatened by the imposition of the Prayer Book. Since opposition to the Prayer Book meant opposition to the liturgical calendar, which was embodied in the Prayer Book, the celebration of even the evangelical feasts fell into disuse among Reformed noncontinental Christians. In 1560, when the Scottish Kirk adopted the Second Helvetic Confession in its *Book of Discipline*, it removed those words that commended the keeping of the evangelical feasts. So while the continental Reformed Christians were free to observe such feasts as they felt enhanced worship, Reformed Christians in Britain stood firmly against such practices as part of their opposition to the political and liturgical expressions of a state church that was not of their choosing.

Particularly strong opposition occurred over the celebration of Christmas, which was associated not only with the Prayer Book, but also with the aristocracy. The rich used the occasion of Christmas to flaunt their money, and Puritans were appalled. As egalitarians, they were opposed to anything that widened the gap between rich and poor. Their opposition to Christmas has earned them bad press through the ages even as their reasons for opposing the lavish expenditures of Christmas have been forgotten.

The Puritans also brought with them to America their opposition to prayer books and liturgical calendars, even though this stance was no longer a part of the struggle for religious liberty. In the years after the Civil War, mention of Christmas and Easter began to appear in the children's Sunday school literature of Congregationalists and Presbyterians. The Dutch and German Reformed had always celebrated these festivals. At the same time came a renewed appreciation of ancient creeds, the Lord's Prayer, and the responsive reading of Psalms. American revivalism provided new, informal styles of worship that resulted in liturgical reform.

Not until the twentieth century, however, did many American Protestants began to observe a liturgical calendar. Only in the mid-nineteenth century did they begin to celebrate Christmas, and not until after World War II were Advent and Lent observed. Although some worship materials published by the various denominations in the first half of the twentieth century included prayers for Advent, Christmas, Good Friday, and Easter, they were generally ignored. Only with the adoption of the ecumenical lectionary in the 1960s was the church year, as such, widely observed.

Most Reformed congregations today try to establish some kind of balance in observing the major days of the church year but also include Stewardship Sunday, Mother's Day, Martin Luther King Jr. Sunday, Memorial Day, Mission Sunday, Church School Recognition Day, Graduation Sunday, and other events that are laid over the structure of the lectionary-based events: Advent, Christmas, Lent, Palm Sunday, Good Friday, Easter, Ascension Day, Pentecost, and All Saints' Day. Such a compromise has the advantage of meeting the people where they are. To try to avoid the obvious festivals of society is pointless. A pastoral style of worship seeks to transform rather than ignore events that are important to the people.

After Vatican II (1962–1965), the desire for closer collegiality among all Christians led to the adoption of a common lectionary and calendar. Many denominations moved to commit to a liturgical calendar, which included Baptism of the Lord, Transfiguration of the Lord, and Christ the King, dates shared with other Christian churches.[2]

The Seasons of the Church Year

It is not surprising that Christian worship, growing as it did out of Jewish worship, should delight in telling, again and again, the ancient stories of faith—now the faith as made known in Jesus Christ. The early church had a simple calendar seen in the Gospels, marked by Christmas (Feast of the Incarnation) and Easter (Feast of the Resurrection); all other time was known as "Ordinary Time." This structure remains the basis of the calendar, which runs as follows:

The Christmas (Incarnation) Cycle

Four weeks of Advent
Twelve days of Christmas
The Day of Epiphany (January 6)

Ordinary Time

A short period of Ordinary Time follows, from January 7 to the Tuesday before Ash Wednesday. This period includes the Baptism of the Lord and concludes with the Transfiguration of the Lord.

The Easter (Resurrection) Cycle

"Forty days" of Lent; Lent begins with Ash Wednesday and includes Passion/Palm Sunday, Maundy Thursday, Good Friday, and Holy Saturday,

which is the Great Vigil of Easter. The three days—Maundy Thursday,
Good Friday, and Holy Saturday—are known as the Triduum, Latin for
"three days."

Fifty days of Easter, which includes the Ascension of the Lord.

The Day of Pentecost, followed a week later by Trinity Sunday, which is in
Ordinary Time.

Ordinary Time

A second period of Ordinary Time extends from the Monday after Pentecost
through the Saturday before the First Sunday of Advent. The last Sunday in
Ordinary Time is called Christ the King. Ordinary Time would include
November 1, All Saints' Day.

Activities, Moods, and Colors of the Seasons

The use of seasonal colors dates back to the church at Jerusalem in the twelfth
century. The traditional seasonal colors have the advantage of long use and
ecumenical agreement.

Advent to Christmas

Advent is the four weeks before Christmas. The Latin word a*dventus* means
"coming," that is, the coming of Christ. Advent is a time of preparation for
Christ's coming to us. One of the Advent terms used through history is the
Aramaic term found in 1 Corinthians 16:22, *Maranatha.* The word is composed of two words run together, and this interesting duality of definitions
speaks to the mood of Advent. *Marana-tha* is the imperative form, oriented to
the future that translates: "Come, our Lord!" *Maran-atha* is the perfect form,
referring to an action completed in the past and translated "Our Lord has
come!" The cry *Maranatha!* in Advent thus speaks to both the past and future
dimensions of the season, evoking remembrance of the words from the
eucharistic celebration: "Christ has died. Christ is risen. Christ will come
again." Our celebrations of Advent, then, do not simply look back to that first
Advent when the Word became flesh; Advent also speaks to the eternally
future dimension, as Christ will come to us again and again.

In some churches, the tone of the season is somber; and the color is purple,
the color of penitence. No Christmas music is allowed until Christmas Eve,
even though as soon as we step outside the church door we hear it everywhere.
Currently there is a rethinking of the mood of the season.

Fourth-century Roman documents indicate that Christmas was celebrated
as early as that century. December 25 was listed as the "Birthday of the Uncon-

quered Sun," and martyrs listed on this feast day include "Christ, born in Bethlehem of Judea."[3] As that became a popularly celebrated feast, it was only natural that a period of preparation should precede it; these preparations can be
traced to prayers in the Gelasian Sacramentary of the eighth century, the oldest known Roman Sacramentary in which the feasts are arranged according to
the ecclesiastical year.

In the early church, the Easter Vigil was the favorite occasion for communicants to become members. The Easter Vigil was preceded by the forty-
day period of fasting called Lent. However, baptism was not conducted on
only that date, and another favorite date for communicants to join came to
be the Feast of the Incarnation (Christmas). Those who were to join the
church on that day also went through a forty-day period of fasting and preparation, starting on St. Martin's Day, November 11; this period of fasting
came to be known as St. Martin's Lent. Because the art and mood of the
Western church in the Middle Ages emphasized the crucifixion rather
than the resurrection, by the seventh century, the practice of the fast and
the penitential period of Advent were blurred and came to be observed by
everyone, not just the communicants. As late as the twelfth century, Advent
was celebrated as a joyous season, but subsequent centuries, emphasizing
the judgment at the second coming, set the time as a penitential period.
(Interestingly, the *Dies Irae* was originally written for the Sunday before
Advent.)

For those churches that don't emphasize the negative, more judgmental
aspects of a second coming, a penitential tone in Advent makes little sense. We
do feel a somberness of mood as we approach the crucifixion during Lent, but
the period before the birth of Jesus is one of joyful expectancy and hope.
Though it is not the festival of joy that Christmas is, it is not a penitential
period either. Some churches have thus begun using Sarum Blue for the season of Advent, a rich blue used in Salisbury Cathedral. (Salisbury, England,
was named Sarum before the Reformation.) Blue is also the color associated
with Mary, who, legend holds, as a young girl wove the hyacinth blue, purple,
and crimson veil (Exod. 26:31) in the Temple that covered the Holy of
Holies—a veil that was to be torn in two at the death of her son.[4] (Cf. Simeon's
prophecy, "A sword will pierce your own soul too." Luke 2:35.)

A popular activity during Advent worship is the lighting of the Advent candles. Four candles are lighted, one each week during Advent. (Sometimes a
fifth "Christ candle," a white one, is lighted on Christmas Eve.) Churches that
use purple candles generally make the third candle rose pink. The four weeks
and four candles do not represent any particular character or quality but rather
are a means of counting to the Day of the Birth. (However, the third Sunday
has traditionally been called "*Gaudete,*" from the first words of the Latin
introit, meaning "Rejoice! Be glad!")

Another liturgical tradition, which we also note in chapter 13, is the use of the Great "O" Antiphons (so called because they begin with the word "O"), a practice that began in the ninth century, probably in Rome, and was popular in the Middle Ages. Each day, from December 17 to 23, one of the antiphons would be sung.

> December 17: "O Wisdom, ordering all things"
> December 18: "O Adonai, burning bush, Law on Sinai"
> December 19: "O Root of Jesse"
> December 20: "O Key of David, scepter over the house of Israel"
> December 21: "O Radiant Dawn, splendor of eternal light"
> December 22: "O Ruler of the Nations, monarch, cornerstone"
> December 23: "O Immanuel, desire of the nations, savior of all"[5]

These antiphons are woven into the text of the popular Advent hymn "O Come, O Come, Emmanuel." Calls to worship can be constructed using combinations of the antiphons; each might end: "The Spirit and the Bride say, Come. Come, Lord Jesus." (See p. 204.) Another ascription that can be used is from the Communion liturgy: "Christ has died, Christ has risen, Christ will come again."

Candles, bulletin covers, processions, a set of Advent banners, and sanctuary decorations will define the quality of Advent. But the most defining activity of the season is the choice of Advent hymns.

Christmas Eve and Christmas Day wear the color of greatest joy: white or gold. Music and scripture celebrate the birth of Jesus Christ. The color red is also appropriate for any season or service. As with Eastertide, the Prayer of Confession, *Kyrie*, and Assurance of Forgiveness are replaced with a Prayer of Adoration and possibly the *Gloria in Excelsis*.

A Short Period of Ordinary Time

A short period of Ordinary Time runs from January 7 through the Tuesday before Ash Wednesday (which is sometimes known as Shrove Tuesday, because of the shriving—confession and absolution—that traditionally took place on this day). Two events may be noted: Baptism of the Lord (the Sunday between January 7 and 13); and the Transfiguration of the Lord (the Sunday before Ash Wednesday).

The Weeks of Lent

Lent is the forty-day period from Ash Wednesday to Easter. (The word *Lent* comes from the Anglo-Saxon *lencten*, to lengthen, which has to do with the lengthening of the days in springtime.) The forty-day length may confuse people who pull out their calendars and actually count the days, because Sunday, being the Day of Resurrection, is never a fast day. Thus the forty days of Lent do not count the Sundays, and there are actually forty-six days from Ash Wednesday to Easter!

The number forty is important in liturgy and is a remarkable number in the Bible.

> It rained forty days and forty nights while Noah was on the ark (Gen. 7:4);
> The children of Israel wandered forty years in the wilderness (Exod. 16:35 et al.);
> The Israelites were under the oppression of the Philistines for forty years before Samson was born (Judg. 13:1);
> Elijah prepared for ministry for forty days and nights (I Kings 19:8);
> Jonah warned Nineveh that it had forty days in which to repent (Jonah 3:4);
> Jesus fasted and was tempted for forty days (Matt. 4:2 et al.);
> There are forty days from Resurrection to Ascension (Acts 1:3).

Numerous proposals have been offered in an attempt to decipher the mysterious meaning of the number forty. In all the explanations no scholars have noted its relation to the primordial number having to do with the length of fetal development: forty weeks from conception to birth for humans. Thus, the number is part of the development of all human life. All of the major incidents in scripture that are based upon the number forty have to do with birth (as a nation of God's people, as a prophet, as the Son of God), rebirth, or second birth (service, ministry).

A dramatic way to prepare for Lent is to observe the "Burial of the Alleluia" at the end of worship on the Sunday prior to Ash Wednesday.[6] (If an Alleluia banner is to be removed from the place of worship on that day and returned on Easter, it should be in place several weeks before the service so that there will be some feeling of loss at its removal.)

The forty days of Lent are a major time of preparation for Christians. As we noted earlier, for the early church, these were the days when catechumens were finally prepared through study and service for baptism. Today, churches that observe Lent often offer special courses in spirituality and study, and special opportunities for service. Lenten retreats are a popular preparation for Easter. Because during this time the church teaches what it believes, saying one of the historic creeds each week in worship is appropriate; if used, the creed may follow the sermon and is introduced with the words: "Let us say what we believe." Generally the congregation stands for the creed.

Ash Wednesday begins the season with its stern reminder that "from the dust we came and to the dust we return: dust to dust, ashes to ashes." A Service of the Ashes on Ash Wednesday invites Christians to think of the season they are entering and receive a cross drawn with ashes on the forehead. In earlier days, sackcloth and ashes were worn during Lent or during times of great penitence or despair. (The ashes used on Ash Wednesday are traditionally burned palm fronds from the previous Palm/Passion Sunday.)

The color of the Lenten season is purple, the color of royalty—and also the color of the robe put on Jesus when he was mocked and beaten (John 19:2); purple has thus become the color of sacrifice and penitence. Elements of rejoicing are removed from the service. The *Gloria* and Doxology are not sung, and the word "Alleluia" is not said or sung. Church bells are not rung, with the exception of hand bells.

Holy Week begins with Palm/Passion Sunday and extends through Easter. Many liturgists avoid making Palm Sunday a day of great triumph: it wasn't. Moreover, since not many people attend midweek services during Holy Week, the church can appear to move emotionally from a joyful Palm Sunday to a joyous Easter, and people will be unaware of the significant interim events. Liturgists recommend a short palm procession that moves directly to a recounting of the events of the Passion.[7] Worship planners can quite possibly build a service around the two-edged sword of adulation and betrayal, moving through the service from the Palm Sunday event (putting this reading at the beginning of the service, followed by a processional hymn) through the events of Holy Week to the Crucifixion. There should be a major reading of the Passion Narrative from the Gospel in the featured cycle that would involve all members of the congregation. (Have one reader be the narrator, one be Jesus, others the major parts such as Judas and Pilate, and the congregation plays all the other roles.) This extensive reading would be included in the bulletin.

Maundy Thursday derives its name from John 13:34, where Jesus washed the feet of the disciples and said, "I give you a new commandment . . . "—in Latin, *Mandatum novum.* Of all services, this setting is the most appropriate for the Lord's Supper. Often the service is held in candlelight; many churches hold a Service of Tenebrae (Shadows) wherein the candles are gradually extinguished at the end of the service, representing the darkness that came over the disciples at the trial, crucifixion, and death of Jesus. (This service is countered by the Service of Light at the Easter vigil.) If a church burns a paschal candle during Lent, it is extinguished on Maundy Thursday and relighted at the Easter vigil.

Good Friday is often celebrated with a service from noon to 3:00 P.M., the time at which Jesus died (see Luke 23:44). Though the Roman Catholic Church and certain other traditions do not celebrate the Mass on Good Friday or Holy Saturday, European Christians commonly celebrate Communion on these days. The color for these two days is either black or red.

The Easter Vigil takes place after sundown on Holy Saturday with the lighting of the new fire. The service is quite different from the traditional

Easter service. Instead, it recounts the holy history of the people of God. Worshipers often have a simple supper together, then process into the church with "new fire," which is used to light the (new) paschal candle. Readings, poetry, dramatic reenactments, banners, hymns, dance, and songs recount (1) the creation; (2) the flood; (3) Abraham's sacrifice of Isaac; (4) deliverance at the Red Sea; (5) Isaiah's promise of salvation offered to all; (6) a reading from Proverbs; (7) Ezekiel's vision of the Valley of the Dry Bones; and (8) Zephaniah's vision of the gathering of God's people. This service may be followed by the reception of new members and the sacrament of Baptism or baptismal renewal, followed by the Eucharist and concluded with the traditional Easter greeting, "Christ is risen."[8] The service moves to Easter, but sometimes concludes just before a full-blown Easter celebration.

The Easter Vigil is very much a part of the history of worship and is an exciting service that requires a great deal of preparation. Some churches that use the Vigil prepare for it all year. To add a service that makes so many demands just before Easter Sunday may be more than many congregations can manage. Congregations may want to give it a try at least once to let them experience this important liturgical occasion and see if they can manage it more regularly.

Easter Sunday is the most important Christian celebration of the year. The color for the day is white. Traditionally the service begins with the Easter acclamation, "The Lord is risen," and with the reply, "He is risen indeed!" The great hymns of Easter give a glorious context to the service. There is no prayer of confession (as there is not for the entire season of Easter) and thus there is no *Kyrie*; the prayer of adoration takes the place of the prayer of confession. The "Alleluia" is returned to the service in symbols and sayings, and the *Gloria* and Doxology are returned to the service. What was taken away from the service is now returned.

The Day of Pentecost

The Easter season (or Eastertide) is sometimes called the Great Fifty Days (*pentekonta* is Greek for "fifty"). The season ends with the Day of Pentecost, which is a jubilant service. The traditional color for the Day of Pentecost is red, but any flame colors (red, orange, and yellow, representing the tongues of fire, see Acts 2:3) are appropriate. Some churches celebrate this day as the birthday of the church, even though Calvin felt that the church extended back to Adam and Eve. Nevertheless, Pentecost was a new start for the Christian community and is an excellent conclusion to the joyous Easter season and the beginning of the long summer season of Ordinary Time. Acts relates how believers of all nationalities gathered in Jerusalem for one of the major Jewish festivals, Pentecost, which celebrates the giving of the Law to Moses on Mt.

Sinai; the giving of the Law defined Israel as a nation. Christians saw the giving of the Spirit of Christ as that which defined the church. (Juxtaposing Law
and Spirit can make for an interesting discussion as well as rich symbolism.)

Pentecost celebrates the giving of the Holy Spirit to be with God's people
forever; symbols of the Spirit (air, wind, water, flames, the dove) are all useful
in designing worship. To set the tone for worship, the first activity on Pentecost Sunday can be a reading of the story of Pentecost from Acts 2.

(Pentecost is also called Whitsunday, particularly in Great Britain, because
it became a popular day for baptisms. The white robes of baptism gave the day
its name.)

Important themes of Pentecost are evangelism and mission—taking the
message of resurrection in word and deed to the four corners of the earth. The
Jerusalem cross, with a small cross in each quadrant, speaks of the gospel going
out from Jerusalem to the four corners of the earth.

The Long Period of Ordinary Time

The Sunday following Pentecost is known as Trinity Sunday, an observance of
the threefold nature of God. After Trinity Sunday comes the second and
longest period of Ordinary Time, from Pentecost to Advent. This is a "period"
rather than a "season" since it does not center on a dominant event or theme.
The color for the period is green, the color of growth, and during this time
congregations grow in faith and service.

Ordinary Sundays sometimes come almost as a relief following the often
strenuous demands of the liturgical seasons. But Ordinary Time is a period
rich with possibilities for those who plan worship. For these days of summer
and early autumn, the lectionary often provides parables that can be explored
with art and drama. In chapter 14, we also suggest Fish and Loaves Communion and Jubilee Sunday. Independence Day and Labor Day are national hol-
idays that suggest activities and appropriate hymns. Worship can be more
casual as life is more casual in the summer, moving to the resumption of regular activities and greater demands in the fall.

As worship planners seek to enrich worship, they will find a vast treasure of
resources as they explore the Christian year. Its observance can be as simple as
the hanging of a parament from the pulpit, or it can involve music, musical
responses, seasonal activities, and so much more. In the Reformed tradition,
the question is whether seasonal activities add to or detract from the proclamation of the gospel and its encouragement to Christian service. Careful
observance of the Christian year can deepen the understanding of the life of
our Lord and the many ways we are called to serve our God.

11

The Wedding

The historic origins of marriage are obscure but certainly reach back into earliest recorded history. Marriage continues to be part of the pattern of human relationships that bind people together in kinship, occupation, and social position. People have historically known themselves in large part by their role in marriage, whom they married, the occupational role of the family provider, and the network of larger family that marriage brought with it.

Marriage can assume a wide variety of forms: polygamy, polyandry, matriarchy, patriarchy; it can be permanent or temporary. Over the centuries, marriage has had a variety of purposes: joining rival clans or families and preventing conflicts; setting up institutional forms for establishing rights and relationships for parents and children; providing cohesiveness and continuity in society. Marriage customs thus have always been important in every culture and have usually been treated as sacred and not to be changed.

Over time, many ancient wedding customs, such as handing over the bride and eating the cake, have become traditional, but these customs no longer maintain their religious meaning—if they ever had any. The betrothal ring took the place of the bride price, and the marriage was based upon mutual consent of the partners and not of their families. Once women had the right to refuse a would-be husband, they gained a level of freedom unheard of by their sisters in other cultures.

The Earliest Issues: Women as Property, Divorce, and Adultery

In the early Roman Empire, the family was patriarchal. The father was not only the head of the family but had all the legal rights; his wife and children had no rights. He could beat them as he saw fit and could even sell them as slaves. He could divorce his wife when she did not please him, especially if she

151

did not produce male heirs. However, during the height of the Empire, when men were away at war, women learned to manage the affairs of the family and began to discover their power.

In the Middle East, patriarchy was also the norm. The Old Testament says little about marriage customs. Marriages were private arrangements and not public religious ceremonies. Most Israelite men had only one wife, but men who could afford the bride price sometimes had more. The monarchs of Israel were polygamous, and the denunciations by the Old Testament prophets suggest that other wealthy males also had multiple wives. Women had few rights; when they married, they were transferred, as property, from their fathers to their husbands. Adultery was forbidden because it violated the property rights of the man—either the woman's father or husband—and even the Ten Commandments place coveting a neighbor's wife on an even footing with coveting his other goods. Although the prophet Micah denounced men who divorced their Jewish wives to marry daughters of the conquerors, divorce was accepted. If a wife committed adultery, her husband could divorce her, and if he caught her in the act of adultery, he could have her put to death (Lev. 20:11). While the Law called for the death of the male who committed adultery, only the husband could demand divorce. If a woman wanted freedom from a marriage, she was required to ask her husband to give her the divorce, and he could, of course, refuse.

By the time of the New Testament, two schools of thought among Jews about divorce had arisen. Rabbi Shammai authorized divorce only for blatantly shameful behavior, such as adultery. Rabbi Hillel permitted divorce for almost anything that displeased the husband. Although Jesus said little about marriage and divorce, what he did say put him in opposition to both rabbinic schools. In Luke's Gospel, his condemnation of divorce is total: "Anyone who divorces his wife and marries another commits adultery, and whoever marries a woman divorced from her husband commits adultery" (Luke 16:18). In Matthew's Gospel, however, there is a different reading: "But I say to you that anyone who divorces his wife, except on the ground of unchastity, causes her to commit adultery; and whoever marries a divorced woman commits adultery" (Matt. 5:32). The exception for adultery was an important change from the hard and fast declaration of Luke. The word translated "unchastity"—in Greek, *porneia* (πορνεια)—can be translated as "immorality" or "indecency" as well as "adultery" or "fornication." Jesus is said to have quoted from the creation account, regarding marriage: "For this reason a man shall leave his father and mother and be joined to his wife and the two shall become one flesh. So they are no longer two, but one flesh" (Matt. 19:5; Gen. 2:24). This citation is interesting. It is nonpatriarchal, for in a patriarchal culture a man does not leave his family; rather the woman leaves her family, joins the man's family, and takes his name. Jesus' use of Genesis seems to suggest that marriage should be neither patriarchal nor matriarchal but an entirely new thing.

Paul stressed the importance of marital fidelity but allowed divorce in some situations. He viewed marriages of Christians to non-Christians as dangerous and in 1 Corinthians 7:12–16 gave his opinion that if a Christian brother or sister was married to an unbeliever who wanted a divorce, he or she might grant it and be free to marry again. Paul advised his readers who were single to stay single (1 Cor. 7:8). He seems to have believed that it was no sin to marry but better to remain single, especially given his expectation of Christ's immediate return.

One searches in vain for any hint of marriage ceremonies in the New Testament. Jewish Christians were probably married according to Jewish customs and Gentile Christians according to Roman custom. As the church spread throughout the Empire, it became more common for Christians simply to marry according to Roman civil rules without any special church blessing. There was no liturgical ceremony. Constantine did try to eliminate the injustices of one-sided divorces by making it illegal for men or women to reject their spouses for trivial reasons.

In 449, the Roman Emperor Theodosius II permitted consensual divorce and expanded the list of acceptable reasons for leaving one's spouse to include robbery, kidnapping, treason, and other serious crimes. He also made it legal, for the first time, for a woman to divorce her husband for adultery. In the sixth century, the Emperor Justinian brought about more changes in the laws of marriage and divorce. According to the Code of Justinian, the basis of marriage was to be mutual affection between the sexes. The Code provided nearly equal grounds for divorce by either husband or wife and, for the first time, the children of dissolved marriages were provided for. The grounds for divorce were extended to impotence, absence due to slavery, and the renunciation of marriage by entering a monastery.

A Brief History of the Wedding Ceremony

The earliest known wedding ceremony itself was very simple and held outside the church. In the usual custom, the father handed over his daughter to the groom in her own family house, after which the bridal party walked in procession to the new husband's home for concluding ceremonies and a wedding feast. No official words were spoken and no blessing given. But late in the fourth century, the custom arose for a priest or bishop to give his blessing to the newly wedded couple during the wedding feast itself or even the day before. As the church became more powerful, it was natural that the clergy would want authority over an institution as important as marriage. Gradually the wedding ceremony developed into a full religious ceremonial in which the priest joined the couple and blessed their union. By the eighth century, religious weddings had become common enough that they were recognized as legally valid. One reason that the church became involved was to mediate the difference in marriage practices between northern and southern Europe. According to Roman custom, marriage was by consent. According to Germanic custom, the giving of the consent came at the betrothal, and the marriage was not complete until sexual intercourse had taken place. It was also the custom for the parents to arrange the marriage years before the couple lived together. Charlemagne reformed such practices by requiring that before the wedding could take place, all proposed marriages had to be examined for legal restrictions such as previous marriages or close family relationships.

By the year 1000, all marriages in western Europe were under the power of and controlled by the church. The collapse of the Roman Empire and resulting breakdown of the civil order contributed to this situation. Holding weddings at the entrance to the church became customary, and generally the service followed a set pattern:

> The priest asked the bride and groom if they had consented to the marriage.
> The father of the bride then handed over his daughter to the groom and gave him her dowry. At times, the priest himself performed this function.
> The priest blessed the ring, which the groom put on the finger of the bride.
> The priest gave the couple his blessing.
> The couple and their families then came into the church itself for a nuptial mass, for which the bride was veiled and blessed.
> At the conclusion of the mass, the priest gave the groom the kiss of peace, which the groom then passed on to the bride.

In the Middle Ages, a theology of marriage began to develop within the church as its clergy began to take a more active role in performing marriages. Christian writers began to say that sexual intercourse for the sake of having children was a positive good. The writings of Augustine were used to develop the idea of marriage as a sacrament. Augustine had taught that marriage fulfilled the theological definition of a sacrament in two ways: (1) It was a sign of the union between Christ and the church; and (2) it was a sacred pledge between husband and wife, a bond of fidelity between them that could not be dissolved except by death. Marriage imprinted the souls of the two people, which permanently united them. The sacramental act was the consent the spouses gave to each other. Theologians claimed that the sacrament gave positive assistance toward holiness in the married state of life, and that the grace given in the sacrament of marriage was fidelity, the ability to be faithful to one's spouse, to resist the temptations to adultery and desertion in spite of the trials of married life. Throughout the Middle Ages, the marriage customs of western Europe did not vary.

Marriage in Reformation Times and After

With the Reformation came new views of marriage. Luther said that he hated divorce, but he admitted that Christ had allowed divorce in the case of adultery, and as a priest, he was inclined to permit it in serious cases that seemed to have scriptural justification. Luther argued that the innocent party should not be forced to suffer for the weaknesses and sinfulness of the spouse. He rejected the sacramental status of marriage, arguing it did not possess the power to create a permanent imprint on the souls of the two parties.

Calvin, like Luther, agreed that marriage was not a sacrament:

> It is enough that marriage should be from God for it to be considered a sacrament, but it is required that there should also be an external ceremony appointed by God for the purpose of confirming a promise such as the promise of salvation that was confirmed by baptism. (*Institutes*, IV.xix.34)

Calvin further rejected marriage's sacramental status because no such ceremony is mentioned in the New Testament and no command is made to all Christians to be married. Calvin believed that marriage laws fell within the jurisdiction of civil authorities, but he contended that governments are morally obligated to make marriage and divorce laws in strict conformity with Christian principles. For him, the only scriptural grounds for divorce were adultery and desertion of one's family, which he likened to pagan behavior; in these two cases, the innocent party should be allowed to remarry.

The Reformers rejected the idea of two states of life: the single, or celibate, and marriage. They insisted that the sexual union was something that God had created and blessed and was the highest estate to which a Christian could be called. As if to illustrate their teachings, both Luther and Calvin married.

The longstanding conflict over who should have control over marriage was more or less given to the state by both Luther and Calvin in spite of their views of the limitations of the state. That conflict has continued throughout the ages as a test of power by the church over against the state, and over time, in different nations, the conflict has been resolved in different ways. In post-revolutionary France and in Mexico, for example, only the state could oversee marriages, while in Spain until very recently, only the church had control.

In the United States today, church and state exist in an uneasy partnership. The state issues licenses and then grants the legal right to the minister to act as an officer of the state for conduct of the service and even the signing of the license. Marriage is the only time when the minister acts as an official of the state.

Marriage and Ministry
in the Church Today

The significance of marriage for the church today is threefold:

1. Marriage connects faith and sexuality. The church always lives with the danger of looking upon sex as a lesser human activity, as if God had not created human sexuality. Marriage as an ordinance of the church forces us to take a serious look at marriage and sexuality as positive blessings from God.
2. The church refuses to let the state have final and complete authority over this very important part of human life. By performing weddings, the church makes a clear statement that marriage has to do with faith and with God, and that the state, while having some business regarding, for instance, issues of health and public safety, does not have the right to determine who can be married. At issue here is the right of persons to marry within the faith by the canons of faith as understood within the various traditions.
3. The church performs weddings because this is an important way of caring for the couple in a crucial life situation. It is ministry in crisis at a time of important transition for the couple and their families. In spite of the joy of the occasion, a wedding is also a time of anxiety and change in which people need the ministry of the church and the assurance of faith. Most people seem to recognize this need for ministry, for they turn to pastors to perform their marriages even when they have no other contact with the church.

In spite of many of the cultural changes that have taken place in the marriage ceremony, some ancient practices continue without our awareness of the history involved. Some practices predate Christianity:

The bridal shower originally provided the bride with her dowry.
The bride feeding the groom a piece of wedding cake at the reception was part of an ancient fertility ritual.
Throwing rice was a symbol of fertility.
Carrying the bride across the threshold was meant to confuse the evil spirits.

Moreover, some customs reflect legal arrangements in the past:

The exchange of rings originally involved ownership of the bride by the groom. The groom's wearing of a ring is a modern phenomenon.

The vows in some traditional form, such as "to have and to hold . . . till death do us part" are part of the legal requirements.

Of course, patriarchal customs abound:

The bride in white, veiled until the end of the ceremony, symbolizes the virginal property of both father and husband.
The father's giving away of the bride to the groom and placing the bride's hand in the groom's also signify her status as property.

Contemporary Social and Pastoral Issues

Because our culture has changed rapidly and radically in regard to sexual mores, many questions still abound today about marriage.

Most pastors are regularly confronted with couples who are already living together before marriage. The two people are on their own, living away from parents as independent adults. In addition, at least one of the two partners likely has already been married before. Divorce is so common that the remarriage of divorced people is an everyday event for Protestant pastors. As women have achieved more social and economic equality with men, the nature of marriage has changed as well. All of these factors mean that the wedding service must not appear to be written for a social setting that no longer exists. Even the simple decision as to which party goes first in the vows, promises, and exchange of rings has important symbolic meaning.

Gays and lesbians are now asserting their right to establish lifelong relationships and to have these relationships blessed by the church. No pastor can expect to avoid the request to preside at a holy union service for a gay couple, at least on occasion, and needs to be prepared with a pastoral response rather than confusion. In some denominations, ecclesiastical laws forbid pastors from presiding at these services. Ministers in these denominations are faced with the difficult choice of violating denominational rules and facing punishment, presiding privately, or refusing to preside.

Certain problems and issues face every pastor who agrees to perform a wedding:

1. *Premarital counseling:* Many people ask, what good does premarital counseling do? The bride and groom agreed to marry long before the pastor was consulted. There is little that any pastor can say or do to dissuade the couple from marriage. Counseling sessions can imply that the pastor approves of the marriage and believes it to be one of great possibility when, in fact, that pastor knows nothing of the sort. Predicting which marriages will endure and which will end in bitterness, anger, and hostility is impossible. The mystery of

human beings is always beyond prediction. What the pastor can hope to accomplish through counseling is to establish a good relationship with the two people so that they may eventually return when they discover problems in their relationship. A good idea is for the couple and the pastor to enter into a contract in which the couple promises to return for a counseling session one year after the wedding.

2. *Economic issues:* The pressure to spend too much on the wedding is tremendous. Often the pressure is especially severe upon those least able to spend. Yet, at the same time, the wedding may be the one time when the couple feels important. Pastors may attempt to discourage lavish expenditures, but they should be careful to respect local traditions and personal reasons that they may not understand.

3. *The centrality of worship:* The wedding is a service of worship, but many couples expect the service to include almost anything but worship. Couples want to write their own liturgy, without regard to the liturgy designed by the pastor, as if it were their private affair. Yet a wedding is the property of the church, not of the bride and groom, in the same way that baptism is not the property of the one being baptized or an infant's parents. Of course, as in every worship service, the pastor must be sensitive to the context. If, for example, the couple comes from different faith traditions, the wedding ceremony should include elements from both traditions.

Ministers have clear rights and responsibilities for every wedding in which they are asked to officiate:

- They have the right to refuse to perform the ceremony.
- They have the right and responsibility to provide premarital counseling.
- They have the responsibility to direct the service.
- The minister has the responsibility of ensuring that the couple meets the requirements for a valid Christian marriage: (1) The man and woman must meet the requirements of the state. (2) At least one person of the couple must be a professing Christian, and ordinarily both should be Christians. (3) Both people need to be aware of the significance of what they are doing, which means that both need to be emotionally mature; neither partner can be coerced or forced into marriage against his or her will.

The Wedding Brochure

Couples who are inquiring about a marriage ceremony should be provided the church's wedding brochure. This brochure, which should be prepared and approved by the congregation's governing body, should state clearly church policy on all relevant issues. The wedding brochure might contain the following information:

1. A clear statement that the minister is responsible for the service and is subject to the mandates of the denomination as well as the policies of the local governing board.
2. A clear statement of the church's theology of marriage and the note that the marriage service is a service of the worship of God.
3. Information regarding facilities, policies, and traditions within the particular congregation. The brochure can answer any number of questions:

Are there any times when weddings are not held, e.g., the week before Christmas, during Lent, during Holy Week, on Sundays?
What is the seating capacity of the sanctuary? What musical instruments are available? Are there limitations as to access for the handicapped?
What parking is available? How many spaces? Is there a special holding location for a limousine?
Are there prohibitions regarding fastening decorations to or moving/removing church furniture? (Thumbtacks, tape, brackets.)
If there are seasonal decorations or banners in the church, can they be removed? Who removes them? Are they to be returned, and by whom?
What is the approximate length of time for rehearsal, who is to attend, and what is the length of the wedding service?
May flowers be placed on the communion table, on the musical instruments?
Is flash photography allowed? By guests? By professional photographers?
Is videography allowed, and, if so, where can equipment be placed?
Is recorded music allowed in the service?
May rice be thrown following the service?
Where may the wedding party dress?
What is the access for the florist? Caterer? Musicians?
Is a sound system provided? Who will operate the system? Can the system make an audio recording?
May receptions be held at the church? What is the capacity of the reception hall? Are champagne or alcoholic beverages allowed? Who caters the reception?

4. A statement about the type of music that is suitable for the wedding service; many churches will allow only music that would be suitable for a service of worship and ask that other selections be used at the reception only.
5. Information regarding the marriage license: When should the license be provided to the minister? (Ideally, several days before the service.) In most situations, the minister is responsible for completing and signing the license, securing the signatures of witnesses, recording the license at the local church, and mailing the license to the county clerk. The minister may want to make and give the couple an unofficial photocopy of the license. The couple has the responsibility to secure for themselves copies of the official, completed license from the county clerk after it has been recorded. Each state has its own laws regarding the pastor's role in providing a legal marriage. Pastors need to know the law.
6. A listing of equipment that the church may provide (at cost or free?) for the ceremony, e.g., candelabra, kneeling bench, guest book stand, candle

lighters, etc. Are there items the church does *not* provide, e.g., candles, wedding programs, etc.?

The Wedding Coordinator

Very small or informal services probably do not need the services of a wedding coordinator. In most cases, however, a wedding coordinator—someone other than the minister or office staff—is helpful in planning the many details of the service: answering questions; scheduling the meeting with the minister; the rehearsal, and the service; and being present at and organizing the rehearsal and the service. Ministers are often at one end of the church when things are happening at the other, and they are unable to coordinate the lineup and start of the procession, to make sure the families are seated, or to return ushers at the end of the service to escort family members out, all of which need to be done. The wedding coordinator becomes an important colleague for the couple and the minister. The coordinator may donate services as a volunteer, or the church may suggest an honorarium. The church should exercise particular care in choosing coordinators, for they become the representatives of the minister and congregation.

What are a coordinator's general responsibilities? At the rehearsal, the coordinator generally assists the minister. The coordinator may also want to be present while the church is decorated. The coordinator is responsible for planning and directing all the elements of the final ceremony itself, under the direction of the pastor.

The wedding coordinator may want to assemble a tackle box with the following items: masking tape, safety and straight pins, needle and thread, scissors, florist's pins, name tags and marking pen, matches, C-60 audio tapes, black pen for license, self-adhesive dots to indicate where members of the wedding party stand, two dimestore rings, a small note pad, and "Post-It" notes.

Fees

Fee schedules for weddings should be clearly determined for active members (probably including children of active members) and nonmembers. Since members continually bear the cost for the maintenance of facilities and salary of the pastor, that nonmembers should be expected to contribute toward the costs of the facilities and services seems only fair. Possible fees include

1. A fee to book the facilities. This fee should be applied to the final cost and is assessed to discourage multiple bookings by wedding parties. Determine

if any of this fee is to be returned if the wedding is cancelled. This fee may be waived for members.

2. Cost of facilities. Facility costs are often waived for members.

3. Cost of musicians. Musicians who are expected to attend the rehearsal as well as the service should be entitled to an extra amount.

4. Equipment costs, such as for candles and printing costs, if the church provides the order of service.

5. Fee for sound technician, if required. If an audiotape is requested, the church should provide the tape. If the church is asked to provide duplicate audiotapes, an additional fee may be noted.

6. Custodial fees.

7. Honorarium for wedding coordinator, if this is not a volunteer position. The fee should be based upon the average amount of time devoted to a service, which is often as much as ten hours.

8. Honorarium for minister. This fee is generally based upon the average number of hours the minister spends on the interview, rehearsal, service, and paperwork. This fee is often waived for members and children of members.

9. Costs related to a church-hosted reception.

All fees (except those paid to the musicians hired by the bride and groom) should be paid to the church prior to the rehearsal.

Creating the Wedding Liturgy

Civil law requires that three declarations or statements be included in every service of marriage: (1) the question asked of the woman, if she will take the man as her husband; (2) the question asked of the man, if he will take the woman as his wife; and (3) the declaration by the person officiating that the man and woman are now husband and wife. People who officiate at services must ensure that these elements are contained in the liturgy.

Beginning ministers are advised to read through various wedding liturgies, particularly their own denominational liturgy, for help in assembling a meaningful service. Copy the liturgy so that the future bride and groom can read it at the interview. The minister can give the final copy to the couple following the service.

Though ministers design the liturgy, they sometimes allow the bride and groom to customize their service by selecting between various options in the service. For example, a couple may decide whether to include the parents in the liturgy by candlelighting or the "giving away" of the daughter or both the daughter and son; they may choose, with the minister's help, the scripture that is included in the service, the vows, the statements with the rings, and the benediction.

Possible elements in the wedding liturgy include

1. Hymns to be sung by the congregation (optional).
2. Opening statement by the minister on the nature of marriage.
3. Brief prayer for illumination.
4. Scriptures that speak to the nature of the marital relationship, faithfulness, and divine love.
5. Other brief readings, responsive readings, or litanies by the congregation.
6. The questions of the bride and groom ("Will you have this woman/man to be your wife/husband?").
7. The permission of the father of the bride or the parents of the bride and the groom (optional).
8. A short prayer for the presence of God in the promises that are to be made.
9. Vows of the bride and the groom. (Sometimes the vows are combined with the questions.)
10. Giving of the rings or other symbols (optional).
11. Lighting of the unity candle (optional).
12. Wedding prayer (asking the blessing of God upon the union as well as the support of families and friends for the marriage), followed by the Lord's Prayer.
13. Declaration of marriage by the minister.
14. Sealing of the marriage by saying, "Whom God has joined together, let no person seek to divide."
15. Benediction.

The Unity Candle

A practice popular in some areas is the lighting of the unity candle, a three-branched candelabra. Prior to the service the two outer candles are lighted; the parents of the bride and groom may do this. At an appropriate place in the service (usually after the exchange of rings), the bride and groom go to the candelabra, take one of the two lit candles and light the center candle.

The minister may use the following words at this time:

> Christ is the light of the world. He has also called individual Christians to be light to the world. And now, as you two join to make this Christian marriage, the community will have a new source of light: the light of Christ, borne by two people, made one in him: committed to Christ, and through Christ to each other. Through all this, the Spirit of Christ will be your strength. He will never leave you nor forsake you. As the Gospel of John says, "The light shines in the darkness, and the darkness is not able to overcome it." Two candles have been lighted representing each of you. Their flames will form the symbol of your new union in Jesus Christ your Lord.

The Wedding Interview

After working out technical questions with the coordinator, the couple meets with the minister. Whether the time with the minister is considered counseling or simply an interview is the determination of the minister, but the nature of the meeting should be clearly indicated to the bride and groom well in advance. Pastors need to be sensitive to the life situation of the couple and what can best be discussed, and they should strive to make the couple feel at ease with the minister and the church, confirm information provided by the wedding coordinator, and answer questions the couple may have. The minister needs to define briefly the nature of Christian marriage and invite the couple to return in the future and talk about the marriage, particularly in times of tension. If the bride and groom are not members of the church, the minister may want to invite them to consider making the place of their wedding their church home.

No matter how many interview sessions take place, one session should be held as close to the rehearsal as possible; otherwise the information garnered by the wedding coordinator may be obsolete! At this formal interview, the minister will review the details of the service and go through the liturgy with the bride and groom. Read through the whole liturgy, since the bride and groom are often so nervous at the ceremony that they have difficulty concentrating on the nuances of the service!

Remind the bride and groom that the wedding is not a performance, attended by an audience, but a service of worship where they are surrounded by friends. No anxiety should be harbored about misspoken lines, unexpected tears or laughter, flowers dropped, or activities that move out of order. The minister will direct the service and see that the couple makes it through, even if the vows must be repeated word by word. Assure the couple that because they are held in such affection by those attending, they can virtually do no wrong at the service.

The minister should confirm the time and place of the rehearsal and wedding and by this time should have the marriage license.

The Wedding Rehearsal

The minister may begin the rehearsal with a short prayer to set the tone and remind participants that they are preparing for a service of worship. The minister should not read the entire text of the service nor practice all the music. The purpose of the rehearsal is to inform the participants how the service will progress, show them where they will stand or sit, and identify their responsibilities.

The minister may want to confirm the details of the wedding with the entire wedding party:

> Remind them of the time of the ceremony. Where will the wedding party dress? Will photographs be taken prior to the service or after? When are the members of the party expected to arrive?
>
> Will there be a guest book? Who will oversee it? (If a long line is waiting to sign the guest book at the time the ceremony is to begin, the wedding coordinator should close the book and ask guests to be seated and sign the book following the service.)
>
> If gifts are brought to the service, where should they be placed? Who will transport them following the service?
>
> Though the members of the wedding party will be busy prior to the service, they should be encouraged not to skip meals. Weddings are notorious events for lightheadedness—often due to nervousness, hunger, or the heat of the candles.
>
> Since ushers may not be familiar with the church and could be called upon to assist in case of an emergency, point out the location of fire extinguishers, telephones, rest rooms, and drinking fountains.

When key people are absent from a rehearsal, have someone stand in for them. Designate someone, most likely the substitute, to orient the absentees as to what has been decided for the wedding.

The Day of the Wedding

By the wedding day, the minister will have completed the appropriate parts of the marriage license; the witnesses can sign it prior to the service as rounding them up following the service may be difficult. Some jurisdictions require that the license be signed with black ink only.

The minister and wedding coordinator determine when everyone is ready to start. The families are then seated, and the long-awaited service begins.

At the conclusion of the service, the minister may give the best man the copy of the wedding liturgy and a photocopy of the as-yet-unfiled marriage license.

Following the Service

After the service, the minister mails the wedding license to the appropriate civil agency. The minister should keep a personal ledger recording all weddings, noting the name of the bride and the groom, the date and place of the service, the number of the wedding license, and the amount of honorarium, if there is one. The essential information from the license should go on file in the official church records.

Weddings are special occasions for every pastor. They can be celebrations of the joy of human love as a symbol of the love of God. Pastors need to be careful to do everything possible to make the wedding a happy occasion. Providing clear information while the wedding is planned and during the rehearsal will make it easier to fulfill everyone's expectations for this most important day.

The previous comments, of course, assume a traditional church wedding. Major variations take place when weddings are held in nonchurch settings and when ethnic customs must be observed. Ministers in these situations must be sensitive and take such factors into account.

12

The Service of Witness to the Resurrection

The resurrection is the heart of our Christian faith, because here we see that there is more to life than we can perceive in our daily lives.

Jesus liked to express his theology in terms of places—but new kinds of places. Indeed, the core of Jesus' teaching, the kingdom of God or heaven, is about a place that is both now and in the future. In John 14, Jesus speaks of his Father's house, which has many rooms, and implies that a room awaits each of his followers. Thus, when the time comes and people are ready, the room will be ready for them. Jesus assures Thomas that he will even come and personally take the disciples to that place. Paul drew numerous analogies, telling how the seed must die before it can come alive, and how there is a place, not made with hands, waiting for the children of God.

All these references point to a new dimension, the dimension of Spirit; whereas in this life, we only begin to live in this Spirit, we will at some future moment move to where the place of the Spirit will be our home.

How can we better understand this phenomenon? We can only use analogies to speak of that which we do not yet know. One analogy of this "multidimensionality of spirit" is the multidimensionality of existences in which we already participate, or have participated, but somehow ignore. For instance, all human beings have already participated in another existence where the terms of our life were entirely different: approximately nine months in a mother's womb. We breathed differently; we were nourished differently. And then, with the considerable efforts of our earthly mothers, we passed into the present existence. We all participated in the existence in the womb, but none of us can remember it and only know of it by noting that in this manner children are born, and concluding that we must have been born this way!

Another analogy is the dual existence we experience daily. We move from human wakefulness to sleep in a process that still baffles scientists. In this sleeping existence, our autonomic nervous system takes over; we breathe differently and we think differently, with dream images. The sleeping existence is very different from the state to which we awake.

If we are already a part of a multidimensional existence, why doubt more: what Christians call the experience of resurrection? Resurrection is different from resuscitation, in which a body dies and then is brought back to life—maybe a little worse for wear, but largely as it was before. A resuscitated body will also die again. We know of the resurrection experience from the resurrection of Jesus. We have learned that resurrection is a deeply personal experience, where identity is not lost but somehow comes to fruition. After his resurrection, Jesus was recognizable, but he did not seem captive to the dimensions of time and space. He greeted his disciples and ate with them, and he promised his presence with them forever.

In some way, we participate in that same resurrection, in that new life of the Spirit. Though death brings sorrow and loss, for Christians also comes a profound realization that it is a movement to a new, good, spiritual dimension, one with God, and certainly not to be feared.

We should approach the service of witness to the resurrection—the funeral service—with this positive outlook. The profound understanding about the resurrection can be a source of comfort and ministry not only to people who most need it, but to people who may be particularly receptive to hearing about the essence of the faith.

The Challenges of the Funeral Service

The funeral, or "Service on the Occasion of Death," is one of the most demanding tasks for pastors because of often unusual circumstances and the emotions that survivors often feel.

- Pastors are called to minister, not only to those who are familiar with the ways of the church, but to those who have never been a part of a church or may even be hostile to it.
- The environment may be the comfortable setting of the usual place of worship or another place, such as a funeral home or cemetery, where the funeral party may have to stand on a steep hillside with wind blowing and rain pouring.
- Death is obviously the end of the relationship with a living person, and loved ones sometimes feel guilt or anger at the one who has died, perhaps at being left alone, or at not having achieved a final reconciliation or farewell. Pastors must acknowledge these feelings and be prepared to offer counsel in this situation.
- The pastor may encounter annoyance or anger about burial practices or the costs of burial. Dying costs a lot of money, and many have made no arrangements, leaving the burden on their families.

- Tensions may exist in the family about the disposition of the body or the division of the estate.
- Pastors may have to deal with funeral directors who are insensitive to the needs of the family and who do not care to recognize that the pastor is in charge of the service.

Seasoned pastors all have horror stories to tell, but through it all we remember that we are privileged to serve at a time of greatest need.

In Preparation

Although most members of a congregation, having attended a funeral before, know how the pastor will handle the service and what facilities and services are available, pastors should continue to inform their congregations of their theology and practices at the time of death. Though this time is full of traditions, pastors nevertheless need to establish helpful practices rather than simply reinforce inherited and antiquated expectations. What's more, pastors and congregations should agree on these practices. Discussion of the following considerations is important:

- *Reception following the service:* If a reception will be held at the church, the persons who will serve the reception need to be designated. Often the board of deacons handles this.
- *Musicians:* Since funeral services are generally held midweek and the church musician may not be available, the church should have available a list of alternative keyboard musicians and soloists. Will the church be charged for musicians' services? Will the church assume these costs for members or ask them to cover the costs? If musicians are to be paid, perhaps the families should pay the church and then the church can forward the payment on to the musicians.
- *Guest registers:* Funeral homes generally offer rather expensive guest registers for the service; congregations can help out by designing and providing simple booklets for guests to sign.
- *Orders of service:* Funeral services generally do not need an order of service, but some people prefer a church-prepared handout to the folders provided by funeral homes. Decide if the church is able to produce these and what the cost, if any, will be. If you do not provide an order of service, have an alternative suggestion for those who request one.
- *Disposition of flowers:* If the service includes flowers and is scheduled late in the week, perhaps the flowers can be used in Sunday worship. Sometimes, however, families ask that the church take flowers out to convalescent homes. This is a big task, and often the flower arrangements are so funereal that they are simply depressing in convalescent homes, unless they are divided up into smaller, more informal arrangements. If the congregation has no volunteers willing to perform this function, pastors should

probably graciously decline the gift of flowers or the responsibility of doing more than disposing of them.

Honoraria or Fees
for Pastoral Services

Discuss fees in advance with funeral directors. A good approach is for a local clergy association to discuss the matter and send a letter to local funeral homes listing participating pastors and stating policies and fees. Ordinarily pastors do not receive a fee for services conducted for active church members or their children. If the family offers payment, the pastor can accept it or not. Often the family, seeing the fees paid to so many, want to thank the pastor in this way. Generally for nonmembers, a fee is charged, collected by the funeral home, and given to the pastor.

What is an appropriate fee? As a rule, pastors devote about four hours to meeting with the family, preparing the service, conducting the committal service and the funeral/memorial service, and doing the additional paperwork. Extra charges can be justified if a pastor must make lengthy trips to service locations and cemeteries, and if the service is on a pastor's normal day off. In all these arrangements, the pastor should consult with the governing body to learn the normal practices and if guidelines are provided.

In cases where a fee is normally charged, the pastor should advise funeral directors that no fee is expected from people who are unable to pay it or would have difficulty doing so.

A Proposed Schedule
for the Day of the Service

On the day of the funeral service, assuming that a committal is taking place, pastors might suggest the following schedule:

> Begin with a rather private committal service with family and close friends; this brief graveside service takes about ten minutes.
> Following the committal, hold a memorial service at the church. This service should be about thirty minutes in length.
> After the memorial service, provide a reception at the church, where family members can meet with guests.

The rationale for this order is that by ending at the cemetery the process concludes on the most depressing note, and the family is often left with the casket as friends move on with their business. A better approach is to put the family on a schedule that does not permit lengthy lingering at the gravesite, but rather encourages everyone to go to the church to celebrate the life of the one they have lost and then enjoy fellowship with family and friends.

Consider a reception at the church instead of at a family member's home. This approach relieves the family from entertaining in a home that has often become less organized because the family was caring for the person in a final illness. Also, family has often come from out of town and is unprepared to have a reception in the home of the deceased. The church can have the necessary catering equipment to host the event. If families would like more elaborate refreshments, the church can suggest caterers that can provide this service at the family's expense.

Some Frequently Asked Questions

1. *What do you do when the deceased has indicated he or she wants no service?*

Some people will protest that they want no service. "Just dump me in the ocean," they say. Pastors need to assure families that the service is not for the dead, but for the living—for those who must contend with the loss of a friend or family member. For those people, funerals or memorial services provide important psychological closure. In the absence of a service, people have a more difficult time saying, "Now it's over. I've got to go on." For many people, grieving is never over. However, in those cases where the family does not want to disregard the modest wishes of the deceased, a short time of prayer with family and friends may be all that is needed.

2. *Who provides what?*

For members, churches normally provide the services of the pastor; copies of the pastoral comments; meeting facilities for the service and reception; a guest folder; basic musical services (but not soloists); the setup, serving, and cleanup of the reception; and simple refreshments and beverages. Families provide the flowers (if desired), possibly the service folder, payment for additional musicians, payment for extra catering, and disposition of the flowers.

3. *Where should the service be held?*

The Presbyterian Directory for Worship suggests that "the service on the occasion of death ordinarily should be held in the usual place of worship in order to join this service to the community's continuing life and witness to the resurrection" (W-4.10003). A funeral home speaks of death; the church speaks of life.

Some families, in an attempt to have a "simple service," suggest that the whole service be conducted at the graveside. But most services are for older people, and their friends tend to be older as well. Moreover, standing for a half hour to an hour on uneven turf in hot sun, rain, or wind can be debilitating. The best place to have a service is in an easily accessible church.

4. Should the body be present?

With the above-suggested schedule, the body is not present. In those services where the casket is present, it should be closed in order "that the attention of the service be directed to God" (Directory for Worship, W-4.10005).

5. Is it appropriate for others to participate in the service?

The service is under the direction of the pastor—something you may occasionally have to remind some funeral directors. Generally the pastor is the sole participant in the service. The pastor reads the scriptures, shares some of the Christian understanding of "life beyond life," comments on aspects of the life of the one who has died, leads the prayers, and generally hosts the service.

Sometimes members of the family ask to speak or other people are asked to speak. Pastors need to be sensitive to the needs of the family but also sensitive to the needs of people who are attending the service. Unless invited speakers are accustomed to speaking in public, their comments often run longer than intended. If several people speak, what they say is often repetitive ("Joe pretty much said what I was going to say, but since I've prepared this talk, I'll go ahead and say it anyway . . ."). If several speakers will be offering comments, each should be assigned a specific and predetermined aspect of the person's life, such as community involvement or professional activities. Remind family members that the service may run longer than they would like if many other people speak.

Inviting people to speak extemporaneously or unexpectedly is often not a good idea. Such requests can lead to embarrassment if no one wants to say anything, or individuals at the service may be embarrassed if others have something to say and they do not. Services can go on interminably even if people are constrained and only speak three to five minutes each. Further, the content of the comments or the awkwardness of the speaker might embarrass everyone.

A point of some tension among ministers is whether or not to allow fraternal, civic, or military rites. Normally these rites should be conducted separately. If the family has a strong desire for such rites, perhaps the pastor can conduct the service in the church and the other organization can be responsible for the committal service.

6. What about music?

Music is the language of the emotions, and pastors can find themselves in trouble without an established policy about appropriate music. All music in worship is expected to direct the worshiper to the worship of God. Romantic or "favorite" songs are generally not appropriate for the service of worship, although they would be quite acceptable at a reception. Be prepared for strange musical requests: one family requested "Smoke Gets in Your Eyes" for a service where the deceased had been cremated.

Live music is symbolically important, so avoid recorded music if possible, although many funeral homes use it exclusively. If you have to use a recording at a funeral home, try to limit the music to before and after the service; don't stop the service to listen to a recorded song. In the church also, try to avoid recorded music, in part because of the possibility of equipment failures.

Because a funeral is a service of witness to the resurrection, the music should be upbeat and joyous without being overbearing, contemplative without being maudlin. Music that is appropriate for a service of worship is appropriate for a funeral. If you wouldn't sing "Somewhere over the Rainbow" in worship, you probably should avoid it at a funeral. Sometimes, however, given the circumstances, a contemporary or show tune might be both appropriate and touching. Services for children can feature children's music. The challenge is to be creative, flexible, and tasteful!

The Memorial Commentary

The concept of a "eulogy" is difficult for pastors. A pastor does not always know the individual or might find it difficult to praise the life of a particular person. Rather than a eulogy, the pastor can give an overview of someone's life without evaluating it. How do you get the information? A group interview with family members often provides information that may have been unknown even to some of them. Provide a finished copy of the remarks to the family.

Assure the family that their comments will be edited, so they should provide as much information as possible, indicating if certain information should not be used. Some families, for instance, are embarrassed by multiple divorces. (The creative pastor can handle this positively, often without mentioning the divorce: "Mabel married Harry Rumford in Philadelphia in 1942; they had two children, Billy and Philomena. In 1956 Mabel met and married Jake Townsend; there were no children in this marriage. In 1970 Mabel and the children moved to Baltimore, where she met Luke Nightshirt; they were married six months after their meeting . . .")

An outline for a family interview for the family might be as follows:

- Full name of person, age, date of birth, place of birth.
- Names of parents, and what occupations they were pursuing when their child was born.
- Brothers and sisters? Where did this person fit in the sibling lineup? (Oldest, youngest?)
- Where was the person raised? What schools did he/she attend? What activities were pursued in school? Whenever there is a move as an adult,

determine the reason for the move. (Health reasons? Job opportunity? Chance to be with family?) This information often provides valuable insight and background.
- College? Which one? What major? What activities?
- What happened after formal education stopped?
- Marriage? Family?
- What next?
- What next?
- Associations or awards?
- Hobbies or interests?
- How would you describe this person to someone who never knew him or her?

Giving the cause, date, or location of death is not necessary.

A Suggested Order of Service

1. The service begins with brief, comforting scriptural sentences. Major portions of scripture will come later.
2. The congregation may sing hymns; if many of the people in attendance do not regularly attend worship, they may be unfamiliar with the hymns, and congregational singing might not be a good idea.
3. A prayer for illumination is read.
4. Following the prayer, selections of scripture should be read. The skillful pastor may weave these together with commentary, indicating how they point to the Christian understanding of life and death, and what insights they provide.
5. If solo music appears in the service, this time may appropriate.
6. There may be a short prayer at the end of the scripture readings, which may be followed by a brief homily if theological comments were not made with the scripture reading.
7. Memorial commentary of a biographical nature by the pastor.
8. Other comments, if family and friends desire to make any.
9. A prayer of thanks for the individual, for God's gifts and promises and the community of faith; prayers of intercession for family and friends; prayers of supplication for faith and grace for those present, concluding with the Lord's Prayer.
10. Benediction.

Breaking the Rules

The suggestions above assume some kind of consistency or pattern, but each funeral is unique. No matter the circumstances, pastors are expected to provide support. Consider these "awkward" situations, none of them uncommon, and what your response might be:

- Various family members are estranged and feel that you are cooperating "with the others" and not with them.
- The ceremony is for a gang member, many of whose acquaintances are so antagonistic toward each other that half the room is ready to fight the other half.
- The family provides conflicting or intentionally inaccurate information about the deceased.
- The deceased has provided money for a pastor to go in and pray with the draped, dead body in the mortuary, and that is to be the only service.
- The family has the casket opened following the service, insisting that unwilling children be lifted up to kiss the deceased.

In certain times the rules don't work, and there are no easy answers. In the end, you and the deceased's family and friends have to depend upon your own kindness, your integrity, and prayers.

In Conclusion

Times of death are difficult for everyone. They are particularly difficult for pastors who know and care for the deceased and are also grieving even as they are expected to lead. But funerals are times when people need help, and that help is a major gift of pastoral ministry.

13

Other Occasions for Worship

Worship takes place in many situations and on many occasions other than Sunday morning. For believers, every moment of life can be some kind of worship as we recognize the relationship between the Creator and the created. Historically, every culture has had ways to sacralize the events of birth, coming of age, marriage, harvest, celebrating a successful hunt, coping with famine and drought, and responding to illness and death, as well as simple liturgies for moments like the lighting of a fire, the coming of dawn and the setting of the sun, and other moments considered important.

Today we have separated the secular from the sacred, and as a result, we have lost the connection between many significant events in life and their ultimate meaning. We have allowed secular rituals to replace the sacred. The ritual of retirement is a good example; another is birthdays. We now celebrate them outside the context of faith. As a faith community, we often settle for one hour a week as the time set apart as holy and sufficient to nurture the souls of believers in the faith. To make the time of faith just an hour in the week is not sufficient for any people. Rather, we need to ritualize all of time, recognizing the presence of God in each moment.

Significant occasions in the lives of individuals and communities require ritualizing in some way. Yet other than the Sunday bulletin, American Protestantism has provided almost no guidance for the ritual needs of people, and often those bulletins may be little more than lists and announcements. Fifty years ago, every member family owned a hymnal, thus providing some guidance for devotional needs. Today the old customs of owning one's own hymnal and singing around the piano are considered quaint and rarely practiced. Although breaking much-needed new ground, the updated resources for public worship that every denomination has produced since the 1980s have only begun to touch the many daily life occasions that could be developed into significant experiences of worship. These resources do not deal with retirement or major vocational change; with moving into a new home and having it blessed; with saying good-bye to a congregation when moving away; with worship occasions for children and youth; or with renewing a marriage, adopting a child, or finalizing a divorce. One important exception is the *Book of Worship* of the United Church of Christ, which provides liturgies for most of these important occasions.

From a long list of possible "other" occasions, or opportunities, for worship, in the following section we discuss three: (1) private worship; (2) opportunities for providing pastoral care in worship situations; and (3) ordination of elders, deacons, and ministers. We have chosen these three different occasions because they represent significant opportunities for worship that are often not included in other resources. We provide guidance for people looking for appropriate resources, and we hope that you may be led to consider how to adapt resources for other occasions that may arise in a congregation.

Private Worship

The Reformed tradition has generally been anxious, hesitant, and suspicious about private worship. Various worship resources have, of course, acknowledged times when Christians should worship in private, but these resources have also warned the reader that such worship must always be held in balance with public worship. The implication is that private worship needs the correcting influence of public worship or it may slip into superstition, idolatry, ignorance, or perversion of some kind. One feels in these warnings a kind of pre-Reformation attitude toward the reading of scripture by the people. Do we not trust our own people to be able to pray on their own without constantly being told how to do it? Too often, Christian people have become afraid of prayer, fearful that because they do not know eloquent language, they are unable to pray.

No such similar warning is ever given about the danger of public worship that is not balanced by private worship, although the danger of perfunctory public worship is very real if people do not bring to it some ongoing experiences of prayer and private devotion. In fact, both private and public worship belong in the lives of all believers. Without public worship as a corrective, private worship can degenerate into a constricted and narrowly self-centered form. Also, without private worship as a balance, public worship can become so perfunctory that it lacks passion and conviction. The daily challenge of discipleship demands and requires some forms of nurture that worship provides.

Daily personal worship may occur in a gathered community of faith, in households and families, or in private. Two primary resources are available for personal worship: scripture and prayer. Scripture can be used in a number of ways. We can read it for guidance, support, comfort, encouragement, and challenge, and use it as a printed pastoral aid. We can also read scripture in order to learn more about its context and thus to hear its message more clearly and accurately. Thus, we can read scripture as an instructional aid, in which scripture becomes our teacher. Scriptures may also be read in a meditative manner, as a guide to prayer and the experience of the holy. Scripture becomes our companion on the journey of faith. As we read, we find God. All three of these ways of reading—as a pastoral aid, as instruction, and as a prompt for meditation—can be done in private.

Most active practicing Christians have some experience with the study of scripture, and as they have heard sermons, they have experienced scripture as a source of encouragement and inspiration. They probably have not had much conscious experience with meditation upon the Word, however. One form of meditation upon scripture, which has a long history among Reformed Protestants, is simple memorization. In order to memorize a text, one must go over and over it, and this repetition shapes the mind and directly influences us. We are what we think. What we feed into our minds will be an important factor in determining the way we think. Familiarity with scripture can significantly counterbalance some of the strong influences of television on our consciousness and the pressure of work, family, and finances.

A second and less familiar form of meditation upon scripture that is also part of our Reformed tradition is *lectio divina*, which means "holy reading." *Lectio* is a form of prayerful reading that grew from the Benedictine monastic tradition and was revived by the Puritans in Great Britain and the Pietists on the continent of Europe in the eighteenth century. *Lectio* is generally made up of four steps: prayer, slow and attentive reading, reflection, and prayer as response.

1. *Prayer:* We approach the text with the genuine expectation that God may speak through the reading, and we call upon God and open the self to the leading of the Holy Spirit. Prayerful reading of scripture seeks to avoid bringing only our own previously held assumptions to the text and seeks to be genuinely ready to receive the Word of God in the text.
2. *Slow and attentive reading:* This form of reading pays close attention to questions, problems, and puzzles that arise in the mind and sees them as clues from God about the meaning of the text. In this stage, we may not finish the text because an issue comes up that needs attention. When this happens, let go of the need to complete the text and move to the third step.
3. *Reflection:* The reader now reflects upon a particular word, phrase, idea, or sentence in the reading—asks what it means, how it speaks to your own situation, what it discloses about you, how it might change you in some way if you really internalize its message. At this time, pay close attention to how God is addressing your life, seeking to discern a divine call to let go of

something or take on something new. In other words, this reflection is a way
of seeking to live under the text.

4. *Prayer:* We conclude as we began: by thanking God for new insight, asking
forgiveness for what may have been uncovered, and praying for a new sense
of direction, perhaps for strength to follow some path that has been
accepted as coming from God. The meditative circle is complete: we have
prayed scripture!

Prayer takes other forms than praying upon scripture. These forms range
from conversations with God—in which we express in words our joys and sor-
rows, our needs, fears, and desires—to prayer that is beyond words and
thoughts, as simple conscious dwelling in the presence of God; to prayer as
performing deeds, social responsibility or protest, or acts of service to others.
Most of us need to expand our sense of prayer and try to discover new ways to
pray that fit our unique selves. One of the reasons that some people are not
comfortable praying is that their method simply does not fit them. No matter
how many promises they make to do better or how guilty they may feel at their
failures, they do not grow comfortable with prayer. They do not enjoy prayer,
but instead perceive it as an onerous duty. When we discover a style of prayer
that fits our personality, we also discover that prayer is something we want to
do because it is fulfilling; in the presence of God, we find our deepest joy.

All of us have dry periods when prayer is very difficult, if not impossible.
Then, above all, we need the assistance of books of prayers so that others'
prayers can become vehicles for our own. Praying through the words of others is perfectly acceptable. The Psalms can also serve as such guides, for they
express universal human emotions and experiences.

Prayer is at the heart of all worship because prayer is communion with God.
Whether in public or in private, the goal of worship is to be open to touch by
the divine, to be inspired to new action or to new ways of thinking about yourself and your world. Prayer opens us to care with God's compassion for the
world around us, as we see other people—even people we have never met—as
of ultimate significance. God opens our eyes and causes us to see things more
clearly, which is both the risk and the possibility of prayer as worship.

Pastoral Care

Because we bring who we are to worship, all of the situations in which we find
ourselves—times of pain and times of celebration—are occasions for worship.
A primary focus for the ministry of the church has always been providing care
to all those who need and seek it. In every culture and every time of history
people have needed healing from physical and mental illness and from various
forms of distress, as well as healing to let go of memories that may have haunted

them. People need the church to help them to endure suffering and pain and to fortify them with the courage to hold fast to their faith in the midst of their struggle. People have always needed also the accompaniment of the church or its representative to assist them in the passage from death to life beyond death. The passing of human life can be a time of worship.

From the time of the New Testament until today, these human needs have remained, and although the outward causes and situations have changed greatly, the basic needs persist. Pastoral care is a continuing ministry that remains a necessity for the church to be the church. We need pastoral care most importantly in the midst of critical life situations. When life seems to be falling apart, when the foundations we carefully erected crack underneath us, when assumptions we made do not work anymore, we desperately need the ministry of the church. Whether that ministry is exercised by the pastor, by deacons or elders, or by other church members may not matter as much as the fact that pastoral care was administered when we needed it.

Two particular crisis situations are nearly universal for the need for pastoral care; both also provide occasions for public or private worship. These situations are (1) services for healing, which respond to the pain and the perplexity of illness; and (2) services of confession and forgiveness, which deal with our sense of hurt and guilt over wrongs committed against us or things we have said or done to others that come back to haunt us.

Healing as Pastoral Care

Healing is one of the most neglected forms of pastoral care, especially by mainstream Protestant churches, in part because it may seem to reflect either superstition and naïve piety of the sort that sees visions of the Blessed Virgin on church walls, or because its connection to the fundamentalist religion of the sawdust trail repels us. Yet, illness poses tremendous challenges for faith. What is the meaning of sickness? What purpose is there in suffering? Why does it happen to some people more than others? Does God will illness and, if so, why? Is it God's will that people be cured? Can the laws of nature be suspended? When we experience sickness ourselves or see it in our loved ones, these questions are much more difficult to answer. They become painful and very important.

These questions are neither new nor peculiar to the modern era. Ancient people asked them also, and the answers they found were often expressed in religious stories and rituals through which they enacted their response to the mystery of life and death, health and sickness. The usual Judeo-Christian response to illness has been to assert that it is a violation of God's good intent, in which health and vitality are meant to be the norm. Such a view is in stark contrast to some other religions, such as Hinduism, in which sickness is to be endured because of actions in a previous life that must be expiated in this life or they will shape the incarnated life to come. In these faiths, nothing can be done about illness except to endure the suffering. The Christian impulse to alleviate suffering and bring healing to the sick rises from our conviction that God's intention is for wholeness for all people.

The connection between sickness and sin is ancient, and the connection survives in some forms both in scripture and the Reformed tradition. Our world cannot be easily divided into physical and spiritual compartments. When one part of life is out of joint, the rest of life is affected. Sin, therefore, affects health, not as punishment from God but as disruption of the self. The relationship between sickness and sin exists because sin infects the whole of life.

The New Testament includes dozens of accounts of Jesus' miracles of healing the lame, the blind, lepers, and the mentally ill. Jesus was known as a healer just as much as he was a preacher, and he commissioned his disciples to preach, teach, and heal. The early church continued the practice of healing, as accounts in the book of Acts indicate. Jesus healed both by the spoken word and by touch, even in one instance through the use of mud made from his own spittle. Paul mentions the spiritual gift of healing as one given for the benefit of the whole community (1 Cor. 12:9–10). The apostle James makes the connection between healing and the use of anointing oil (James 5:13–16).

What happened to healing in the years between the New Testament and the Protestant Reformation? After the close of the New Testament period, references to healing are scarce. *The Apostolic Tradition of Hippolytus of Rome* (A.D. 215) contains a prayer over oil that was brought to be blessed. Some fourth-century documents imply that oil was blessed for the purpose of curing illness. In 416, Pope Innocent I responded to another bishop who asked whether James 5:13–16 referred to the physically ill and, if so, how the anointing should be practiced. Innocent replied that it was his understanding the passage did speak about the faithful who are sick and can be anointed with the oil that is prepared by the bishop.[1]

Well into the middle ages, the church used oil for healing. Usually the anointing was done by a priest. The dying did not request anointing but rather, in anticipation of death, requested confession and Holy Communion. People who received the sacrament of penance on their deathbeds were, however, also anointed. Because most serious illnesses were fatal, priestly anointing was given increasingly to the dying, but through the eleventh century, the prayers still asked for physical recovery as well as forgiveness of sins. The approach to anointing began to change in the twelfth century. Since anointing was rarely given to people who were expected to recover, the prayers for healing gradually disappeared from the ritual and were replaced by prayers that spoke only of remission of sins and the hope of salvation. Anointing became the sacrament of preparation for the life to come and came to be known as the Last Rites.

By the time of the Reformation, healing ministry had all but disappeared from the church, and the sacrament that had begun as ministry to the sick was now administered only to the dying. What spiritual healing was done took place on the fringes of the church, at shrines, on pilgrimages, and with holy persons whose presence seemed to inspire healing. The church was always suspicious of these events.

Because of the strong emphasis upon healing in the New Testament and because they saw no evidence of the healing ministry in the church of their own time, the Protestant Reformers concluded that healing was a gift of God given to the early church in order that it might be planted, a gift that was later withdrawn. Calvin was explicit about this: "But that gift of healing, like the rest of the miracles which the Lord willed to be brought forth for a time, has vanished away in order to make the new preaching of the gospel marvelous forever. Therefore, even if we grant to the full that anointing was a sacrament of those powers which were then administered by the hands of the apostles, it now has nothing to do with us, to whom the administering of such powers has not been commended" (IV.xix.18). The church accepted this point of view for centuries and thus ignored the possibility for spiritual healing as part of its ministry.

Protestants have pioneered medical science, been open to such radical actions as performing autopsies, and generally encouraged physical healing as a ministry of the church. Hospitals were always part of the church's missionary activities. But only in the last few decades has healing returned to most of the Christian church, through a combination of Jungian psychology, holistic medicine, frustration with medicine's inability to heal many diseases, and the charismatic movement. Vatican II restored the ritual of healing to the Roman Catholic Church, indicated that "extreme unction" should more fittingly be called "anointing of the sick," and directed the rewording of prayers to include specific situations of illness for which these prayers might speak: terminal illness, the illness of a child, illness with expectation of recovery, illness in which there is great pain. The Council also directed that there should be communal occasions when a group could gather in the church for anointing. Through these actions, the church returned the emphasis of the ritual of anointing to strengthening one for recovery rather than forgiving one in preparation for death. The priest now says: "Through this holy anointing, may the Lord, in his love, help you, with the grace of the Holy Spirit. May the Lord who frees you from sin save you and raise you up."

The Episcopal Church's *Book of Common Prayer* (1977) includes a ritual for "Ministration to the Sick" that can be adapted for either private or communal usage just before Communion is celebrated. This ritual was the first non–Roman Catholic effort to restore healing to the ministry of the church, and was followed in 1986 by the United Church of Christ, which included an "Order for Healing for Congregational Use" in its *Book of Worship*. This service provides for anointing those who cannot come forward or even be present by saying, "Those who desire to be anointed for spiritual healing may come forward. If you wish us to come to you, raise your hand or ask your neighbor to identify you for us. You may come for yourself or you may come as a channel of God's healing power for someone else."

The Presbyterians included a "Service of Wholeness for a Congregation" and a "Service of Wholeness for an Individual" in the 1993 *Book of Common Worship*. Both services have the option of including Communion. They also offer the choice of the simple laying on of hands or the laying on of hands and anointing with oil. For the laying on of hands without the use of oil, a prayer may be offered:

May the Spirit of the living God, ever present with us now, enter into your body, mind, and spirit, to transform you and bring you healing from all that keeps you from being the person God wants you to be, in the name of Jesus the great healer, Amen.[2]

A change of perspective clearly has already taken place that now encourages anointing of the sick and takes seriously the relationship between the spiritual and physical in healing. Special services now occur in churches of nearly every denomination and across the spectrum of theological positions.

Confession and Forgiveness

Confession can take three different forms: (1) public prayers of confessions in which the whole congregation confesses together, (2) private prayer made by the individual to God directly and personally; and (3) confession to another person done to unburden the conscience in anticipation of words of forgiveness.

1. *Public confession.* The early church practiced public confession in the context of the worship of the gathered community. This public confession was an acknowledgment that Christians continued to need forgiveness even though they had been redeemed by Christ. By the third century, the practice of reconciliation of sinners known to the community began to take more definite shape. People who wanted to rejoin the community were to go to the bishop and confess their sin. They were required to perform acts that demonstrated their seriousness and symbolized their sorrow for sin. Such acts of penitence included fasting, prayer, and giving alms to the poor. The rigor of this method

of public discipline as a form of penitence gradually declined after the legalization of Christianity.

Calvin restored to corporate worship the ancient practice of the public prayer of confession. He made this corporate prayer normative for every service of public worship. The prayer of common confession became a standard feature of Reformed worship and the assurance of pardon a major source of spiritual consolation for Reformed Christians. In recent years, the assurance of pardon or declaration of absolution has lost some of its power. Pastors do not always realize how central this act is to the spiritual life of the people. Fear of clericalism is the usual excuse used to justify not offering the public declaration of pardon, but in the absence of a pastor forcefully declaring forgiveness without ambiguity, the people are left with an uneasy feeling of guilt.

2. *Private Prayer.* The second form of confession open to all Christians is private prayer. By themselves, people are free to unburden themselves of their personal guilt and know that they receive the mercy of God promised in Christ Jesus. In private prayer, people can name sins that they would be unable to admit in a public setting. Public prayers of confession must of necessity be general and inclusive. By its very nature, private prayer can be more deeply personal and specific than any other form. There are times when private prayer is not enough, when we need to tell another human being what we have done, and have that person reassure us that we are forgiven.

3. *Private Confession.* In private confession, one confesses sins out loud to another person. By private confession the church sought to assist people to resolve their personal guilt and was thus an expression of pastoral care. Although begun as a voluntary practice, by 1214 private confession was declared a sacrament and required at least once a year, always before receiving Holy Communion. Perfect contrition, caused by the grace of God, was needed for sins to be fully forgiven, but people could never tell whether their contrition was perfect enough to merit forgiveness.

In the late Middle Ages a legalistic understanding of private confession developed, and the words of absolution by the priest were viewed as the one thing needed to obtain forgiveness. This emphasis on absolution was in response to the anxiety of many people about whether their contrition was complete enough. Confession, contrition, and the assigned penance (prayers, fasting, or good deeds) were required for the sacrament to be helpful, but were not essential for its validity.

Luther and Calvin reluctantly attacked the sacrament of penance, and both grounded their attack on their pastoral concern for people. Calvin was more muted in his criticism of this sacrament than any other: "I judge the ancient observance which Cyprian mentions, to have been holy and wholesome for the church, and I would like to see it restored today. This more recent practice, although I dare not disallow it or speak too sharply against it, I nevertheless deem less necessary" (IV.xix.14). He believed that the practice of laying on of hands, though a ceremony ordained by people rather than God, at least "ought to be classed among things indifferent and outward exercises—things that are indeed not to be despised, but that ought to occupy a lower place than those commended to us by the Lord's word" (IV.xix.14). Because of the abuses associated with confession, Calvin considered that the practice of required confession produced more evil than good, but he wished to continue confession as a voluntary practice because of its importance as a pastoral tool. Calvin recognized that people need to unburden themselves of those things for which they are sorry, but he was concerned that required confession led either to the practice of treating confession lightly and making confession superficial or to a sense of hopelessness. He insisted that forgiveness not be tied to the practice of remembering and declaring one's sin to a minister even when that person performs the office with humility and the recognition of limits. The certainty of binding and loosing does not lie within the competence of earthly judgment, he argued, because the minister of the Word can absolve only conditionally at best. No one but God can know the state of the person's mind and heart, and God is the one who forgives.

Like Luther, Calvin urged people to go to their pastors for spiritual relief and solace. At the same time, he maintained that such confession must be free, to be commended only to those who know that they have need of it. Confession to the pastor was always a voluntary form of pastoral care within the Reformed tradition. Confession could also be made to an elder or to any other church member. One of the chief purposes of the elders was to assist the pastor in providing this form of pastoral care. Elders visited the people in their homes and listened to them, hearing their joys and concerns and also their confessions.

Thus, although joining Luther in rejecting penance as a sacrament, Calvin certainly did not mean to cut Christians off from the spiritual benefits that result from unburdening their souls to a pastor or other Christian: "For it often happens that one who hears general promises that are intended for the whole congregation of believers remains nonetheless in some doubt, and, still a troubled mind" (III.iv.14). Because the practice of confession became totally voluntary, the individual was the only judge of the content of what was to be revealed and also had complete freedom of choice as to the person who would serve as the confessor. The principle that Calvin lays down is absolute freedom: "we should lay our infirmities on one another's breasts, to receive among ourselves mutual counsel, mutual compassion and mutual consolation" (III.iv.6). The only reason for selecting a pastor to unburden oneself is that it is the pastor whose "duty it is, both publicly and privately, to comfort the people of God by the gospel teaching" (III.iv.6).

One setting for confession to a pastor persisted long after the practice had generally fallen into disuse. On the Sunday before the Lord's Supper was celebrated, Calvin would announce that those who wished to receive Communion were required to inform him of their desire and arrange for a time for consultation, especially if they were not known to him or there was some suspicion about their manner of life that had been brought to his attention. He gave three reasons for this practice: first, to instruct believers more carefully in the faith; second, to assist those in need of correction; and third, to comfort any who were troubled by guilt.

Visiting with the pastor or an elder before coming to the sacrament of Communion remained a Reformed spiritual practice for many years and is still a source of solace and healing for Reformed Christians in some parts of the world: France, Germany, and Korea, for example.

The principal purpose of making confession to a pastor was to provide help for people in dealing with their guilt, facing their sin, and accepting the grace and forgiveness of Christ. Calvin did not hesitate to pronounce words of absolution when people confessed their sin. Many Reformed pastors today, however, are wary of anything that might suggest that they have any particular status as mediators between God and the people. Yet a great many people desperately need a clear and direct assurance of forgiveness. They may be feeling extraordinary guilt so that general statements are not sufficient to satisfy their need; they need another person to say, without any hesitation or reservation, "You are forgiven" in order to be able to receive that good news.

Now that mandatory confession has been relaxed as a rule in the Roman Catholic Church, Protestants may be able also to relax their fear of this practice. The introduction of services of repentance and forgiveness in new worship materials may enable such practices to take place more readily. Pastors can indicate to parishioners that they are available for services of reconciliation. The results are likely to be surprising. Hear, for example, the following example of strong words that might be spoken by the minister in declaring the pardon of God for the individual:

God's love is all-encompassing. That love is stronger than our sin. The mercy of the Lord is from everlasting to everlasting.
I declare to you that you are forgiven, in the name of Jesus Christ.
May the mercy of God,
strengthen you in all hope
and by the power of the Holy Spirit
protect you in eternal life.[3]

In an age of anxiety and guilt, this form of pastoral care can provide tremendous help to people who do not know how to live with unforgiven sin and unhealed memories. A service of reconciliation may enable us to move beyond nondirective counseling into a form of spiritual guidance that is not afraid to use the resources of Christian faith.

In all of these ways, the restoration of some spoken and personal forms of confession can open the windows of our souls to experience the grace of God in ways that involve silent meditation, healing touch, and expressed forgiveness. We will all be healthier and spiritually stronger as we begin to practice these gifts.

Services of Ordination and Installation

In most Reformed churches, ministers, elders and deacons are ordained, and ordination is thus a ritual that is observed more frequently than in those traditions in which only ministers are ordained. The same essential service is used for all three ordinations, implying an equality of ordination. Reformed churches do not make the distinction between clergy and laity that other traditions do, but rather distinguish between church officers, including ministers, elders, and deacons, and church members. Elders and deacons are not laypeople because they have been ordained, but neither are they clergy. Services of ordination and installation are occasions for recognizing the value of these ministries alongside the ministries of pastors.

The word "ordain" comes from the Latin, *ordinare*, which means "to order," and refers to the ordering of ministry, that is, to appointing certain people for particular tasks. The idea of a number "set apart" is seen in the special position given to the twelve disciples of Jesus; then "the seventy" were chosen to go on a special mission (Luke 10:1). Following the resurrection, the apostles assumed an even greater role. As the size of the Christian community grew, the Twelve found that they needed help with their task, and seven men were chosen as deacons (Acts 6). They stood before the apostles, who prayed and laid their hands on them. This simple, primitive rite has become the norm for ordinations of Christian officers since that time.[4]

Soon it was not just the apostles whose ordination prayer for the gift of the Spirit was seen as efficacious. In Acts 13:1–3, we read that Barnabas and Saul were commissioned with laying on of hands and prayer by the prophets and teachers at Antioch. In 1 Timothy 4:14, Paul reminds Timothy, "Do not neglect the gift that is in you, which was given to you through prophecy with the laying on of hands by the council of elders." In this case, the administration of ordination was clearly in the hands of a presbytery, or council of elders. In 1 Timothy 5:22, Paul warns, "Do not ordain anyone hastily." Ordination is not simply for a local community or congregation but for the whole church, acting through its ministers; thus special care should be taken in this "setting apart." The rite was considered necessary for receiving the gifts of the Spirit—and probably the authority—to undertake the new office and work.

The New Testament lists the different tasks of ministry. In 1 Corinthians 12:29–30, Paul speaks of apostles, prophets, teachers, healers, those with various responsibilities in leadership, and those who speak in tongues. Although scripture does not indicate if each of these is an ordained office, Paul argues that one office is not greater than another, but all are part of the "body of Christ."

The terms "bishop" and "presbyter" often seem interchangeable in the New Testament, although in 1 Timothy 3:1–7, a list of qualifications is set forth for a bishop; in Acts 11:30, an administrative question is sent "to the elders" for their information and possible consideration, suggesting that the office of elder was already operative. Through the centuries, bishops increasingly became the ones who were responsible for the laying on of hands, thus continuing an apostolic tradition or succession, although the term "apostolic" has a much broader meaning: being able to trace a direct line back to one of "the Twelve."

By the Reformation, considerable suspicion had arisen about placing authority in the hands of any one individual; thus the presbytery, acting as bishop, became responsible for the ordination of ministers who, in turn, oversaw the ordination of the elders and deacons elected by particular congregations. The ordination of these ministers, elders, and deacons continued to be for the whole church, although now the "whole church" had a far different meaning, as various ecclesiastical bodies organized and came to recognize only their own ordinations. The recognition of ordination is one of the major topics of ecumenical conversations in this new century, and the mutual recognition of ordinations of other denominations is an important step toward unity in Christ.

Ordination today is seen as setting a person apart for a particular and necessary task of ministry. Thus, in the Presbyterian Church, one who is ordained as a deacon is not thereby ordained as an elder, and one ordained as an elder is not thereby ordained as a minister.[5] Each function has a particular task, and each office is invested with particular responsibilities requiring distinct gifts, defined by the church constitution.

The service of ordination for elders and deacons occurs more frequently in churches than the ordination of ministers and usually follows a standard procedure. Generally the service is included in a regular service of worship and involves a brief exposition of the scriptural authority for the offices, constitutional questions asked of the people to be ordained, the laying on of hands by all present who have been ordained (including those from other congregations), prayer, and welcome. The local congregational governing body sets the date for the ordination, and the pastor of the congregation conducts the service.

People to be ordained as ministers must have met all denominational requirements, including completion of a theological degree, and must have a validated call to ministry. A governing body examines the candidate. Since the candidate may be ordained by one governing body and installed into the office of pastor by another, great care must be taken to ensure that all the steps to ordination are followed. A mentor who will help a candidate through this process is most useful; such a mentor may be a member of the denominational committee that supervises the ordination process or a beloved pastor or member of the candidate's home congregation.

The service of ordination for a minister in the Presbyterian Church (U.S.A.) must follow the procedures below, which may also apply to other Reformed denominations:

- For both ordinations and installations, the governing bodies approve the date, place, and time.
- Participants in the service(s) are approved by the governing bodies.
- A commission or representative, acting on behalf of the governing body, is designated to ask the constitutional questions.

Generally the candidate has the privilege to invite at least some of those people who will participate in the service. The constitution that has jurisdiction over the candidate may require that a sermon be given. A representative from the governing body will ask the constitutional questions. Then the candidate will kneel, if able, for the laying on of hands by ordained pastors and elders. The governing body representative offers the prayer of ordination and then declares the minister ordained to the particular office. Those people who have laid on hands greet the newly ordained minister. Then optional features may include a charge to the minister and a charge to the congregation where the minister will serve. Because this service involves many people, communication is critical. Everyone who is involved in any way should be fully informed as to what has been planned.

In the case of ministers, both ordination and installation services are conducted by the particular governing body that has jurisdiction, not by the local congregation. Though the ordination and installation of a minister may be held during a regular service of worship, in order to allow other ministers to attend, these services are usually held at a separate service.

Services of installation that occur after the minister has already been ordained follow the same outline but omit the laying on of hands and the prayer of ordination. The service is held at the place to which the minister has been called. The constitution as well as the governing body sets out requirements, and local expectations should be honored as well.

Services of private prayer, healing, forgiveness, and ordination are special occasions for worship beyond Sunday morning, as are weddings and funerals. There are many other such occasions: the commissioning of a person for a particular responsibility for service in the community or church, the celebration of wedding anniversaries and services of renewal of marriage, celebrations of the adoption of a child, acknowledgments of the end of a marriage. All of the most important events in life are appropriate occasions for holding up to God our thanksgiving, our need for guidance, our commitment as disciples. These components are all part of worship.

14

The Style of Worship

We are living in a time of cultural transition. People no longer dress up for occasions, such as the theater, that were once thought of as very formal. Casual dress and language are taken for granted. People seldom make music in their homes; pianos are disappearing. Organ concerts draw only senior citizens, and even symphony orchestras are struggling to hold on to an aging audience.

Reformed congregations are caught in the middle of this cultural shift. They have tried to hold on to traditions that no longer have broad appeal. The average pastor is caught between the desire to minister to the older folks who pay the bills and, at the same time, to attract the young, who are the church's future.

Churches across the nation are putting massive efforts into designing services that are relevant and accessible to worshipers, especially people under fifty, who are so largely absent from most Reformed congregations. Many people under fifty who have no church experience are, in fact, intimidated by church styles that are foreign to them: they know no hymns, are uncomfortable with liturgical language, and are put off by the formality of the pastors and people. The "creative" or "contemporary" worship, which appeared in the 1960s, has reemerged in new forms in the hope that it will bring younger members to aging congregations. But since many established congregations are filled with members who have been there for years and like things the way they are, some churches feature two services, one called "contemporary" and another "traditional." Unless churches have sufficient staffs to design these services, often the energy is thrown into one of the two services, leaving the other bereft. What often results is that young families attend one service and the older folks attend another, splitting the congregation. In many of these situations, worship—which is meant to unite us as the One People of God—divides.[1]

Another such division in worship comes from separation into "seeker services" and "believer services." Seeker services are designed so that those who have no background in the church will not only feel welcome but recognize music and language styles with which they are comfortable. No hymns are played on organs, nor are there pastors in robes or liturgical symbols. The music is "easy listening," with simple words often projected on screens, pastors moving around with hand-held mikes, and the meeting having the ambiance of a folksy, friendly gathering. Believer services, rather than observing the Lord's Day, are often consigned to a midweek evening and may be little more than Bible studies with a few songs and prayers. Further, indications are that few people who attend seeker services move on to the believer services.

Churches must reach out to people who do not know the language and traditions. Such an outreach is necessary if the church is to survive in this new century, but the church must not so accommodate itself to the styles and beliefs of the unchurched that it loses its ability to lead and teach. In the midst of unprecedented technological changes, need the church feel that those who come to it are incapable of learning new forms? Under these circumstances, Christian worship risks being conducted at the lowest common denominator, which is not necessarily a radical return to Christ-centeredness.

Another problem involves equating novelty with relevance. New and unexpected elements in worship can make for excitement, but having continually to design or invent new gimmicks exhausts worship planners. If the most creative liturgists in the nation are unable to design novel liturgies week after week, how bleak it becomes when people with far less talent and far fewer resources try to accomplish this.

No wonder worship leaders do so much shopping for new materials; they are desperate. Their best efforts are not appreciated by the "old guard' and not innovative enough to welcome outsiders. Efforts to develop "blended" worship services, which introduce elements of the new into an otherwise traditional service, tend to satisfy few. New people are still bored, and longtime members are upset by the changes. Many pastors feel themselves caught in a no-win situation; worship, which was once a great time of congregational bonding, has become a field of conflict. No wonder many of our brightest and best pastors burn out so quickly!

But the tide may be changing. Demographic studies indicate that younger worshipers are seeking both a sense of the holy and more traditional formats in worship. Both the Eastern Orthodox Church and the Episcopal Church are experiencing a wave of new, younger members desperately seeking this combination. So what are we to do?

A Worship Trinity:
Festival, Mystery, and Rationality

In our efforts to be relevant today, we should remember that worship must contain three elements: festival, mystery, and rationality. If any one of them is too little present, the result is often an unmet hunger in the people and a sense of dissatisfaction.

Festival

A note of joy and the involvement of the senses is a proper part of all worship, yet these characteristics are frequently missing in Reformed congregations. Understanding reverence to mean only solemnity inhibits festivity. Reverence *can* include laughter, applause, delight, and enthusiasm. Lowered voices, hushed greetings, and futile efforts to quell the spirit of spontaneity in children can have the result of stifling the natural. In worship, we are enacting good news, and our worship should somehow acknowledge that. A festival is marked by song, conviviality, color, drama, dance, food, laughter, and remembering. We celebrate important occasions by having a feast.

Of course, celebration can be threatening, for it cannot be made orderly. Celebration may not even fit into the procrustean sixty minutes allotted for worship. Some people have a hard time celebrating while sitting in pews, staring at the back of others' heads. Celebration may also not fit within the confines of a printed bulletin, for some elements of spontaneity often arise. Part of the fear of festival may be our fear of ourselves, our bodies, our feelings, and our fear of touching or being touched by others. We are often afraid that if we let our guard down even a little, a whole set of needs will come tumbling out that we have spent a lifetime suppressing.

Mystery

The mysterious or mystical is another necessary element of worship. One of the most damning criticisms made of the church today is that it isn't religious enough; people are increasingly turning to Eastern religion in a effort to reach that which is under and beyond them. Worship must break through the ordinary, everyday world of the five senses, for this break arouses a sense of mystery, a sense of being grasped by the sacred.

So long as we remain in a state of the ordinary, our common sense keeps us safe, rational, and distant. We see nothing that is not literal. We may like or dislike what is happening, but as spectators we are removed from it. A proper function of worship is to help us experience the holy and be transformed by that experience. Like the festive, the mystical is a threat to our sense of control. Mystery defies our ordered, predictable patterns.

A key to the development of the mysterious is practicing the discipline of silence. Our moments of silence are often far too brief to allow us to be grasped by a sense of mystery. They are hardly long enough for us to collect our thoughts. All too often we fear silence, and to avoid discomfort we try to cover it with organ music. Silence is highly personal. Silence may embrace in us that which we cannot share, yet we may be able to share that very silence—as Quakers do.

Rationality

The telling of the story of holy history involves the mind and cannot be minimized. The historic content of the Christian faith must be re-presented in every age. The spoken word may be more powerful today than at any time since the Protestant Reformation. We live in a culture in which we are deluged by electronic media, and we may yearn for words spoken in person by a living human being.

Without the rational, worship can be an end in itself, an emotional experience that does not translate into life. The task of prophets is to translate the tradition into the modern idiom in such a way that the prophet may point directly to the situations in which we find ourselves and open us to hear a word from the Lord.

Each of these three elements—festival, mystery, and rationality—belongs in worship. The three great families of Christendom are each often said to emphasize one of these three features over another: Orthodoxy emphasizes the festive; Roman Catholicism, the mystical; and Protestantism, the rational. Within Protestantism itself, Pentecostalism seems to emphasize the festive; Anglicanism, the mystical; and the Reformed tradition, the rational. Any effort to renew worship today should concentrate on identifying elements of these three components that are missing and stressing them without surrendering the values already present. For example, if Reformed Protestants were to let their tradition of an educated and scholarly approach to scripture be given away in an effort to find popularity, such a trade off would be unfortunate indeed. The Reformed tradition has many—often unexplored—resources to strengthen the faith of people who seek God.

Practical Suggestions for Enriching Worship

We have magnificent resources. As Reformed Christians we can draw upon four thousand years of Judeo-Christian tradition. The most successful worship occurs when leaders sensitively design a framework for liturgy with which their congregations feel comfortable, then continue to bring in or design resources that not only enliven the service but allow worshipers to participate in the rich heritage of faith.

How can worship planners bring about this synergy? In a number of ways, and we offer here but a few suggestions:

- For a celebration of the Lord's Supper on Maundy Thursday, you can incorporate elements of the ancient Jewish Seder— elements that may date back to the Exodus.
- For Reformation Sunday, enlist the services of a bagpiper and use prayers of the Reformers as well as questions from the Shorter Catechism. (Specific suggestions are included in this chapter.)
- For Advent, use the Advent wreath and the Great "O" Antiphons.
- In mid-summer, celebrate the Lord's Supper using the "Feeding of the Five Thousand" as a motif, and decorate the sanctuary with large paper fish and loaves of bread. (Suggestions are included at the end of this chapter.)
- A service featuring the story of Jonah could include a short play presented by the children of the congregation and feature symbols of water, ships, and fish.

Don't forget the church bulletin, which is one of our most underused resources. Use the bulletin to present background information and a theological rationale for worship activities. Further, by printing a "Prayer Before the Service," one can include timeless prayers from our tradition as well as contemporary sources. Some churches ask members to draw illustrations to be used as cover art each week; with inexpensive color printers, this technique can present wonderful results at a reasonable cost.

Using the Lectionary and the Church Year

The combination of the lectionary and the church year provides rich themes for worship. Industrious worship committees and worship leaders can plan a full year, spacing activities throughout the year to keep interest high. Some examples of how you might do this are as follows:

Advent. Use the four Sundays of Advent to light the Advent candles and gradually decorate the sanctuary for Christmas. Decorations and seasonal music will provide rich resources for the services. You may want to have a special get-together, perhaps a potluck supper, during which the music of Advent and Christmas can be sung, as there never seems to be enough time in the service to sing all of the great music. Another popular activity is the "Hanging of the Greens," a service in which the sanctuary is decorated for Christmas.

Christmas. Most congregations have their own traditions for this season, which includes Epiphany; the star and symbols of the magi are appropriate for Epiphany. Though Christmas is a rich and busy season, many of its activities (caroling, children's pageants, providing food for the needy) take place outside of worship. A generous dose of Christmas music in worship may be all that is needed to define the season.

The baptism of our Lord in January is a good time to remember our own baptism. You might want to place a large bowl of water at the entrance to the sanctuary, possibly with small stones or clear glass marbles in it, suggesting that people who enter the church touch the water and remember their baptism (have towels handy).

A Sunday remembering Martin Luther King Jr. is a good time to remember the ministry and ideals of Dr. King as well as the ministries of other Christians of color. Including spirituals is a good idea for this service, which must seek to be faithful to King's ideals.

Burial of the Alleluia. At the end of the service on the last Sunday before Lent, include the short "Burial of the Alleluia," (included in this chapter) and remove an Alleluia banner from the sanctuary; then decorate the sanctuary with purple: paraments, ribbons on flags, stoles, banners, candles.

During Lent, it is traditional not to use the word "Alleluia." Remove the *Gloria* and Doxology from the liturgy and silence the church bells. In Lent the service can include short dramatic vignettes that speak to the passion themes.

To make and use a Lenten prayer wreath, take an eight-foot wooden pole and drill three sets of holes at the top. Through these holes insert three purple ribbons, approximately ten feet in length; the result is six ribbons, five feet long. (Inch-wide purple T-shirt material is an excellent alternative for ribbon.) Attach a twelve to fifteen-inch grapevine or willow wreath as a crown, using ribbon to secure the wreath. Attach the ends of the poles to pews using a bracket device you have manufactured, or mount them on banner stands. Fill a basket with five-foot lengths of cord or narrow ribbons and put it in an easily accessible place. Throughout Lent, invite worshipers to tie cords or ribbons to the wreaths to represent particular prayer concerns and ask other worshipers to pray for these unnamed concerns. The wreaths can be decorated with flowers and bright ribbons for Easter.

St. Patrick's Day. Though most Reformed Churches do not celebrate St. Patrick's Day, some congregations use this opportunity to remember the

Celtic heritage, singing such great hymns as "Morning Has Broken" and "Be Thou My Vision" and including Celtic prayers in the liturgy. Apt parallels for exploration include Abraham leaving his homeland and Patrick leaving his. (It's interesting to note that Patrick was not Roman Catholic and Irish but Celtic and British!)

Palm/Passion Sunday. Decorate the church lavishly with palms (if you have access to them) or other greenery. Distribute small crosses made from palm fronds. Have a procession of children singing a Palm Sunday hymn. At the end of the service, include an extended reading of the Passion narrative from the Gospel of the current cycle. Use three readers: one as a narrator, one as Jesus, one for all the other voices: Pilate, Judas, etc. Ask the congregation to read the lines assigned to the group voices.

Maundy Thursday. Provide a service of Tenebrae. Throughout the sanctuary, light numerous candles, which will be extinguished during the service. You may want to use a paschal candle, which will be the final candle carried out or extinguished, to be relit on Easter Eve or Easter Sunday and to burn throughout the season of Eastertide. In your Communion liturgy, you may want to use elements from a Jewish seder.

Easter. Make the first activity the return of the Alleluia banner, carried in a joyous procession. Feature the word "Alleluia" prominently in the liturgy. Flowers and color emphasize the joy of resurrection morning. The great hymns of Easter are almost all the celebration you need. The *Gloria* and Doxology are returned to the liturgy. No prayer of confession or *Kyrie* is used during the season; rather, the people say a prayer of adoration.

Eastertide. Some churches feature what is known as the "Gospel Procession,"[2] which can be staged in any number of ways. Instead of reading the Gospel from the usual place, place a lectern in the center of the congregation. At the time for the reading, the congregation sings one verse of a hymn, e.g., "Alleluia! Sing to Jesus" (tune: HYFRYDOL), as the reader goes to the lectern. The reader is accompanied by someone who brings up the great Alleluia banner behind the reader. Alongside the reader might be others holding pennants with Easter symbols, e.g., the triumphant Lamb of God. Still others might hold processional torches. At the end of the reading, the reader says: "This is the word of the Lord!" and the congregation responds, "Thanks be to God." As the procession returns banners and people to their places, the congregation sings a second verse of the hymn. Each year a different hymn might be chosen, but for continuity, the same hymn should be sung at the beginning and end of the Gospel Procession during the seven weeks of Eastertide.

Pentecost. Use symbols for the Spirit, flames, and water. Decorate the sanctuary with red geraniums or steel conduit poles, which hold gossamer

streamers/ribbons of red, orange, and yellow. Have a "wind chime procession," with those in the procession carrying T-shaped frames from which wind
chimes or Noah bells are suspended. Some congregations arrange for a dove,
butterfly, or balloon release outside, following the service.

Sunday near the Fourth of July. Consider an old-fashioned hymn sing, followed by an ice cream social.

Mid-summer Communion. Use the fish and loaves (miracle of the multipli-
cation) as a theme for the liturgy (liturgical suggestions are provided in this
chapter); use red-and-white checkered napkins and
tablecloths for a picnic feel, and serve the bread in baskets; recall again the stories where Jesus fed his disciples on the shore of the Sea of Galilee following the
resurrection. Make a 'T' by using a ten-foot bamboo
pole with a three-foot pole lashed at the top. From one
arm of the 'T', drop a two-foot cord to which is
attached a large paper fish. From the other end of the
crosspiece, hang another cord with a large fishhook,
made from a clothes hanger; on the hanger, hang a
large chunk of bread. Nets and glass floats can also be
used as decorations.

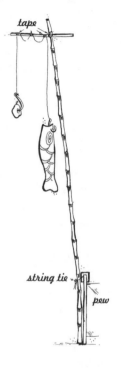

Jubilee Sunday. During summer, host a Jubilee Sunday that everyone can make their joyous praise to God.
Ask people in the congregation (particularly young
people) who play instruments to select a hymn to perform for the congregation. Order plastic kazoos, and
have the children distribute these from brightly berib-
boned baskets—with free instructions for the older
folks as to how to play them; select several hymn verses
that everyone can play on the kazoos. Use Psalms
147–150 for elements in the liturgy. Invite people to
come dressed in shorts and Hawaiian shirts!

Reformation Sunday. Celebrate our Reformed faith, and an appropriate
symbol is the rooster! The rooster proclaims the new day just as the Reformation proclaimed the new day of faith! Tartan pennants throughout the sanctuary can remind worshipers of the contribution of the Scottish Reformed tradition. This is a good Sunday to sing the psalm tunes, e.g., "Now Israel May
Say," "The Lord's My Shepherd," and two or three others.

Thanksgiving Sunday. Feature the traditional fruits of the harvest and the
great Thanksgiving hymns.

Christ the King. The last Sunday in the liturgical year, coming near to
Advent and Thanksgiving, can probably best be celebrated with such hymns

as "All Hail the Power of Jesus' Name" and "Crown Him with Many Crowns."

Most of these festival Sundays will be celebrated annually, but room is available in the church year for special celebrations that can be prepared for one-time use. Combine drums and shaker instruments with bright African colors and music for a joyous celebration. If yours is a largely Anglo or African-American congregation, Hispanic music and decorations, as well as Asian music and art, can both aid worship and sensitize us to the contributions these peoples have made and make to our community of faith.

In any service, it is important that the themes and motifs permeate the entire service, in both music and liturgy, not just the decorations. Sometimes an observance is so minimal—with the minister dolefully intoning, for example, "Today is Reformation Sunday," then having nothing else in the liturgy reflecting the theme—that even the initial comment is a waste of time!

Because of the widespread use of the lectionary, the same themes are explored around the world on the same day, so numerous materials are available for churches. The celebration of the church year also provides a vast array of study materials that suggest numerous liturgical activities. Certainly special themes and decorations should not overwhelm the service or overpower the fact that we gather to worship our God. But the Psalms lead us to believe that our God enjoys a little hallelujah once in a while.

A church that has had little in terms of liturgical enrichment should not suddenly undertake a full-blown celebration every Sunday. If your church has been rather staid, move slowly. The sensitive development of materials takes time—and must be accompanied by gentle and constant education of a congregation as to why we do what we do on special Sundays and during liturgical seasons. One way to provide this consistent, low-key education is to insert information regularly in the bulletin as an ongoing education in liturgy, explaining the rationale for new worship activities. Computers allow us to do this easily.

What's more, we should have a reason for what we do! If what we do does not lead people to an understanding of the joy and fullness of our God and the life of faith in Jesus Christ, then we have no reason to do it. Yet even as the same furniture in a room may be rearranged to provide relief from tedium yet continue to serve the same functions, so the elements of the service of worship can be rearranged to bring new delight—and even cause for wonder—to the worshiper.

Resources for Seasonal Worship

The following are some seasonal resources that can be adapted to the local situation.

Lighting the Advent Candles

Lighting the First Candle of Advent

During these weeks of Advent, we prepare the way for Christ's coming.
✠ **We hear the voice crying, "In the wilderness,
prepare the way for our God."**

✠ *Sing "Advent Candles" as the first Advent candle is lit.*

Light the light in dark-est _ night! Ad-vent can-dles burn so _ bright! Prepare our hearts, pre-pare the _ way, pre-pare our-selves _ for _ Christ-mas day!
"Glo - ri - a," the an - gels sing, "Come, pre-pare _ for _ Christ your King."

Light up-on the _ Ad - vent _ way, light our hearts _ for Christ-mas day.

As the mighty are thrown down and the lowly lifted up,
we prepare for God's "great reversal . . ."
✠ **Nations shall beat their swords into plowshares
and their spears into pruning hooks.
Nation shall not lift up sword against nation,
neither shall they study war again. (Isa. 2:4)**

Lord, we await our Savior's coming—bringing peace.
✠ **"Gloria," the angels sing, "Come, prepare for Christ your King."
Light upon the Advent way, light our hearts for Christmas day."**

Lighting the Second Candle of Advent

During these weeks of Advent, we prepare the way for Christ's coming.
✠ **We hear the voice crying, "In the wilderness,
  prepare the way for our God."**

✠ *Sing "Advent Candles" as the first two Advent candles are lit.*

As the mighty are thrown down and the lowly lifted up,
we prepare for God's "great reversal . . . "
✠ **Wolves shall dwell with lambs,
  leopards shall lie down with young goats,
  calves and lion cubs will feed together,
  and little children will take care of them. (Isa. 11:6)**

Lord, we await our Savior's coming—bringing friendship with creation.
✠ **"Gloria," the angels sing, "Come, prepare for Christ your King."
  Light upon the Advent way, light our hearts for Christmas day."**

Lighting the Third Candle of Advent

During these weeks of Advent, we prepare the way for Christ's coming.
✠ **We hear the voice crying, "In the wilderness,
  prepare the way for our God."**

✠ *Sing "Advent Candles" as the first three Advent candles are lit.*

As the mighty are thrown down and the lowly lifted up,
we prepare for God's "great reversal . . . "
✠ **The wilderness and the dry land shall be glad,
  the desert shall rejoice and blossom;
  like the crocus, it shall blossom abundantly,
  and rejoice with joy and singing. (Isa. 35:1)**

Lord, we await our Savior's coming—when heaven and earth shall sing.
✠ **"Gloria," the angels sing, "Come, prepare for Christ your King."
  Light upon the Advent way, light our hearts for Christmas day."**

Lighting the Fourth Candle of Advent

During these weeks of Advent, we prepare the way for Christ's coming.
✠ **We hear the voice crying, "In the wilderness,**
  prepare the way for our God."

✠ *Sing "Advent Candles" as the four Advent candles are lit.*

As the mighty are thrown down and the lowly lifted up,
we prepare for God's "great reversal . . . "
✠ **The Lord will give you a sign.**
  Look, the young woman is with child
  and shall bear a son,
  and shall call him Immanuel, that is, God is with us. (Isa. 7:14b)

Lord, we await our Savior's coming—born of a maiden.
✠ **The people who walked in darkness have seen a great light;**
  those who lived in a land of deep darkness,
  on them has light shined. (Isa. 9:2)

✠ **"Gloria," the angels sing, "Come, prepare for Christ your King."**
  Light upon the Advent way, light our hearts for Christmas day."

For Advent: The Great "O" Antiphons

The seven Great "O" Antiphons are so named simply because they all begin with the word "O." They all use terms that refer to an aspect of Christ's nature. In Latin they are *O Sapientia, O Adonai, O Radix Jesse, O Clavis David, O Oriens, O Rex Gentium*, and *O Emmanuel*. For centuries the antiphons were sung before and after the Magnificat at Vespers on the seven days from December 16–22, with *O Virgo Virginum* added on December 23. The date and composition of the Antiphons are unknown, but they were already in use in the eighth century. They were used as the basis for the beloved Advent hymn "O Come, O Come Emmanuel."

Call to Worship (The Great "O" Antiphons, Nos. 1 and 2)

O Wisdom, from the mouth of the Most High!
You reign over all things to the ends of the earth;
come and teach us the way of wisdom.
✠ **Lord Jesus, come soon.**

O Lord, and Head of the house of Israel,
you appeared to Moses in the fire of the burning bush
and gave him the Law on Sinai;
come with outstretched arm and ransom us.
✠ **Lord Jesus, come soon!**

The Spirit and the Bride say come!
✠ **Amen! Lord Jesus, come soon!**

Call to Worship (The Great "O" Antiphons, Nos. 3 and 4)

O Root of Jesse, rising as a sign for all the peoples,
before you earthly rulers will keep silent,
and nations give you honor:
Come quickly to deliver us.
✠ **Lord Jesus, come soon.**

O Key of David, Scepter over the house of Israel,
you open and no one can close,
you close and no one can open:
Come to set free the prisoners who live in darkness and the shadow of death.
✠ **Lord Jesus, come soon.**

The Spirit and the Bride say come!
✠ **Amen! Lord Jesus, come soon!**

Call to Worship (The Great "O" Antiphons, Nos. 5, 6, and 7)

O Radiant Dawn, splendor of eternal light, Sun of Justice:
Come, shine on those who live in darkness and in the shadow of death.
✠ **Come, Lord Jesus.**

O Ruler of the Nations, Monarch for whom the people long,
You are the Cornerstone uniting all humanity:
Come, save us all, whom you formed out of clay.
✠ **Come, Lord Jesus.**

O Emmanuel, our Sovereign and Lawgiver,
Desire of the nations and Savior of all:
Come and save us, O Lord our God.
✠ **Come, Lord Jesus.**

Let us proclaim the mystery of faith:
✠ **Christ has died. Christ is risen. Christ will come again.**

For the Sunday Before Lent:
The Burial of the Alleluia

Since the time of Pope Alexander II (1060), the Alleluia is discontinued during Lent and not heard again until the Great Vigil of Easter. In France, Normandy, and Germany, evidence has been found of a minor service for the beginning of Lent called "The Burial of the Alleluia." During the penitential weeks of Lent, the Alleluia was put aside and the themes of examination and confession were stressed. In some services, a coffin was provided for the Alleluia, with the knowledge that it would rise again with Christ at Easter and be the first word said or sung on that morning. In other churches, the Alleluia was symbolically banished by removing an Alleluia banner.

Alleluia—or its more Hebraic form, "Hallelujah"—is part of the international, timeless, truly universal language of Christian worship. Like that other Hebrew word, "Amen," the expression is familiar to countless generations of worshipers. Alleluia has become a song of the Christian heart to which no mere vernacular phrase can do justice. The Alleluias of medieval plainsong, Handel's Hallelujah Chorus, and innumerable hymns have found in this word the "language of the soul." By not saying "Alleluia" during Lent, we prepare to return it with renewed feeling and understanding when Easter, the "Feast of Feasts," arrives.

Sanctuary preparations for the service would include an Alleluia banner, perhaps another banner proclaiming "Watch and Pray," purple paraments, a paschal candle and matches, ribbons for flags, and purple stoles for pastor and choir.[3]

The Burial of the Alleluia

Reader 1: "I heard a great voice of many people in heaven saying, Alleluia! Salvation and honor and power be to the Lord our God. And again they said, Alleluia!" (based on Rev. 19).

Reader 2: The Lord reigns, clothed in majesty. Alleluia!

Reader 1: Alleluia! Give praise to the Lord our God and give your worship, for God alone is holy. Alleluia!

Hymn: "Praise the Lord, God's Glories Show" (Tune: LLANFAIR)

Reader 2: Alleluia! God is Lord of life, and in God's raising Christ from the bonds of death, the Lord has conquered that ancient enemy.

Reader 1: Our Lord said, "Soon I will leave you, and where I am going, you cannot come. But I will return to you, and you shall follow me afterward."

Reader 2: Peter said to him, "Lord, why cannot I follow you now? I will lay down my life for you."

Reader 1: Jesus answered, "Will you lay down your life for me? Truly, I say to you, the cock will not crow until you have denied me three times. But let not your hearts be troubled; believe in God, believe also in me" (based on John 14).

Reader 2: It was necessary for him to go so that we might receive him back more completely.

Reader 1: He is with us wherever we may go. Even when we feel most distant from him; he is with us—even in the valley of the shadow of death. [Let us read together from Psalm 139.]

Psalm 139 *(read in unison)*

✠ **O LORD, you have searched me and known me.**
   You know when I sit down and when I rise up;
      you discern my thoughts from far away.
   You search out my path and my lying down,
      and are acquainted with all my ways.
   Even before a word is on my tongue,
      O LORD,
   you know it completely.
   You hem me in, behind and before,
      and lay your hand upon me . . .
   Where can I go from your spirit?
      Or where can I flee from your presence?
   If I ascend to heaven, you are there;
      if I make my bed in Sheol, you are there.

If I take the wings of the morning
  and settle at the farthest limits of the sea,
even there your hand shall lead me,
  and your right hand shall hold me fast.
If I say, "Surely the darkness shall cover me,
  and the light around me become night,"
even the darkness is not dark to you;
  the night is as bright as the day,
  for darkness is as light to you. . . .
How weighty to me are your thoughts, O God!
  How vast is the sum of them!
I try to count them—they are more than the sand;
  I come to the end—I am still with you.

Reader 2: Take the Alleluia from us.

Reader 1: Take down the colors of rejoicing and replace them with purple, the color of penitence and preparation.

Reader 2: If we are to rise with Christ, we must die to our old selves. [*The Alleluia banner is removed, the paraments are changed from green to purple, and the paschal candle is lighted.*]

Reader 1: The Alleluia is gone. The colors of joy are put away. No more shall our hearts sing Alleluia until that day when our Christ is raised Son of God in power.

Reader 2: We await that morning and count the days.

Reader 1: Watch and pray.

Reader 2: Watch and pray that we will not enter into temptation.

Reader 1: Watch and pray that we will be found ready when our Christ returns.

Reader 2: *[Let us pray]*
God of light, you suffered the pains of darkness for us.
Lead us through this time of preparation and make us ready.
We cannot know when you will return,

for you have told us that your coming
will be as unexpected as that of a thief in the night.
So help us to use this time—and all our time —
to prepare ourselves to serve others as you served us.
Come again, Lord Jesus. Maranatha.
Come and save us. Amen.

Hymn: "Swiftly Pass the Clouds of Glory" (Tune: GENEVA)

Benediction
We have worshiped our God and been reminded of all that the Lord has done
for us. In our lives, we will work to share this love.

✠ **We have put away the Alleluia, for there is a time for everything, and
we prepare ourselves for the mystery of Christ's passion. It is the time
to consider the depths of God's love and human sinfulness—and how
God's love is triumphant.**

Grace, mercy, and peace from God the Father, God the Son, and God the Holy
Spirit be with us all.
✠ **Amen.**

Gospel Procession for Eastertide

[The following is an example of what should be printed in the bulletin. Instructions for the Procession are printed on p. 199.]

(All who are able may stand for the Gospel and the hymn, which surrounds the reading of the Gospel.)

✠ **Come, Christians, join to sing Alleluia! Amen!
Loud praise to Christ our King; Alleluia! Amen!
Let all, with heart and voice, before his throne rejoice;
praise is his gracious choice; Alleluia! Amen!** (Tune: MADRID)

[Introduction to the Gospel: On the day of the Resurrection, two of Jesus' disciples walk to the village of Emmaus, seven miles from Jerusalem. A man joins them and somehow makes sense of the events of the week. He joins them for supper, and when he breaks the bread, they recognize him.]

Gospel Lesson: Luke 24:13–35 *(stand)*

The Word of the Lord!
✠ **Thanks be to God!**

✠ **Praise yet our Christ again; Alleluia! Amen!**
Life shall not end the strain; Alleluia! Amen!
On heaven's blissful shore His goodness we'll adore
singing forevermore, "Alleluia! Amen!" (Tune: MADRID)

The Feeding of the Multitude

Call to Worship

The crowds had been with Jesus for three days, listening with excitement as he taught them of the love of the heavenly Father.
✠ **"Master, we have fed upon the Word, yet still we hunger."**

The disciples were impatient and said: "Send them away. It is impossible for us to feed so many." But Jesus would not hear of it and asked them: "What do you have? Feed them from what you have." And they were fed. Christ fed his people with bread and fishes. From a broken loaf and a chalice of wine they were fed. From fish roasted on the shore on that resurrection morning, from a meal at table on the Emmaus road, from quail and manna in a wilderness, they were fed.
✠ **"Bread of heaven: feed us till we want no more."**

✠ **Hymn: "The Day Is Long and Evening Comes"**[4] **(Tune: ELLACOMBE)**
1. **The day is long and evening comes,**
   and still we would hear more.
   O feed us now before we fall,
   feed us here by the shore.

   Refrain: Whether bread and wine from your table,
      fish and loaves upon the shore:
      O speak your word, O holy Christ,
      and we will want no more.

2. **The five small loaves and two small fish**
   were brought by just a boy.
   So bless and use the gifts we bring
   for all needs, for all joy. (Refrain)

Prayer of Confession

✠ God our Father, we do not trust you as we should.
  On those too rare occasions when we do follow you to the mountain,
  we lose sight of all that you have given to us
  and start worrying about what we do not have.
  We do not truly believe that you will take care of us;
  we do not believe in miracles, in transformation.
We wonder what good are the few fishes and loaves
  when there are so many to feed.
We wonder what good is the testimony of a few believers
  in a world, which has so many voices, declaring false gospels.
We wonder what good are a few acts of generosity
  in a time that is filled with so much unkindness.
God, make us part of your miracles.
  Transform the little that we have and are into something useful:
  food for the starving,
  life for your people,
  love for the lonely,
  light for those in darkness.
We ask these things in Jesus' name. Amen.

The Assurance of Forgiveness

God's love is a miracle.
A few fish and loaves fed the multitudes,
and there were baskets left over.
That same power can transform us.
We bring our inadequacies, our failings to the Master,
and he changes them:
we become his useful, redeemed people.
The miracle of Christ's love is that we are changed, transformed,
and made whole:
sufficient to do his work.
Brothers and sisters: I declare unto you,
and we ought to declare unto one another,
that in Jesus Christ we are forgiven.
✠ Thanks be to God. Amen.

Invitation to the Lord's Supper and Opening Words

The people had been with Jesus on the mountainside for three days, listening to him teach. It was inevitable then that they should be hungry—surprising that it should be three days before they should be aware of their hunger! The disciples would have sent the people to their own homes since they knew they could never feed so many as this. But Jesus knew how weak the men and women were, and he knew they would have fainted on the way; so he told the disciples to feed the people.

"But how?" the disciples honestly asked. Did the Lord have any idea how much food would cost for such a multitude? And even if they had the money, where would they buy so much food? But the Lord still insisted that the disciples feed the crowd.

And so they went among the people to see what food was there. In three days, if there had been some food, surely it would have been eaten. But they discovered a small boy whose mother had packed a picnic lunch for him. In it were five barley loaves and two fish, and he was willing to share it!

Jesus took the bread and the fish, and when he had given thanks, he broke them and gave them to the people; and everyone had enough to eat—and more!

And still the Lord commands us to feed his people. "But how?" we honestly ask. We do not have the money. And even if we had the money, we do not have the personnel, or the time, or the strength. Our Christ, however, will not accept such an answer. And we are sent among the people to find those—even children—who will share the little they have. Thus, the miracle is worked again and again through the blessing of the Savior.

Prayer of Consecration

God our Father, as Jesus transformed the loaves and the fishes on that Judean hillside, take the bread and the wine, set on this table, and transform them for us: that they will be more than simple elements, that they will feed us until we want no more. Hear these our prayers, for we ask them in the name of the One who is able to work such great miracles, even the changing of ourselves: Jesus Christ our Lord. Amen.

The Breaking of the Bread (*read before the distribution of the bread*)

On the night on which he was betrayed, our Savior took the bread, and after having given thanks, he broke it and said "Take, eat, this is my body which is broken for you."

(After the bread is served, the congregation prays in unison):

✠ **Lord, we take your broken bread and are made whole.**
  We give you our lives—and are given them back in return.

The Pouring of the Wine

In the same way our Savior took the cup after supper, and, when he had given thanks, he gave it to his disciples saying, "All of you drink of this, for this cup is the new covenant in my blood, which is poured out for you and for many for the forgiveness of sins; whenever you drink it, do this in memory of me."
(After the wine is served, the congregation prays in unison):

✠ **Lord, you poured our your life for us.**
  Now fill us with your life so that we may serve you all our days.

The Blessing

We have been to the mountain with the Lord and he has filled us again.
✠ **We have been to the Table of the Savior and received Jesus Christ our**
  Lord.

Go out into the world as people who are part of a miracle.
✠ **We are changed; may the love, which we share, make miracles happen**
  to others.

Let us praise the Lord.
✠ **Thanks be to God: and to God's Son, Jesus Christ!**

Jubilee Sunday

The following information may be printed in the bulletin for Jubilee Sunday:

"For God's foolishness is wiser than human wisdom, and God's weakness is stronger than human strength" (St. Paul, 1 Cor. 1:25).

The theological rationale behind Jubilee Sunday is that all of us, no matter how humble, have the means to praise our God. Whether we have great voices or not—or can play deftly upon demanding instruments or just hum in a kazoo—we can still participate in the joyous worship of our God.

We wanted a celebration where children could participate as freely as the adults; where no music would be rejected because it was not "up to musical standards"; where most of the music was immediately accessible due to its ease or familiarity. We wanted a sense of something of the Feast of Fools and the medieval celebration of Midsummer's Day. We put all this together for our Jubilee Sunday: a once-a-year celebration filled with mirth, color, and humor; a day when we abandon our more formal standards and less comfortable clothing and get together to celebrate the merriment and goodness of God in our lives. Enjoy yourself, enjoy your friends, enjoy making music, and enjoy God!

Prayer before the Service

O God, give us a song: to break the power of darkness
and lead us joyfully into the day.
O God, give us a song: to show us your direction in our work,
then courage to do it.
O God, give us a song: to sing of your love that protects and befriends us.
O God, give us a song: when we are deserted, cheated, demeaned, forgotten.
O God, give us a song: as night comes, as darkness envelops,
when we find it difficult to find your light.
O God, give us a song: when the future of years is no longer ours,
when all we will have is your song, eternally.

Call to Worship (from Psalms 33, 108, 100)

All of you who are God's people, shout for joy for what the Lord has done!
✠ **You that follow God's way, praise the Lord!**
  Give thanks to the Lord with harps,
  and sing to God with stringed instruments.
  Play your harps as best you can, and shout for joy!

Our confidence is in the Lord; therefore, we will sing and praise our God!
✠ **Wake up, my soul! Wake up, my harp and lyre!**
  I will wake up the sun with my songs that tell of God's constant faithfulness, which reaches near to the skies.

Sing to the Lord, all the earth! Worship the Lord with joy!
Come before God with happy songs!

✠ **Enter the temple gates with thanksgiving**
   and into its courts with praise.
   Give thanks and praise to God.

For the Lord is good!
✠ **The love of God is eternal,**
   and the faithfulness of God lasts forever.

Prayer of Confession

There is a song that you have placed within me, Lord.
✠ **But I do not sing very often.**

There is joy in the world you have hidden.
✠ **But I seek other treasures, which are empty and vain.**

There are those who cry out for my help.
✠ **But I seek my own peace and comfort instead.**

You have given me Christ as my Savior.
✠ **But I cannot have another as Lord as long as I am Lord.**

Lord, have mercy.
✠ **Christ, have mercy.**
Lord, have mercy upon us.

Assurance of Forgiveness

Our notes are flat when there is not enough breath.
Our lives are empty until they are filled with the wind of the Spirit.
Our vision is dim until we see with the light of Christ.
Brothers and sisters, the One who gave us Jesus Christ
did so in order that we might turn and live.
Believe the good news: in Jesus Christ, we are forgiven.
✠ **Thanks be to God. Amen.**

A Responsive Psalm of Praise (Psalm 150)

Praise the Lord!
✠ **Praise God in the sanctuary; praise God in the mighty firmament.**

Praise God's mighty deeds; praise God's marvelous greatness!
✠ **Praise God with trumpet sound.**

Praise God with lute and harp.
✠ **Praise God with tambourine and dance.**

Praise God with strings and pipe!
✠ **Praise God with clanging cymbals; praise God with loud clashing cymbals.**

Let everything that breathes praise the Lord!
✠ **Praise the Lord!**

Prayer for Illumination

O God, let your words fill our hearts,
your Spirit fill our souls,
and your songs fill our voices,
so that we may ever be your people.
✠ **Amen.**

Prayer of Dedication

✠ **Lord, you have given us songs and laughter and joy.**
  Take our gifts and change them
  so that others may sing and laugh and know you, too. Amen.

Reformation Sunday

Call to Worship with Rooster Motif

As dawn breaks, the rooster cries to all who slumber: Awake and sing!
✠ **The night, with its shadows and fears, is over.**
  The creatures of the dark withdraw into hiding,
  unwilling to face the brightness of the light;
  for God is light, and in God there is no darkness at all. (1 John 1:5)

Awake and sing,
for each day our Savior gives us a new day:
with the hope of wholeness, and activity, and joy!

We press on to that high calling.

✠ **From out of the darkness, God created light.**
  From our brokenness, our Savior makes us whole.
  From our poverty, the Spirit lifts us to riches!

As a hen gathers her brood under her wings, (Matt. 23:37)
so our God gathers us together to be the church.

✠ **Let us combine memory and vision,**
  but most of all love, to be that people.
  Hear the song: awake and sing!
  Let our new day of faith begin![5]

Hymns that may be played by bagpipes if they are used in this service:
"Lord, Thy Glory Fills the Heaven" (HYFRYDOL), "Come, Christians, Join to
Sing" (MADRID), "All People That on Earth Do Dwell" (OLD 100TH), "Amaz-
ing Grace" (AMAZING GRACE), "O Thou, My Soul, Return in Peace" (MAR-
TYRDOM), "The Lord's My Shepherd" (CRIMOND).

Prayer of Confession (by John Calvin)

✠ **Grant, Almighty God, that as thou urgest us daily to repentance,**
  and each of us is also stung with the consciousness of his own sins,—
  O grant, that we may not grow stupid in our vices,
  nor deceive ourselves with empty flatteries,
  but that each of us may, on the contrary, carefully examine his own life,
  and then with one mouth and heart confess that we are all guilty,
  not only of light offences, but of such as deserve eternal death,
  and that no other relief remains for us but thine infinite mercy,
  and that we may so seek to become partakers of that grace
  which has been once offered to us by thy Son,
  and is daily offered to us by the Gospel,
  that, relying on him as our Mediator,
  we may not cease to entertain hope even in the midst
  of a thousand deaths,
  and we may be gathered unto that blessed life,
  which has been procured for us by the blood of thy only Son. Amen.[6]

Assurance of Pardon (adapted from a statement by John Knox)

As we believe in one God,
so do we believe that, from the beginning,

there has been and now is and to the end of the world shall be one church . . .
by faith in Jesus Christ.
This church is catholic, that is, universal,
but it contains the elect of all ages, of all realms, of all tongues, invisible:
known only to God. . . .
The message of the church is that we are called, saved, and forgiven:
in Jesus Christ our Lord.
✠ **Thanks be to God. Amen.**[7]

Prayer for Illumination (by John Calvin)

Grant, Almighty God,
that as almost the whole world give such loose reins to their licentiousness,
that they hesitate not either to despise or to regard as of no value thy sacred
     word,—
grant, O Lord, that we may always retain such reverence
as is justly due to it and to thy holy oracles,
and be so moved, whenever thou deignest to address us,
that being truly humbled, we may be raised up by faith to heaven,
and by hope gradually attain that glory which is as yet hid from us.
And may we at the same time so submissively restrain ourselves,
as to make it our whole wisdom to obey thee and to do thee service,
until thou gatherest us into thy kingdom, where we shall be partakers of thy
glory, through Christ our Lord.
✠ **Amen.**[8]

Questions from the Catechism

*[The Westminster Shorter Catechism of 1649 was the means by which our spiritual
forebears learned their theology. In 107 questions and answers, the Catechism sought
to lay out the basic tenets of the faith. The following questions have to do with how
God's Word is received in worship.]* [*]

Q. 88. What are the outward means whereby Christ communicateth to us the
benefits of redemption?
✠ **The outward and ordinary means whereby Christ communicateth to
   us the benefits of redemption are his ordinances, especially the Word,**

*Churches that use a different catechism can substitute it here.

sacraments, and prayer, all of which are made effectual to the elect for salvation.

Q. 89. How is the Word made effectual to salvation?

✠ **The Spirit of God maketh the reading, but especially the preaching, of the Word an effectual means of convincing and converting sinners, of building them up to holiness and comfort, through faith unto salvation.**

Q. 90. How is the Word to be read and heard, that it may become effectual to salvation?

✠ **That the Word may become effectual to salvation we must attend thereunto with diligence, preparation, and prayer; receive it with faith and love; lay it up in our hearts; and practice it in our lives.**

Prayer of Dedication

O heavenly Father, which art the fountain and full treasure of all goodness,
we beseech thee to show thy mercies upon us thy children,
and sanctify these gifts which we receive of thy merciful liberality;
granting us grace to use them soberly and purely,
according to thy blessed will;
so that hereby we may acknowledge thee to be
the author and giver of all good things;
and, above all, that we may remember continually
to seek the spiritual food of thy word
wherewith our souls may be nourished.
✠ **Amen.**[9]

Benediction
(used at the Highland Games at Grandfather Mountain, North Carolina)

May the blessing of light be on you—light without and light within. May the blessed sunlight shine on you and warm your heart till it glows like a great peat fire, so that strangers may come and warm themselves at it, and also friends. And may the light shine out of your two eyes like a candle set in the windows of a house, bidding the wanderer to come out of the storm.

And may the blessing of the rain be on you: the soft, sweet rain; may it fall upon your spirit that all the little flowers may spring up and shed their sweetness on the air. And may the blessing of the great rains be on you; may they beat upon your spirit and wash it fair and clean and leave there many a shining pool where the blue of Heaven shines—and sometimes a star.

And may the blessing of the earth be on you—the great, round earth. May you ever have a kindly greeting for those you pass as you are going along the roads. May the earth be soft under you when you rest out upon it, tired at the end of a day; and may it rest easy over you when, at the last, you lie out under it. May it rest lightly over you that your soul may be off from under it quickly, and up, and off, and on its way to God.

And now may the Lord bless you all, and bless you kindly. Amen.[10]

These are samples of services that can be used throughout the year to bring new life and interest to worship. While all of them are new, each is based on our roots in the Bible and the Reformed faith. It is a rich tradition that the creative liturgist will enjoy exploring.

Notes

Chapter 1: The Characteristics of Reformed Worship

1. James Hastings Nichols, *Corporate Worship in the Reformed Tradition* (Philadelphia: Westminster Press, 1968), 88–89.
2. Ibid., 175.

Chapter 2: From the New Testament to the Reformation

1. The Gospel of John deals with the new understanding of the Temple as giving way to Christ as the dwelling with God among human beings by putting Jesus' Temple cleansing at the very beginning of his ministry. John reports Jesus saying, "'Destroy this temple, and in three days I will raise it up' . . . [b]ut he was speaking of the temple of his body" (John 2:19, 21). John presents another good example of early Christian preaching. The two lessons are Exodus 16, the story of the manna in the wilderness, and Isaiah 54:13, "And your children shall be taught by the LORD."
2. Henry Bettenson, *Documents of the Christian Church* (New York and London: Oxford University Press, 1947), 93.
3. Irenaeus, *Against Heresies*, Book IV, cited in Bettenson, *Documents*, 105.
4. Because the language used is male, the role of presider seems to have been restricted to males alone by this time, or at least in the knowledge of Hippolytus.
5. Cited by Joseph Martos, *Doors to the Sacred: A Historical Introduction to the Sacraments in the Catholic Church* (Garden City, N.Y.: Doubleday and Company, 1982), 256.
6. Ibid., 70.

Chapter 3: From the Reformation to Today

1. Cited by Bettenson, *Documents*, 280.
2. Ulrich Zwingli, "On the Lord's Supper," from *Zwingli and Bullinger*, trans. G. W. Bromiley (Philadelphia: Westminster Press, 1953), 108.
3. Ulrich Zwingli, "On Baptism," from *Zwingli and Bullinger*, 156.
4. Bard Thompson, *Liturgies of the Western Church* (New York: Collins World, 1961), 178.
5. Cited by Thompson, *Liturgies*, 187.
6. John Calvin, "Treatise on the Lord's Supper," in *Calvin: Theological Treatises*, trans. J. K. S. Reid (Philadelphia: Westminster Press, 1954), 163.
7. Ibid., 164.
8. Ibid., 165.
9. Ibid., 165.

10. Ibid., 165.
11. Ibid., 166.
12. *Book of Confessions,* The Scots Confession, 3.21.
13. Ibid.
14. Thompson, *Liturgies,* 370.

Chapter 4: The Sacrament of Baptism

1. *Book of Confessions,* Heidelberg Catechism, 4.065.
2. *Book of Confessions,* 7.094.

Chapter 5: The Sacrament of the Lord's Supper

1. *Book of Confessions,* 3.21.
2. John Calvin, *Calvin: Theological Treatises,* trans. J. K. S. Reid (Philadelphia: Westminster Press, 1954), 136.
3. Arlo Duba, "Theological Dimensions of the Lord's Supper," in *Worship in the Community of Faith* (Louisville, Ky.: Joint Office of Worship, 1982), 100.
4. *Book of Confessions,* 3.21
5. *Book of Confessions,* 6.167.
6. Brian A. Gerrish, *Grace and Gratitude: The Eucharistic Theology of John Calvin* (Minneapolis: Fortress Press, 1993), 125.
7. *Book of Confessions,* 4.075.
8. Gerrish, *Grace and Gratitude,* 20.
9. *Book of Confessions,* 7.284.
10. *Book of Confessions,* 9.52.
11. *Psalter Hymnal of the Christian Reformed Church* (Grand Rapids: Christian Response Publications, 1987), 855.
12. Note: Every time boldface type is used in a response, the part is spoken by the people.
13. See the entire text of the Reformed *Sursum Corda* on pp. 33–34.

Chapter 6: The Service for the Lord's Day

1. John Burkhart, *Worship* (Philadelphia: Westminster Press, 1982), 18.
2. Jeffrey S. Gaines, unpublished church bulletin, used by permission.
3. James C. Huffstutler
4. James C. Huffstutler
5. James Robie
6. James C. Huffstutler
7. Jeffrey S. Gaines
8. Nan Jenkins

Chapter 7: Music

1. Quoted in Cecil Northcott, *Hymns in Christian Worship* (Richmond, Va.: Ecumenical Studies in Worship #13, John Knox Press, 1964), 8.
2. E. Werner, "Music in the Bible," *Interpreter's Dictionary of the Bible,* vol. 3 (New York: Abingdon Press, 1962), 458.
3. Dom Gregory Dix, *The Shape of the Liturgy* (London: Dacre Press, 1945), 326f.
4. Matthew Spinka, *John Hus at the Council of Constance* (New York/London: Columbia University Press, 1965), 231f.
5. Quoted in E. E. Ryden, *The Story of Christian Hymnody* (Rock Island, Ill.: Augustana Press, 1959), 58.

6. Ibid.
7. Harold J. Grimm, *The Reformation Era* (New York: MacMillan Co., 1954), 163.
8. Charles Garside Jr., *Zwingli and the Arts* (New Haven/London: Yale University Press, 1966), 45.
9. Charles Garside Jr., "The Origins of Calvin's Theology of Music: 1536–1543," (monograph) in *Transactions of the American Philosophical Society*, vol. 69, part 4 (Philadelphia: Independence Square, 1979).
10. W. Stanford Reid, "The Battle Hymns of the Lord: Calvinist Psalmody of the Sixteenth Century," in *Sixteenth Century Essays and Studies*, vol. 2, ed. Carl S. Meyer (St. Louis: Foundation for Reformation Research, 1971), 38. Herein after called "Battle Hymns."
11. Garside, "Origins," 6f.
12. Ford Lewis Battles, *The Piety of John Calvin: An Anthology Illustrative of the Spirituality of the Reformer* (Grand Rapids: Baker Book House, 1978), 27.
13. Ibid., 8.
14. John Calvin, *Institutes of the Christian Religion*, ed. John T. McNeill, Library of Christian Classics (Philadelphia: Westminster Press, 1960), III.xx.895.
15. Garside, "Origins," 14.
16. Battles, "Piety," 138.
17. Walter Blankenburg, in "Switzerland and France," in Frederich Blume, *Protestant Church Music: A History* (New York: W.W. Norton and Co., 1974), 518.
18. Frank Dobbins, on "Loys Bourgeois" in the *New Grove Dictionary of Music and Musicians*, vol. 3, ed. Stanley Sadie (London/Washington: Macmillan Publishers, Ltd., 1980), 112.
19. Ross J. Miller, *John Calvin and the Reformation of Music in the 16th Century*, (Dissertation at the Honnold Library, Claremont Colleges, 1970), 137.
20. Blankenburg, "Switzerland and France," 531.
21. Ibid.
22. Quoted in Garside, "Origins," 18.
23. Ibid., 43.
24. Ibid., 53.
25. Battles, "Piety," 139.
26. Reid, "Battle Hymns," 55.
27. Marva Dawn, *Reaching Out without Dumbing Down* (Grand Rapids: Wm. B. Eerdmans Publishing Co., 1995), 170f.
28. *The Presbyterian Hymnal: Hymns, Psalms and Spiritual Songs* (Louisville, Ky.: Westminster/John Knox Press, 1990).

Chapter 8: Prayer

1. John Calvin, *Institutes of the Christian Religion*, III.xx.29.
2. James C. Huffstutler.
3. Jeffrey S. Gaines.
4. Jeffrey S. Gaines.
5. James C. Huffstutler.
6. James C. Huffstutler.
7. James C. Huffstutler
8. *Book of Confessions*, Presbyterian Church (U.S.A.).
9. James C. Huffstutler.
10. James C. Huffstutler.
11. Howard Rice.
12. James Robie.
13. James C. Huffstutler.

14. Jeffrey S. Gaines.
15. James C. Huffstutler.
16. James Robie.
17. James C. Huffstutler.
18. Jeffrey S. Gaines.
19. Brian Gerrish, *Grace and Gratitude* (Minneapolis: Fortress Press, 1993), 50.
20. Nan Jenkins.
21. Nan Jenkins.
22. *Book of Common Worship*, 81.
23. James C. Huffstutler.
24. James C. Huffstutler.

Chapter 9: The Setting of Worship

1. Edward A. Sovik, "Notes on Sacred Space," *The Christian Century*, March 31, 1982, 363.
2. Ibid., 363–64.
3. John Manners in the Introduction to *The Oxford Illustrated History of Christianity* (Oxford/New York: Oxford University Press, 1990), 8. See Calvin's *Institutes*, Library of Christian Classics (I.xi.12).
4. Manners, Introduction, 9.

Chapter 10: The Church Year

1. The Second Helvetic Confession, *The Constitution of the Presbyterian Church (USA)*, Part 1, *Book of Confessions*, 5.226.
2. For historical information tracing the development of the liturgical year, we are indebted to Harold M. Daniels, in the Introduction to *Liturgical Year*, Supplemental Liturgical Resources, vol. 7, (Louisville, Ky.: Westminster/John Knox Press, 1992).
3. See the discussion on page 42f., in *Liturgical Year* (Supplemental Resource No. 7).
4. See "The Protoevangelium of James" in Edgar Hennecke, *New Testament Apocrypha*, vol. 1, Gospels and Related Writings (Philadelphia: Westminster Press, 1963), 380.
5. Note the layout of the great "O" antiphons in the *Book of Common Worship*, 166ff.
6. See chapter 14, p. 206, for the Burial of the Alleluia.
7. *Passion* is Latin and means "suffering," referring to the last days of Jesus' life, particularly the crucifixion. *Pasch* is Greek and means Passover and refers to the redemptive death *and* resurrection. The *paschal* event is the Easter event.
8. Instructions for the Easter Vigil are found in the *Book of Common Worship* and *Liturgical Year* (Supplemental Resource No. 7).

Chapter 13: Other Occasions for Worship

1. Joseph Martos, *Doors to the Sacred* (Garden City, N.Y.: Image Books, Doubleday, 1982), 373.
2. Howard Rice.
3. Howard Rice.
4. Biblical scholars are aware of the difficulty of defining the terms "disciples" and "apostles." Sometimes "disciples" refers to all believers; at other times it seems to refer to the Twelve, or a small band who may have accompanied the Twelve. At times the term "apostle" means one of the Twelve; at other times it seems to refer to any who seem to have early authority as a result of having some rela-

tionship to the Twelve or to Jesus. Paul considered himself an apostle with apostolic authority.

5. Since the United Church of Christ ordains only ministers in most congregations, some of these comments do not pertain to that denomination.

Chapter 14: The Style of Worship

1. Marva Dawn, *Reaching Out without Dumbing Down* (Grand Rapids: Wm. B. Eerdmans Publishing Co., 1995).

2. This idea comes from Arden Mead, Creative Communications for the Parish, in St. Louis, Missouri.

3. See *Alive Now!* (March–April 1979), where Elizabeth Platz gives background of the service and a simple reconstruction. Fr. Robert Neily contributed other information here.

4. James C. Huffstutler.

5. Roosters: God's Church Bells. One Sunday in worship I was struck with the power of Jesus' imagery of a "hen gathering her brood under her wings" (Matt. 23:37) and wondered if that might be a useful symbol around which to shape a liturgy. Then, at a Presbytery Worship Committee meeting, the Rev. Elaine McRobbie mentioned something she had noted at the World Council of Churches' Ecumenical Institute in Bossey, Switzerland. She told how, during the Reformation, the Reformed churches used the symbol of the rooster rather than the cross; she had a photograph of a wrought iron rooster mounted on the outside wall of a church in Gruyere. That was all I needed. I remembered a restoration at St. Giles Kirk in Edinburgh where the rooster weathercock was brought down from the roof so that it could be repaired and it was, for a short while, on display at eye level.

I wrote a text and persuaded a musician friend to set it to music. Then I had one of our artists in the congregation design some graphics. Now all that had to be done was to create the liturgy.

But then I paused: How could I authenticate any of this? Elaine had suggested that the reason the Reformed churches stopped using the cross was because most crosses were crucifixes, and that clearly became the symbol of the Roman Catholic Church; further, those were times when each side had little compassion for the other, and many Reformed Christians had been humiliated and forced to kiss a crucifix. So the symbol they adopted was the rooster.

What did it mean? A rooster or cock is mentioned in scripture twice; one reference has to do with the denial of Peter; the other is in the Proverbs (30:31), which uses the strutting rooster as a symbol of pride. But surely the Reformed churches had something else in mind; they wouldn't have made a negative symbol, one of denial or vanity, a symbol for the Reformation!

When I could find no mention of the rooster as a symbol of the Reformed churches, I contacted my mentor, Dr. Jane Dempsey Douglass—then professor of church history at Princeton Theological Seminary—who, my friend Jack Purdy suggests, "knows everything." Jane listened patiently and said she really knew nothing of such use of the rooster. She was familiar with certain churches, such as the Hungarian Reformed, adopting alternative symbols (the star), so it was not beyond reason; still, she was not aware of the use of the rooster. She assured me she would work on it.

Jane consulted with a fellow faculty member at Princeton, Karlfried Froehlich, an expert in medieval and Reformation iconography, who could not confirm the use of the rooster by Protestants as opposed to the use of the cross by Catholics. Dr. Froehlich did send along Latin hymns by Anselm and Prudentius from the fourth century, which include the use of the rooster as one who calls believers to the approach of the new day. That was exactly what I believed the iconography must represent: the call to awake to the new day of faith, the new life in Christ: a completely positive symbol. But I didn't have my verification.

Another friend, Dana Babb, remembered a wrought iron rooster at Louisville Theological Seminary, so I phoned the seminary and ended up talking to Dr. Johanna Bos and hit pay dirt; she recalled how, as a girl growing up in Holland, she had seen the roosters on the tops of the Reformed churches. You could tell the faith of a church—or even a whole town—by the use of the rooster or the cross. Perhaps the use of the rooster was a geographical phenomenon, which was not universal, but it was and is used. Subsequent observation of photographs turned up numerous instances of the rooster atop Protestant churches.

Actually, the reformers didn't trust symbols much, so one should not come away with the idea that churches at the time of the Reformation were rich in symbolism. The veneration of statues and the abuse connected with jewel-encrusted reliquaries and golden altars were objects of scorn for them. So virtually all creative energy went into music, and what a rich treasury we have because of it.

We hope our choice and use of symbols will lead worshipers to a deeper understanding of faith rather than serve as a focus, which sidetracks believers. In worship, as in all else in the church, we will reform and keep being reformed by the living God who works among us. JCH

6. Calvin, "Commentaries on the Twelve Minor Prophets," in *Calvin's Commentaries*, vol. 14, trans. John Owen (Grand Rapids: Baker Book House, 1981), 20.

7. Adapted from a statement by John Knox from The Scots Confession, found in *Book of Confessions* 3.16, "The Kirk."

8. Calvin, *Commentaries*, vol. 14, 57f.

9. From "The Works of John Knox," ed. David Laing (Edinburgh: James Thin, 1895).

10. In the public domain.

Bibliography

Andrews, James E,. and Joseph A. Burgess, eds. *An Invitation to Action: The Lutheran-Reformed Dialogue, Series III (1981–1983)*. Philadelphia: Fortress Press, 1984.

Baird, Charles W. *The Presbyterian Liturgies*. Grand Rapids: Baker Book House, 1957; originally published, 1856.

Barkley, John. *The Worship of the Reformed Church*. Ecumenical Studies in Worship, No. 15. Richmond, Va.: John Knox Press, 1967.

Battles, Ford Lewis. *The Piety of John Calvin*. Grand Rapids: Baker Book House, 1978.

Benoit, J. D. *Liturgical Renewal*. London: SCM Press, 1958.

Bettenson, Henry, ed., *Documents of the Christian Church*. New York and London: Oxford University Press, 1947.

Blume, Frederich. *Protestant Church Music: A History*. New York: W. W. Norton and Co., 1974.

Burkhart, John. *Worship*. Philadelphia: Westminster Press, 1986.

Calvin, John. *Institutes of the Christian Religion*. Edited by John T. McNeill. Vols. 1 and 2. Philadelphia: Westminster Press, 1950.

———. *Calvin: Theological Treatises*. Translated by J. K. S. Reid. Philadelphia: Westminster Press, 1954.

———. *Devotions and Prayers of John Calvin*. Compiled by Charles E. Edwards. Grand Rapids: Baker Book House, 1954.

Chinn, Nancy. *Spaces for Spirit: Adorning the Church*. Chicago: Liturgy Training Publications, 1998.

Christian Reformed Church, *Psalter Hymnal*, Grand Rapids: Christian Reformed Publications, 1987.

Church of Scotland. *Book of Common Order of the Church of Scotland*. Edinburgh: Saint Andrew Press, 1994.

Cross, F. L. and E. A. Livingston. *The Oxford Dictionary of the Christian Church*. 3d ed. Oxford: Oxford University Press, 1997.

Cullmann, Oscar. *Baptism in the New Testament*. Translated by J. K. S. Reid. London: SCM Press, 1950.

Daniels, Harold, editor, with Daniel B. Wesler, Cynthia A. Jarvis, Arlo D. Duba, and Melva Wilson Costen. *Worship in the Community of Faith*. Louisville, Ky.: The Joint Office of Worship of the Presbyterian Church in the United States and the United Presbyterian Church in the U.S.A., 1982.

Davies, J. G. *A Dictionary of Liturgy and Worship*. London: SCM Press, 1972.

Dawn, Marva J. *Reaching Out without Dumbing Down: A Theology of Worship for the Turn-of the-Century Culture.* Grand Rapids:William B. Eerdmans Publishing Co., 1995.

Dix, Dom Gregory. *The Shape of the Liturgy.* London: Dacre Press, 1945.

Doran, Carol, and Thomas Troeger. *Trouble at the Table: Gathering the Tribes for Worship.* Nashville: Abingdon, 1992.

Driver, Tom F. *The Magic of Ritual.* San Francisco: Harper, 1991.

Duck, Ruth. *Bread for the Journey.* New York: The Pilgrim Press, 1983.

Garside, Charles Jr. *Zwingli and the Arts.* New Haven/London: Yale University Press, 1956.

———. "The Origins of Calvin's Theology of Music: 1536–1543," monograph in *Transactions of the American Philosophical Society*, vol. 60, part 4. Philadelphia: Independence Square, 1979.

Gerrish, Brian A. *Grace and Gratitude: The Eucharistic Theology of John Calvin.* Minneapolis: Fortress Press, 1993.

Grimm, Harold J. *The Reformation Era.* New York: Macmillan Co., 1954.

Hageman, Howard. *Pulpit and Table.* Richmond, Va.: John Knox Press, 1962.

Hennecke, Edgar. *New Testament Apocrypha*, vol. 1: Gospels and Related Writings. Philadelphia: Westminster Press, 1963.

Heron, Alasdair I. C. *Table and Tradition.* Philadelphia: Westminster Press, 1983.

Iona Community, *A Wee Worship Book.* Edited by John Bell. Glasgow, Scotland: The Wild Goose Worship Group, 1989.

Jones, Cheslyn, Geoffrey Wainwright, and Edward Arnold, eds. *The Shape of Liturgy.* New York: Oxford University Press, 1978.

Kingdon, Robert. "The Genevan Revolution in Public Worship." *The Princeton Seminary Bulletin*, new ser., 20, no. 3 (1999).

Leith, John H. *An Introduction to the Reformed Tradition.* Atlanta: John Knox Press, 1977.

Long, Thomas. "Reclaiming the Unity of Word and Sacrament in Presbyterian and Reformed Worship." *Reformed Liturgy and Worship* (winter 1982).

Luther, Martin. *Luther's Works* (vol. 53, Liturgy and Hymns). Edited by Ulrich S. Leupold. Philadelphia: Fortress Press, 1965.

Macleod, Donald. *Presbyterian Worship: Its Meaning and Method.* Atlanta: John Knox Press, 1965.

Martos, Joseph. *Doors to the Sacred: A Historical Introduction to the Sacraments in the Catholic Church.* Garden City, N.Y.: Doubleday and Company, 1982.

Maxwell, William D. *A History of Christian Worship: An Outline of Its Development and Forms.* Grand Rapids: Baker Book House, 1982.

McKim, LindaJo. "Hymnody," in *Encyclopedia of the Reformed Faith.* Edited by Donald McKim. Louisville, Ky.: Westminster/John Knox Press, 1995.

McManners, John, ed. *The Oxford Illustrated History of Christianity.* Oxford and New York: Oxford University Press, 1990.

Miller, Ross J. *John Calvin and the Reformation Music in the 16th Century.* Unpublished diss., Claremont Colleges, 1970.

Nichols, James Hastings. *Corporate Worship in the Reformed Tradition.* Philadelphia: Westminster Press, 1958.

Northcott, Cecil. *Hymns in Christian Worship*, Ecumenical Studies in Worship #13. Atlanta: John Knox Press, 1964.

Otto, Rudolf: *The Idea of the Holy.* London: Oxford University Press, 1953.

Presbyterian Church in the United States of America. *The Book of Common Worship.* Philadelphia: Office of the General Assembly/Board of Christian Education, 1946.

Presbyterian Church (U.S.A.). *Book of Common Worship*. Louisville, Ky.: Westminster/John Knox Press, 1993.

———. *Book of Confessions*. Louisville, Ky.: Office of the General Assembly, 1995.

———. *Book of Order*, Part 2, containing the Directory for Worship. Louisville, Ky.: Office of the General Assembly, 1999.

———. *Liturgical Year*, vol. 7, Supplemental Liturgical Resources. Louisville, Ky.: Westminster/John Knox Press, 1992.

Presbyterian Church (U.S.A.) and the Cumberland Presbyterian Church. *Book of Common Order*. Louisville, Ky.: Westminster/John Knox Press, 1991.

Presbyterian Hymnal: Hymns, Psalms and Spiritual Songs, The. Louisville, Ky.: Westminster/John Knox Press, 1990.

Reid, W. Stanford. "The Battle Hymns of the Lord: Calvinist Psalmody of the Sixteenth Century," in *Sixteenth Century Essays and Studies*, vol. 2. Edited by Carl S. Meyer. St. Louis: Foundation for Reformation Research, 1971.

Rice, Howard L. *Reformed Spirituality: An Introduction for Believers*. Louisville, Ky.: Westminster/John Knox Press, 1991.

Rice, Howard L., and Lamar Williamson Jr., eds. *A Book of Reformed Prayers*. Louisville, Ky.: Westminster John Knox Press, 1998.

Routley, Erik, ed. *Rejoice in the Lord: Reformed Church in America*. Grand Rapids: Wm. B. Eerdmans Publishing Co., 1985.

Ryden, E. E. *The Story of Christian Hymnody*. Rock Island, Ill.: Augustana Press, 1959.

Sadie, Stanley. *New Grove Dictionary of Music and Musicians*. London and Washington: Macmillan Publishers, Ltd., 1980.

Sheldon, Robert M. "A Theology of the Lord's Supper from the Perspective of the Reformed Tradition." *Reformed Liturgy and Music*, XVI, 1 (winter 1982).

Sovik, Edward A. "Notes on Sacred Space." *The Christian Century* (March 31, 1983): 363.

Tamburello, Dennis E. *Union with Christ: John Calvin and the Mysticism of St. Bernard*. Louisville, Ky.: Westminster John Knox Press, 1994.

Thompson, Bard. *Liturgies of the Western Church*. New York: Collins-World Publishing Company, 1962.

United Church of Christ. *Book of Worship of the United Church of Christ*. New York: Office for Church Life and Leadership, 1986.

———. *The New Century Hymnal*. Cleveland: The Pilgrim Press, 1995.

Webber, Robert E. *Blended Worship: Achieving Substance and Relevance in Worship*. Peabody, Mass.: Henderson Publishers, 1994.

Webber, Robert E. *Worship Old and New*. Grand Rapids: Zondervan Publishing Company, 1994.

Werner, E. "Music in the Bible," in *Interpreter's Dictionary of the Bible*. Vol. 3. New York: Abingdon Press, 1962.

White, James F. *Protestant Worship: Traditions in Transition*. Atlanta: John Knox Press, 1989.

Willimon, William. *Worship as Pastoral Care*. Nashville: Abingdon, 1982.

Wolfe, Janet E. *Worship: Reformed and Ecumenical: A Comparative History of the Changes in Texts of Worship Resources Developed since 1961 in the Presbyterian Church (U.S.A.) in Light of Ecumenical Models of Worship*. Ann Arbor, Mich.: UMI Dissertation Services, 1998.

Zwingli, Ulrich, *Zwingli and Bullinger*, Translated by G. W. Bromiley, Philadelphia: Westminster Press, 1963.

Index